JACK SCARROTT'S PRIZE FIGHTERS
Memoirs of a Welsh Boxing Booth Showman

Lawrence Davies

Peerless Press
2016

JACK SCARROTT'S PRIZE FIGHTERS

First published in Great Britain by
Peerless Press
P.O. Box 4352
Cardiff CF14 8HS
Wales

First printed July 2016
Copyright © Peerless Press

All rights reserved. No part of this publication may be reproduced, stored in a retrieval system, or transmitted in any form or by any means, electronic, mechanical, photocopying, recording or otherwise, without prior permission of the copyright holder, nor otherwise circulated in any form, binding or cover other than which is published, and without a similar condition, including this condition, being imposed upon the subsequent publisher.

ISBN : 978-095703-423-5

For my mother, Mary
With all my love

Clockwise from back right – Jack Scarrott, Jim Driscoll, Llew Edwards, Jimmy Wilde, Percy Jones, Ermin Long

Contents

Introduction	1

Fifty Years of Boxing in South Wales
Memoirs of a Welsh Boxing Booth Showman

Part 1	13
Part 2	21
Part 3	27
Part 4	32
Part 5	38
Part 6	44
Part 7	49
Part 8	54
Part 9	62
Part 10	68

Part 11	73
Part 12	78
Part 13	84
Part 14	89

Jack Scarrott's Prize Fighters

Chapter 1	Fothergill Street	95
Chapter 2	Martin Fury vs. Jack Hearn	105
Chapter 3	William Samuels	117
Chapter 4	William Samuels vs. Bob Dunbar	127
Chapter 5	Shoni Engineer vs. Tom Books	139
Chapter 6	Shoni Engineer vs. Dublin Tom	147
Chapter 7	Death on the Mountain	171
Chapter 8	William Samuels vs. Toff Wall	179
Chapter 9	William Samuels vs. John L. Sullivan	191
Chapter 10	Shoni Engineer vs. Jem Guidrell	199
Chapter 11	Shoni Engineer vs. John O'Brien	207
Chapter 12	Boxing Booth Days	215
Chapter 13	William Samuels in the Lion's Den	225
Chapter 14	Shoni Engineer vs. William Samuels	235
Chapter 15	Scarrott's Boxing Booth	243
Chapter 16	Doctor William Price	251
Chapter 17	Dangerous Jack and the Japanese Strangler	261

Introduction

In the days of the mountain fighters of South Wales, bareknuckle boxing had always been conducted from the safety of a bloody 'spot', a 'hollows' or maybe a 'patch', a place hidden from view and usually inaccessible without a steep climb up a sharp gradient to a spot on the mountains concealed from the sight of the towns and villages below. For a few it might be remembered that it was once a place where a relative who has since faded into the mist of time was said to have once spilled his own blood and that of his challenger for forty rounds or more at sunrise on a Sunday morning, and that perhaps the performance of the men was deemed good enough for a bucket to be sent around for 'nobbings' or donations from the spectators to show their appreciation of the victor afterwards. Today little more than a hollow on the mountainside would now be found, forgotten by all and overgrown with weeds and bracken. At the end of the 19th century it would have been a well-known place of ill-repute, where bareknuckle champions of town and village had competed for mountain fighting glory.

Time has not been kind in recording the earliest days of the Welsh prize-ring, and there are no memories of the early days of Welsh boxing that were recorded in writing that could begin to rival those of Jack Scarrott, perhaps the most famous of the fairground boxing booth showmen of his day. Jack Scarrott was approached by William Hughes, a journalist of the South Wales Echo and Express to tell his tale in 1936, when he was sixty six years old. Having been unable to read or write, Jack Scarrott's dictated story was printed shortly afterwards in the form of fourteen serialised weekly instalments, under the title of 'Fifty Years of Boxing in South Wales'.

By this time there were few, if any personalities of the time, that could perhaps even boast of having been present from the earliest days of the boxing careers of so many of the early Welsh fighters, or could recollect central incidents from the last days of the bare-knuckle men known as the 'mountain fighters'. Few had been so centrally placed to be able to tell us of some of the fights, battles, rivalries and achievements of some of the main ring men of these early days. Even more tantalising is the fact that John Scarrott stood amongst the foremost boxing booth showmen of his time, and had a key role in assisting the development of some of the first true gloved boxing champions of Wales, many of whom owed their earliest victories to the schooling and hands on education that they received in 'Scarrott's Pavilion'.

'Showman' is perhaps the key word to understanding the nature of Jack Scarrott's tale. While Jack Scarrott later gravitated more fully to the role of boxing promoter proper, his earliest memories are those of a boxing booth 'showman'. The beginnings of the art of boxing, bare-knuckle fighting, was not for the eyes of the general public in Wales, and began in these secretive patches, the 'bloody' spots and ominously named 'blood hollows' hidden in flat bottomed nooks between mountains or secreted in woody patches where they sought to settle scores, determine potential champions and prepare fighters for championship matches. Here, out of reach of the agents of the law, fist fighting was at first used a means to settle arguments, which had often begun in the depths of the coalmine between colliers, or to determine who might be considered amongst the most skilled fighters in their locality. Knowledge of many of these early 'champions', and the many battles in which they measured their skill and ability are now lost to us. Certainly there were likely to have been local 'champions' of a sort even before the days of William Charles of Newport, who is stated to have been widely known as having been the 'Welsh champion' in the early part of the 19th century.

Even at this time, boxing as an entertainment had featured as an entertainment on the fairground, which is where the majority of the later gloved boxers of South Wales would receive their start in the boxing trade. With the slow adoption of the first true set of modern boxing rules, the Marquis of Queensbury rules, showmen like Jack Scarrott found there was an new angle for money-making which had previously been denied to them by the underground nature of a fighting art that had been shunned as sinful by the church and universally condemned as the 'sport' of the underclass. Most prize fights comprised a brutal, bloody brawl that now failed to find the well-heeled amongst its patrons, even outside the relatively small geographic area of the South Wales valleys. In Wales, as in England, fist fighting had been largely consigned to the pastimes of the working classes, along with other blood 'sports', such as dog fighting, rat killing, and cock fighting.

With the founding of a more widespread series of rules, the working man of South Wales began to witness the growth of 'gloved' boxing as a sport and pastime, and boxing became accessible to a larger section of the population through the boxing booths. By restricting the length of a match to a set number of timed rounds, the likelihood of a match resulting in serious injury or even death was also theoretically reduced, opening the door to the fairground showman as a provider of boxing 'entertainment'. Previously, the organisation of a bare-knuckle fist fight had been something that was organised either behind closed doors, usually by accommodating pub owners in a private back room, or perhaps by those seeking to make their money through backing one fighter against another on the side of a mountain at dawn.

Even before the time of Jack Scarrott, the fairgrounds had proved to be one of the highlights of not only the local area but also the annual calendar, with crowds of spectators having been attracted to see the entertainments on offer from miles around. The mixture of humanity that might be witnessed on the fairground was an assemblage unlikely to be seen anywhere else in day-to-day life, miners rubbed shoulders with town councillors and local officials, travelling people and van owners could

Jack Scarrott in 1936 when relating his life story

be found buying their wares from the cheapjack stalls alongside the townspeople, while those in search of exotic diversions could offer over their coins to watch snake-charmers, strong men and freak shows, and witness the marvels of the bioscope, the forerunner of moving pictures.

It can be imagined that a spectacle as thrilling as a boxing match found eager and willing spectators in a setting such as this, and was usually tolerated by the police, if not the local churchmen who were duty bound to resist the spread of boxing as a legitimate form of entertainment. For many, the fair was one of the few local 'holidays' that might be enjoyed by all, with many of the earlier fairs having first been organised as a means to trade and barter goods from different parts of the country. In time the fairground would move from a necessary vehicle for trade towards something more approaching a 'pleasure' fair, where multiple entertainments jostled for space and tried to get the working man to part with what little money their employment might allow them to spend besides that which had been allocated for their day-to-day needs. Early pioneers of the Welsh fairground boxing ring, such as William Samuels, played an important role in bringing boxing before the general public in the days before there was anything resembling a permanent venue where boxing contests could be held.

This is not to say that William Samuels and Jack Scarrott were the only boxing 'showmen' of note, there were many others, most of which have not been lucky enough to have been remembered perhaps as well as they should. The booths of Charlie North, Felix Scott,

Sullivan, Frank Gess, Taylor and Jack Gage were just a few of the many boxing booths that would tour the South Wales valleys and sometimes even further afield, that have since slid into obscurity. Famously, the very first booth that the British boxing historian will no doubt be familiar with is that of the very first champion, James Figg, whose booth features prominently in the engraving by Hogarth of Southwalk Fair. By Jack Scarrott's time, the booth had changed very little in its basic composition, other than the fact that it had ceased to be an open stage, with entertainment on display for anyone able to crane their neck sufficiently to see above the crowds in front to see. The fairground boxing booths of Scarrott's early days were little more than a canvas tent, often with a small wooden platform in front for the booth owners 'champions' to be paraded, hoping to interest the crowds enough to entice them to part with an entrance fee to enter the tent proper. Here they could witness either an 'exhibition' between champions or a genuine 'contest', although the lines between the two often appears to have been blurred in the event a true battle was being brought off secretly.

There are few recollections of these early days of the boxing booth of any great length and substance recorded in writing, and so to truly understand the days of booths such as Jack Scarrott's, the boxing historian must study the newspapers of the time to try and understand the origins of a sport that have often been overlooked in modern times. For Jack, it is clear that boxing and true showmanship go hand in hand, and his story creates no end of problems in distinguishing fact from fiction, and tall tales from accurate recollections. Tricks to overstate the quality of one minor champion or another intermingle with stories of some of the biggest boxing stars to have emerged from his booth, and arguably in some key instances, a few of the foremost fighters to have come from South Wales at this time.

Despite Jack Scarrott having been name-checked in the records of virtually all the most familiar of Welsh boxing champions to some degree, some having gone on to either national or international acclaim, time has overlooked the story of John ('Jack') Scarrott himself, who has since passed from memory into legend, and then afterwards only recalled in the brief footnotes of the boxing idols who he helped on the path to success. Jim Driscoll and Jimmy Wilde are two champions that are still remembered today by boxing historians and enthusiasts across the globe, but it is fair to say that others have long been forgotten. Who now remembers the powerful punch of Tom Thomas, the first British middleweight champion, who claimed his solid gold Lonsdale belt in 1908? Or Billy Morgan, the Swansea champion, whose list of victories could probably only be rivalled by the number of court appearances for roguish behaviour in his home town? The list of 'back-timers' to have dealt with Jack or have featured in his booth or on those of his rival operators is even greater. Who else but Scarrott would be able to remember intimate details from the lives and careers of such notables as Shoni Engineer, Dai St. John, John O'Brien, Sam Butcher, or recall a local one-time champion fighter of such notorious character as Pete 'Dublin Tom' Burns?

There are even older surprises be found amongst Scarrott's memories, 'Sam Lane' is remembered only as a belligerent challenger, but was more familiar perhaps to some of the bare-knuckle fighters of the time as Bob Dunbar, claimant of the lightweight Welsh crown, and recognised as one of the greatest fighters ever produced in Wales up to his time. Morgan Crowther, who was once a name that appeared in the scandal notes and police court reports of newspapers throughout Britain, and a champion featherweight bare knuckle fighter who had been chased by policemen throughout the land, is also name-checked in Jack Scarrott's memoirs. Even more surprising is the wealth of memories regarding William Samuels, probably the greatest of the forgotten ring-men of South Wales and a flamboyant hero of the earliest remembered days of the Welsh knuckle fighters. Samuels was undoubtedly the most famous Welsh knuckle-fighter and boxing promoter of his generation.

The difficulty for the historian is to separate fact from fiction, and favoured fighters from those that are remembered less kindly. Scarrott is never completely impartial in his judgements. This is mainly because, for Jack, like so many other showmen-promoters, boxing was first his occupation, and afterwards his business. Naturally, he takes a defensive stance against many of the other men to have ventured into what Jack sees as his 'domain', with rival showmen such as Fred Gray and Frank Gess coming in for scant recognition for their services to boxing, whether justified or not.

The birth of boxing in Wales owes massively to the fairground. Even fifty years before Scarrott's earliest days of running a boxing booth, champions were made and defended their crowns on the fairground fields of South Wales, through taking on a continual stream of challenges from the crowd. The experienced boxing booth owner could reap considerable financial reward through the entrance fees paid over by those eager to witness a fighter defend his honour within the booth tent. It appears to have been a common practise for many of the fairground booth men to have served for some time as a boxing booth troupe member before having decided to try his hand at the booth trade himself. In truth, it was often only the booth owner that made the real money, and represented a natural step forwards for the man who had learned the ins and outs of the trade as a booth boxer himself. The mountain fighters themselves were a different breed, hardened by their lives in the dark, with pick and shovel. Frustrated by the hardship of daily life, it was always 'on the mountain' that quarrels were settled. To lose a few teeth, or to potentially suffer a few more facial scars at the hands of a booth boxer in order to put a well-known man down, was payment enough for most and worth the cost in order to be able to say, I defeated the champion of the boxing booth.

Sifting through a disordered series of memories covering a lifetime spent on and around the fairgrounds of South Wales is no easy task, and one that is complicated by the lack of comprehensive coverage of Welsh boxing at this time in the Welsh newspapers. Unfortunately the newspapers of this period would take a fairly hard stance against boxing having been a legitimate sport, and so what few reports exist often leave a fragmented understanding of the world of Jack Scarrott and his peers.

The lack of media coverage in the Welsh newspapers is mainly due to the fact that, particularly in the early days of knuckle-fighting as opposed to boxing, there was little support for a 'sport' that had grown out of an illegal prize-fighting scene conducted by hard-nosed men in secretive lonely spots in defiance of the local authorities. As such, any form of combat, even when public interest had moved on from actual prize-fighting to gloved boxing, had come to represent one of the most sinful forms of recreation for the majority of newspaper editors. Many of these men found their sensibilities enforced by the chapel-going local government representatives – with many of the leading lights in moral matters also having had a business interest or investment in the newspapers themselves. Quite often key fights only appear to have been reported in the newspapers in the event of a scandal or a tragedy, such as a death within a makeshift ring, or at one of the many 'bloody spots' or 'hollows' in the hills above the South Wales coalfields.

Despite having often been a few years out of date with his recollections, it is astonishing testimony to Jack Scarrott's personal memory that his story is confirmed by what limited newspaper coverage exists. It is also something of a tribute to the foresightedness of William Hughes, the journalist who recorded Jack Scarrott's story for prosperity. It is true to say, that without the roadmap more or less afforded by the recollections of Jack Scarrott we would know very little of the early ring-men of Scarrott's time today. By printing the whole and complete serialised memoirs of Jack Scarrott, it is hoped that the commentary that follows, based on further research, will help provide a more complete view of the remarkable story of Jack Scarrott, a self-made entrepreneur, who brought many Welsh boxing champions to prominence. He surely deserves to be remembered as a great showman, boxing pioneer and storyteller over half a century after his death.

Fifty Years of Boxing in South Wales
Memoirs of a Welsh Boxing Booth Showman

Part 1

Fifty years I've been in the game, mister, and all that time I've been right here in the mining valleys. I know every town and village in South Wales, and I knew every boxer worth calling a fighting man they ever turned out. Dai St. John, Tom Thomas, Jim Driscoll, Freddy Welsh, Johnny Basham, Jimmy Wilde, Percy Jones, and many more that were before their time. I knew them all, and a good few started with me in my booth. I was scrapping for a living in a boxing booth before I started a booth on my own, and I was only about twenty one when I started on my own. Believe me, the life of a booth boxer in those days was tough. Mountain fighters! That's what they called the miners who used to fight bare-knuckle on the mountains. To tell you the truth, mister, we booth boxers were afraid of them.

The pubs were very small places with very rough crowds

They used to come to the fairgrounds from the collieries with their gangs with them, most of 'em half drunk, and the very sight of them was enough to freeze the heart out of a bull terrier. Broken noses, black eyes, cauliflower ears, lumps knocked off 'em. If they heard that there was a well-known champion in a boxing booth at a particular fair they'd walk fifty miles to have a go at him. And they'd bring their crowd with them. Often the whole crowd would turn up half drunk, and I've known them to try and break into the caravans. They were out to lick us booth boxers. Very often when you were boxing one of them and you were backing before his punches, watching out for a chance to get in the k.o., you'd get a punch from behind from one of his pals. The difference between the fairgrounds in South Wales today and what they were fifty years ago – it's like being in another world. Education and the churches and chapels have done that.

You might not believe it, but about the roughest place in the valleys in those days was Ferndale. Treorchy, Tonypandy and Bargoed were almost as bad. I remember a riot in my booth at Ferndale 48 or 47 years ago. It was only over a shilling which somebody put in the cap when we made a collection for an old mountain fighter and which somebody else took out, but before you could say Jack Robinson everybody was fighting through and through, and my booth was on the floor. Men were hitting other men and not knowing who they were hitting or why. Two mountain fighters started it, and the crowd had nicknames for both of them. One they called Shoni Engineer – his real name was John Jones – and the other Dai Brawd. Shoni Engineer became a famous fighter, and I'll have a lot to tell you about him. Anyway, Dai Brawd hit one of the booth men, and when Shoni Engineer asked him in Welsh what he was doing, he said he'd do the same to Shoni, and that started it.

The pubs at this time were very small places with very rough crowds. There were more Bristol men than Welshmen in some parts of the Rhondda at this time, and there was many scraps between them. Fifty-two years ago there was a terrible fight in the Mardy Hotel between a Bristol gang and a Welsh gang. It was on Christmas Eve, and I remember looking in and seeing them fighting all over the pub and out in the backyard. Four or five of the worst were taken on a milk float to Ferndale with policemen on top of them holding them down. Talking about the rough 'uns fighting in the pubs, old Mr. Trehearne of the Butchers' Arms in Pontypridd had a wonderful way of handling 'em. He was a great character, he was. All the ruffians from Pontypridd and the valleys used to gather at the Butchers' Arms on Saturdays and particularly on Mabon's Day – that was the Monday's holiday once a month which 'Mabon' got for the miners and which they named after him.

Mr. Trehearne had his own way of dealing with them. Fights used to take place in the big bar, but Mr. Trehearne always took it very calm. When a fight started he'd come into the bar from another part of the house and ask, 'What's going on here!" "So-and-So and So-and-So are goin' to have a fight." "Right," Mr. Trehearne would say, "Lock the doors, draw the blinds, and put everything out of the way. Now get on with it." He used to let 'em go on for three or four rounds until one of them showed signs that he'd had enough, and then he'd

The Butchers Arms on right near the horse drawn cabs

stop it and say, "Now open the doors and get on with your drinks, boys."

There was a rough crowd in Pontypridd on Mabon's Day. It was on one of those days that a policeman was kicked to death on the steps of a pub by the station. People talk about boxing today being a brutal sport. They don't know nothing at all about it. They ought to see some of the bare-knuckle fights I saw when I was a boy. The very first fight I ever saw was about sixty years ago, when I was a very small boy – I'm now sixty nine. When I was going on an errand for my mother near a place called Black Pill, on the Mumbles road, I saw a crowd of gypsies, and I heard there was going to be a fight between a gypsy named Jack Hearn and a man named Martin Fury. The gypsy women, who were afraid of trouble, were asking for somebody to go for the police to stop the fight, but the gypsy men wanted the fight to go on.

Well, they stripped and got at it. Hearn was a very fine man, about 15 stone in weight, about 5ft. 10in. in height, and all strength and ruggedness from head to foot, while Fury was only about 11st. 6lb. None of the gypsies could believe that Hearn could be beaten, for he had licked all the gypsy fighters that came his way, and those gypsies in those days didn't fight for money, for there was nobody about to offer them purses, but just for the love of fighting.

But this Fury turned out to be a very fast fighter and clever. He kept on ducking and dodging in and out, and playing on Hearn's face, until it was dreadfully swollen and battered. They must have fought for an hour and a half, but how many rounds I don't know, for a round

*Martin Fury beat Jack Hearn so badly
that he blinded him in both eyes*

lasted until a man went down, but Fury beat him up in the face so bad that he blinded him in both eyes. The gypsy women were now shouting to go for the police, and the fight was stopped, but a gypsy shouted, "We will lance his eyes and get him to see, and he can fight again." They did it, and the fight went on, but Hearn was blinded again, and the man could fight no more. Five minutes after the fight the police came, and an old gypsy woman said to them, "My dear men, you're too late."

And they talk about boxing as they carry it on today being brutal! I remember a worse bare-knuckle fight than that in a field off the road between Whitland and Carmarthen between William Samuels – he was a Swansea man and a famous boxer and showman – and a man named Sam Lane. I'm going to tell you about this fight, and also about the time Samuels caused a riot at the Irish fete at the Sophia Gardens, Cardiff.

Part 2

The most remarkable bare knuckle fight I ever saw was fought sixty years ago in a field off the road between Whitland and Camarthen between two rival boxing booth proprietors, William Samuels, the famous Welsh champion, and a man from Scotland named Sam Lane. Samuels knocked out Lane until everybody thought he was dead, but after Lane came round the fight was re-started. Samuels being willing, and Lane blinded Samuels.

William Samuels, who was born in Swansea, was a great fighter and a great showman. In fact, I think he may have been the greatest fighter of his time in the whole of the country. Though not over-big – he was about 5ft 9 inches in height and weighed between 12 stone and 13 stone (*168-182 lbs*) – he had a wonderful muscular development and was tremendously strong. He was a weight lifter and an acrobat as well as a boxer, and his wife used to give exhibitions of weight-lifting, such as lifting two 56lb. weights up by her hair. Another of her feats was to allow her husband to break large stones which were placed on her chest with a sledge-hammer.

William Samuels boxed against the great John L. Sullivan at the old Philharmonic Music Hall in Cardiff and he fought Tom Vincent of Plymouth, the West of England champion, when he was 65 years of age, and I think he made a draw of it. Samuels was very jealous of any rival boxing booth proprietors that came on his ground, and when there was any clash he always wanted to fight. He and Sam Lane had been clashing several

William Samuels, Heavyweight Champion of Wales

times before they had it out in this fight off the Whitland – Camarthen road. There was a number of showmen on the spot, and I was there as a boy. I remember hearing John Studt and his brothers Henry and Jacob – they were famous showmen – talking about the fight. John Studt said to Henry Studt, "This man will be too clever for Samuels." But Henry said, "Samuels will be too strong for him."

For dangerous punching Samuels was the greatest fighter I ever saw. He was never known to hit a man out with a punch on the jaw. It was always the pit of the stomach he went for, and that stomach punch of his put paid to everybody it landed on. When the fight between Samuels and Lane started, Sam Lane, who was taller and had a longer reach, tried to box in and out, but Samuels forced his way in to close quarters and landed his stomach punch with such terrible force that Lane fell down dead out. They sent for brandy and rubbed him, but out he remained till everybody thought he was dead. Samuels himself attended to him and did his best to bring him round.

At last they brought him round, and everybody thought that the fight was over, but Lane said, "Samuels, you were a lucky man to land that punch but I don't think you can do it again." He repeated this several times to a large crowd of showmen and other people who had collected there, and Samuels said "If you're not satisfied you can have another go." So they stripped and got at it again, and this time they must have fought twenty five or twenty six rounds. Lane was boxing at long range and hitting for the face, while Samuels was trying to land with his favourite solar-plexus punch.

They kept at it, smacking in punch after punch until they'd fought pretty near all over the field. But men can be blinded in bare knuckle fights by playing for the face, like Martin Fury blinded the gypsy Jack Hearn and as Tom Sayers blinded Heenan, "the Benicia Boy" – I've been to Farnborough where they fought. Well, that's what happened to Samuels. We could see that Lane was gradually blinding him, and it was a question whether Samuels could get that stomach punch in again before he went completely, but he failed to land it. He fought on until he couldn't see at all, and the crowd shouted "Shame" and "Stop it." But Samuels was still strong, and he was all pluck from head to heel. He said, "Lance both my eyes." They did so, let out a lot of blood, until they got him that he could see again, and they went on fighting until he was again blinded.

But it was Samuels who won in the long run. He said to Lane "You've licked me this time, for I can't see, but I'll fight you again in a month's time for £50 a side." They fought again several times, though nothing like as savage as the first fight, but Samuels kept on challenging Sam Lane until he drove him clean off his pitch. When I was a boy there was a bit of a riot in Bill Samuel's booth at Abercwmboi. It was 3d. to go in, and I had only a penny, but I got in under the canvas. A man named Dai Magee from Aberdare told Samuels, after he'd put a man out in the third round, that he could not do that to him. "Step up," says Samuels, and with his usual punch in the wind he put this Dai Magee out in quicker time than the other – about a round.

The large crowd started hooting and booing Samuels, but he faced 'em like a lion. He told them he didn't care for all of them and that he'd lick the three best men in the county of Glamorgan. There was a match made for Samuels to fight a man called Ivor Gwynn, of Pontylottyn, for £5 a side with bare knuckles, and the fight was held on the Deri Mountain near Fochriw. Samuels had not a single supporter in the crowd, but he not only seconded himself but rested Ivor Gwynn on his own knee between the rounds. It was a minute rest after each knockdown. Samuels knocked him out in eight or ten rounds. To show you the temper of the crowds on the Welsh fairgrounds in those days I'll tell you what happened to a man named Fred Gray, a Londoner at the Treorchy Fair. This was about the greatest fair in Wales, and shows from all parts of England used to visit it. There'd be boxing, weight-lifting, lady dancers, and all sorts of entertainments. The man who had the letting of the places on the fairground was Mr. John Studt, and he was only supposed to let one boxing booth come there, but we found out there were three.

There was old William Samuels, a man named Harry Stokes, and this Fred Gray. Gray, who called himself a champion, used to give displays of swordsmanship and exhibitions of boxing with his wife. Boxing with his wife might have gone done all right with the crowd in the place where he came from, but the Welsh crowd wouldn't have it. "Never mind about boxing with a woman" they shouted, "we've got plenty of men in the Treorchy for you to box with."

Gray smelt trouble. He was afraid of the crowd and he wouldn't meet the mountain fighters. So he came to an agreement with Harry Stokes, who was a clever boxer, to have the loan of his booth boxers, and I was one of them. We had to do the job properly and take on all comers, and Gray, Stokes and Samuels made a good profit out of that fair.

Part 3

When the famous English boxer, Jem Smith, came to Cardiff, William Samuels was there to challenge him. "Who is this man who is offering money to anyone who can stand up against him?" says Samuels. "Who are you?" asks Jem Smith. "I am William Samuels, the champion of Wales, and I'm here to have a go at you."

Smith had with him a pupil of his called "Toff" Wall, and Smith said to Samuels, very sarcastic and haughty like, "My man, I'll have nothing to do with you. I have a novice who will be here tomorrow night and he'll fight you. If you'll stand six rounds in front of "Toff" Wall I'll give you £10 and a gold watch. The match was made, and it was the talk of Cardiff. Smith and his men were appearing for a week at the old Panopticon Music-Hall. The cheapest seat for the fight cost two shillings, but the place was packed to suffocation. All the crowd were in favour of Wall and the excitement was terrific. Samuels for once had the worst of it. He immediately rushed to close quarters, but Wall would not join in a mix-up and he boxed in a very tricky way. Twice he ducked under Samuels when Samuels was rushing at him and lifted him clean up so that he tamped on the boards like a football. In the fourth round he knocked Samuels over the ropes and into the band. Then Samuels' wife went half off her head because Samuels was getting the worst of it, and all the crowd were shouting for Wall. She started hitting out right and left at the men around her. There was a tremendous uproar and a number of police rushed in and stopped the fight.

Jem Smith, English Heavyweight Champion

Before this happened Jem Smith had fought 106 rounds in France with Jake Kilrain. Soon after his fight with "Toff" Wall, Samuels' took his booth to the Hibernian fete and gala, at the Sophia Gardens, Cardiff. A large Cardiff gang got around him and started leering at him about his fight with "Toff" Wall. Samuels wasn't the man to stand for that sort of thing, and he shouted to them from the front of his booth that he'd fight any three men they'd got in Cardiff. They kept on shouting abuse at him until he got so mad that he jumped down amongst them and dropped a few of them, giving them one punch apiece.

Then he got back on the booth and made them an amazing offer. He shouted out, "Where is the six best men you've got in Cardiff?" and offered to stop the six best men they could put forward in 20 minutes or forfeit £10. Six men volunteered to have a go – I forget their names – and Samuels put down his £10. The people crowded into the booth until it was pretty nearly crushed to the ground. Samuels charged a shilling for admission, while the other booths were only charging two pence. But the crowd were only too glad to pay the shilling, and there was no room for all of them inside the booth. One of the men who came forward was a great favourite with the Cardiff crowd – I can't remember his name – but he went the same way as the rest of 'em. How long do you think it took Bill Samuels to lay the six out? He got to work with the usual punch to the stomach, and he had the whole half dozen out in 12 minutes.

When he was past his prime I saw a great fight between him and a famous Rhondda boxer called "Shoni Engineer" whose real name was John Jones and who came from Treorchy. It was at Neath fair, and I think it would be 48 years ago come next September. This was a huge annual pleasure fair and all the prominent showmen of England and Wales used to make their way there. Samuels had his booth there, and there was another booth there owned by a man called Jimmy Day, of Plymouth. Samuels had a number of Welsh fighting men with him, and Day had Shoni Engineer, Sam Butcher, Bill Lane, of Cwmavon, and myself. Samuels started to tell us how quick he could lick the lot of us, and kept on challenging us day after day, for this fair lasted pretty nearly a week. Now I'm sure that Shoni Engineer was at that time the level best 10 stone 10 lb. man in England, and he had been sparring a lot with Samuels. So I said to him, "Look here, you're much the younger man, you've boxed with him so often that you know his style, and I feel sure you could lick him in ten rounds."

Shoni Engineer took up Samuels's challenge, and they were matched for £25 aside over ten rounds. Both were famous fighters, and we soon found that we'd have such a crowd that no boxing booth would hold half of them. So we arranged with a circus proprietor named John Scott to have the fight in his circus. We charged half a crown for admission and had a big crowd. A showman named Lloyd Roberts and a Liverpool boxer called Fitzpatrick seconded Samuels, and in Shoni Engineers corner were Sam Butcher, Bill Lane, Jimmy Day and myself assisting. I said to Shoni, "Box him at long distance and look out for that right hand stomach punch." After a delay because Samuels wanted three minute rounds while we wanted two's, they got at it and fought a wonderful fight which ended in a draw. In Samuels's time there were a number of fighting men in Cardiff. There was Pete Burns – him that they called "Dublin" Tom – and Jack Northey, but the greatest man up to that time was John O'Brien, who was the nearest man to the champion of the world among the middleweights.

I'll tell you about O'Brien's fights against Shoni Engineer, Dai St. John, Alf Ball, Felix Scott the negro, Dublin Tom's fight against Shoni Engineer, and Shoni's fight against Tom "Books" at Treherbert, which was stopped when the police arrested the whole lot of them. The police also arrested a good few when they stopped the fight between Shoni and Guiderell, of Bristol, at Patchway, in Gloucestershire, and I'll have something to tell you about that, for I was there.

Part 4

When John O'Brien, the best man Cardiff had produced up to his time, knocked out the old showman and boxing booth proprietor Lloyd Roberts, Cardiff people started to take notice of him and he was matched against Shoni Engineer for £100 aside. They fought at Heol-y-cyw near Bridgend and O'Brien put Shoni Engineer out in six rounds. O'Brien became middle-weight champion of England and beat a wonderful lot of men. He was matched to fight Frank Craig, the "Coffee Cooler" for the middle-weight championship of the world, but the Coffee Cooler was taken ill with sciatica and the fight was called off.

O'Brien put out Alf Ball in four rounds at the National Sporting Club when they were matched for £500 aside and the purse, but Felix Scott, a negro, put O'Brien out in three rounds. Then O'Brien and Shoni Engineer toured South Wales with a boxing booth, and they came to the annual Neath fair, which is over a hundred years old, and in the old days always drew a very large crowd. In front of our booth was John O'Brien, Shoni Engineer, Bill Lane, the Cwmaman mountain fighter, and myself. Who should come up but old Dai St. John bringing a big and very rowdy crowd with him. Dai chucks out a challenge to O'Brien, and as O'Brien had been hard at work on the booth all day, Dai St. John made him look flat and practically put him out, but later on O'Brien beat him when they met at the N.S.C. O'Brien had been in the army, and Dai St. John was on the reserve of the Grenadier Guards. Dai was a fine built young man, about 15 stone in weight and standing six

John O'Brien, Welsh Middleweight Champion

feet in height. He came from Resolven. Dai was killed in the South African war, and I think it was at the Battle of Belmont. We were told he killed half a dozen Boers with the bayonet and was just throwing another over his shoulder on the point of his bayonet when he was shot through the head.

Tom Burns ("Dublin Tom") another Cardiff boxer, and Shoni Engineer were matched to fight for £100 aside at Heol-y-cyw, the same place that Shoni and O'Brien fought about fifty two years ago. The fight was for the championship of Wales, and both men were put into first-class condition and smuggled away easily, for in those days we had to look out for the police. It was a bare knuckle fight, and they fought with spikes in their shoes because it was such a cold and frosty morning, Shoni won on a knockout in the sixteenth round. It was owing to me that Shoni Engineer and Tom "Books" fought at Treherbert, although I was only a youngster at the time. Tom "Books'" real name was Tom Davies, but they called him Tom Books because his father kept a bookseller's shop at Pentre. I came across old Lloyd Roberts, who said he was up against it because he wanted to float a fight between Shoni Engineer and Tom Books at Treherbert and was short of £5 to build a boxing booth.

Lloyd Roberts wasn't much of a showman then, but he had swing boats, Aunt Sally's and coconut shies. I was a boy talking to a man, but I got him out of the hole. I said "You've got a van worth £30 and there's a timber merchant at Ystrad who'll give you £5 worth of timber if you leave him the van as security." Lloyd Roberts did so and the booth was built opposite the Treherbert police

Dai. St. John – The Resolven Giant

station. Lloyd Roberts asked me to lend a hand to look after the booth and I was delighted with the job. The fight was to be over twenty rounds under the Marquis of Queensbury rules. The crowd was rowdy, and I saw there was a very large number of people there. There were a lot of chapel people there, preachers and deacons. This was I think, the first boxing match to be held at Treherbert, and the chapel people were all dead against what they called a brutal exhibition and they were asking where the law was and why didn't the police stop it.

The police did stop it after they had fought six or seven rounds, hammering away like blacksmiths. In about the eighth round Tom Books put his foot in it. He walks out of his corner, drops the boxing glove off his right hand – and gives Shoni a terrific smash right on the jaw with the naked fist. That done it! Bare fist fighting was against the law, and the police jumped into the ring and stopped the fight. They arrested the fighters, the seconds, the timekeeper, the referee, and everybody else they could think of who had anything to do with the fight. They were all fined very heavy, and it gave boxing a very bad name, it being the talk of the Rhondda and South Wales, but some of the rebels in the Rhondda still kept on mountain fighting.

Tom Books settled in Resolven and became an official at a colliery and the deacon of a chapel, but poor Shoni Engineer came to a bad end. He got into some street fight in Cardiff and was knocked down. His head struck against the kerbstone and he died. The police also stopped Shoni Engineer's fight with Guidrell, of Bristol, the West of England Champion, when they met at Patchway, Gloucestershire. The fight should have been held a few days before on the Cardiff moors, but the police interfered. There were thousands of Bristol men at this fight in Gloucestershire and hardly any Welshmen. These Bristol chaps were about the toughest crowd I've ever seen. They'd have murdered us men from Wales if they'd only been able to pick us out in the crowd. There was myself, Sam Butcher, "Jockey" Saunders, Sam Hughes, and I think, Sam Wiltshire, of Cardiff, with Shoni Engineer. Shoni put Guidrell out several times but the Bristol crowd wouldn't allow that the fight had been won. They just kept Shoni waiting while they got Guidrell round and then re-started the fight. Their idea was Guidrell just had to win and they didn't care anything about rules.

We were glad when the police came and stopped it and glad to get from there. The police arrested the boxers and others, and I was told that when the case came on at Gloucester the jury disagreed the first time, and the second jury said "Not guilty." The old farmer who owned the field where the fight was, caused a lot of fun at the assizes by saying he didn't mind 'em trespassing because he enjoyed the fight so much.

Part 5

I've seen a very famous champion – I think he was a world champion – knocked out with a pop bottle by one of his own friends. But he was a champion walker, not a fighting man. It was about the year of the Diamond Jubilee and big sports were held at Llwynypia in the Rhondda in one of the hottest summers I've ever known. There was pony racing, foot racing and walking matches. An old showman and boxing booth proprietor named Charlie North entered for the walking match. He was an Irishman and he came on the track wearing green stockings and with two boxing gloves tied to his belt as mascots. I don't know whether there's anything in this mascot idea, but old Charlie North – I knew him well – was most remarkable lucky that day. This famous walker – I forget his name but I'm almost certain he was a world's champion, was competing and they handicapped him something terrible. The match was over two and a half miles walking round the field, and old Charlie North, who was over 50, had pretty near a mile start. Others had half a mile and there were professionals who had about a quarter of a mile.

This champion had a heart-breaking job but off he went at a terrific rate under a sun hot enough to broil him, and the crowd was very excited, wondering if he could do it. In the last half mile this man had passed 'em all except old Charlie North, and by and by Charlie gave in and flopped down by the side of the track, green stockings, boxing gloves, and all, puffin' and blowin' like a grampus. On comes this champion, but he was that done in that he was totterin' and lurchin' along, staggerin' from one side of the track to the other, and only half in his proper senses. Seeing the state the poor man was in one of his friends rushed to a stall where they sold lemonade, got a bottle, stuck the marble in, and ran on to the track to spray lemonade over this champion to bring him round. He swung the bottle over his head to spray him and – believe me or believe me not, mister – the bottle flew out of his hand, hit the champion on the head, and in the state he was in it knocked him dead out. Seein' this, old Charlie North picked 'isself up and staggered on to win the race.

There is an art to being a showman, and sometimes we put some pretty smart fakes across the public. I'll tell you how I put on my booth an enormous big Negro as "The Wild Man" and a little chap from Maesycwmmer that I painted up yellow as "The Japanese Strangler". I met this Negro when my caravan was on the way from Tonyrefail to Gilfach Goch. The road was bad and I got him to help the horses to pull the caravan along. He couldn't speak a word of English and couldn't make me understand what his name was or where he come from, but I think he'd come on a boat from somewhere to Cardiff and lost the boat. At Gilfach Goch I put him behind the booth to keep the boys from coming under the canvas, and he were big enough and ugly enough to scare away a troop of monkeys, let alone boys.

We kept him with us for a few days, and then I saw that he was having a good look at the scraps on the booth. One day I made him understand that I'd like to see him try a bit of boxing and I got the gloves on him. He didn't know a boxing glove from a turnip, but he was tremendously strong and dangerous, and I said "You're

WORLD'S FAIR. BOXING SALOON

Conducted by the old veteran Prof. Charles North, Jack Engineer (Champion of Wales), Peter Burns (better known as Dublin Tom), Robert Wilkshire (light weight champion), James Day (9st. 6lb. champion of Plymouth), Sam Hughes, Cardiff (late of Birmingham), and a host of others will appear.

Charles North Boxing Saloon Advert, 1889

the man for the job." I said to the missus, "This man is a champion. He can beat all the Welshmen that come along." She said "Get rid of him before he murders us in our beds or gets us killed by the crowd on account of him." I said "Woman, there's a fortune in him." It was at Pontycymmer I showed him on the booth first, and I'll tell you how I did it. I hung up a great big bone from the carcass of a horse in front of the booth, and then I fetched out the Negro. He looked uncommonly ferocious. In fact he was the ugliest featured man I've ever seen in my life. And this is what I said to the crowd, and they were looking at him with their eyes and mouths wide open.

"You see this black man? He's an uncivilised savage, a wild man. He can't speak English and can't tell us what his name is or where he comes from, but we call him 'Dangerous Jack.' Any man who likes to box him takes him on at his own peril. He's dangerous. We don't let him ramble about the streets. When his turn is over he's put behind bars like he was a lion in a menagerie. Like a lion or a tiger he won't eat civilised food. It's no good offering him tea and buns. Raw meat is the only food he'll eat, and he prefers horseflesh. You see that bone? He's just gnawed eight or ten pounds of raw horseflesh off that for his dinner. We'll do our best to see fairplay, but I warn you that as soon as you put 'em up in front of him he'll be for you like a mad bull, and he knows no rules or regulations."

But these Welsh mountain fighters weren't easily scared, and in a good many places we showed at they took him on. They did their best to put him down but he kept hitting and slashing away at them in a style of his own, and he put six so-called champions out in one week. I remember when I was showing at Monkey Island, Caerau, they fetched a Welsh miner they called "Dai Rush" from the Caerau Colliery to lick Dangerous Jack. Dai said "Myn uffern i, I can beat all the ------- black men that ever came from the wilds of Africa," and Jack just looked across the ring at him. Dai Rush set about him until at first there was only one man in it, but by and by Jack gets home with some of his slaughtering wallops and out goes Dai. A Porth chap they called Tom Scadan, a nice fellow and a good boxer, thought Jack was an easy job, but Jack put him out with one right-hand swing.

I had Dangerous Jack for about a year, and then he found a ship and went back to his own country. On the road between Crumlin and Pontypridd we picked up a young fellow who was very small, but had extraordinary muscles. He made friends with the boxers I had on my booth, and he followed us to the Pontypridd fairground. We kept him as an amusement for the crowd, for he could sing and dance and play the mouth organ. This jiu-jitsu was being talked about a lot and I got a bright idea. He looked something like a Jap, so we painted him yellow, shaved off his hair except for one lock on the top of his head, and put him on as Yuko Sako, from Yokohama, the Japanese strangler. He used to pretend to write things in Japanese on bits of papers and chuck them to the crowd, but they were just scribbles and scrawls that all the Japanese in creation wouldn't have made anything out of. After taking a lot of tankins at the start he became a good boxer, so good that we were offering a pound to any man of about his size that could stand him for three rounds. At Porth he laid a man named Mog Wilde of Trebanog, dead out after swopping a few punches, and when Wilde's brother said, "If you've put my brother out you can't do it to me," Sako put him out as well. Sako became a great draw, but he got that cheeky that there was no living with him and we had to sack him. He wouldn't do what he was told for anybody.

Part 6

The first time I started a boxing booth on my own – it was at Robertstown, Ynysybwl – I got into hot water with some gypsy women. The champion fighters of the Ynysybwl neighbourhood at that time were two chaps named Ianto Cwmavon and Twm Parry. Some young gypsy fellows came along on the first night and asked for the governor, and I let them have a go on the stage. I don't think they understood what kind of scrappin' there was waiting for 'em and they took terrible tankins from the mountain fighters. They got black eyes, swollen lips, and so on, but when I gave 'em eighteen pence apiece they seemed quite satisfied. This was on a Saturday night and next morning, walking down from Ynysybwl to Pontypridd I passed the gypsy encampment that these lads belonged to. The lads said, 'There's the man of the boxing booth," and an old gypsy lady gave me such a dressing down for letting these boys get knocked down.

After all, I only let 'em have a go at what I'd been doing myself as a youngster, and I was not much more when I started my own booth, which I made in the Mill Field, Pontypridd. Why, mister, I remember being on a booth at Brecon Fair, when every boxer on the stage was beaten to a standstill and we had to close down, and I was the youngest of them. There was on that booth besides myself Harry Stokes, Jack Eynon, Tug Wilson, of Leicester, and Bob Griffin of Birmingham. They were all useful, but the crowd fairly knocked us to pieces, and I had the worst hiding of the lot. A tremendous number of big, strong, rugged fellows came at us one after the other – farm labourers, miners, steel workers, and I don't know

Joe Collins (Leicester), better known as 'Tug Wilson'

what else – and by four o'clock we had to shut down the show. But the crowd didn't get it all their own way as a rule, and I remember once some gypsies, who had made up their minds to half-kill us catching a very bad cold, and it was through me that they got it.

It was at Abergavenny Races, and it goes back the best part of fifty years. It was an open race course for showman and gypsies of all kinds, and there were fighting men there in galore. There were drinking saloons there too, and there were many desperate fights there the day before the races. Old Charlie North and John Stokes were there with their booths, and I was boxing for Stokes. After knocking around the race course for a bit to find out what the crowd was like, I went and had a very serious talk with Stokes. "About the roughest and most dangerous lot I've ever struck," said I, "and you'll have to get bigger men than you've got now to meet 'em. We'll stand a bad chance against these gypsies and big, strong, rugged fellows".

"There are gangs of gypsies all talking about what they're going to do to us at the booths. There are chaps here who don't know their own strength, and we'll have to get bigger and better men than we've got to beat 'em. And I've got in my mind the very men we want, the brothers Butcher of Talywain."

The two men I was speaking to Stokes about were Arthur Butcher, Talywain, who had done some time in the police, and his brother, William, who'd been in the army. They were both fine men, six feet or more, and weighing about 14 stone.

Stokes said "How will we get them?" and I said, "I'll fetch them tonight." So I walked ten miles to Talywain and told the Butchers all about it. I explained to them that a lot of the worst blackguards and some of the most savage fighters in the country would be all out to wipe the floor with us booth boxers the next day. "When they come targetin' against us, we want you two to be there to take 'em on," says I. Mister, they were as delighted as if I had come to invite them to a feast. They promised they'd stand in front of the booth for one day, and they put me up for the night. We landed at the races next morning about ten o'clock. The first races started at twelve, and we tried to get the crowd to come to the boxing booth in the interval between the races. The gypsies were waiting in gangs for the booths to open, and there were some big 'uns among them. There were six of us on the booth and one or two were dummies, show hands put up to make a show but didn't know much about boxing.

Stokes was a very clever boxer, but I said to him, "You must remember you're only a small man and I'm not very big myself. We must put the brothers Butcher against the gypsies."

Stokes then shouts out to the gypsies: "Here are two men, the brothers Butcher, who can beat any of you. A pound to any man who can stand Arthur Butcher for four rounds." A gypsy named Sam Price shouted back, "Keep your money, I don't want it. I'll fight him for nothing." Gangs pushed into the boxing booth to see this fight, and almost straight after the start Butcher hit him not only over the ropes, but clean out of the tent, and there was a very big hole in the canvas where the gypsy went through. Back he comes to finish the fight, and he and Arthur Butcher fought toe-to-toe with their arms going like piston rods, with the gypsies waving their sticks and hooraying their man like as if they'd gone mad.

They were using awful language and hurling threats at us, and I told 'em to keep better order. As the fight went on we saw that the gypsy was very strong at close quarters, swinging in wicked punches from all angles and we advised Butcher to stand off and box him. Butcher did so and got in a blow in the stomach which steadied him a lot. I said to Butcher, "Just hit him once again in the same place," and in the fourth round Butcher did so and put paid to him. The gypsy was carried out to a gypsy encampment on the race ground and he was not properly right till the next day. We didn't have such a great lot of trouble with them after that.

Part 7

Jim Driscoll was one of the cleverest boxers the ring has ever known, and he was a very nice boy, but I saw him lose his temper once. I had my booth at Treorchy, and I had boxing for me Jim Driscoll, Boyo Driscoll, George Dixon, Tom Thomas, a boy named Burke and a Swansea boy named Darkie Thomas. But there was a rival boxing booth alongside of us, run by men from the North of England. We were not interfering with them, but they were interfering with us. They were saying I didn't know anything about running a boxing booth, and how they could lick all my men. At last they got Jim Driscoll so wild that he made one spring off our booth and on to theirs. And when he got there he didn't pick and choose – he just let go at whichever of them happened to be nearest. Then there was some strong showman's language used, and they started hollerin' to me to get Jim back, but I told 'em they should behave themselves and make sure they knew what they were talking about.

We got Jim away after he'd left his mark on a couple of 'em and that night their booth was empty, while we had a tremendous crowd to see a fight between Lewsin Roderick, the old Blaenrhondda mountain fighter, and Gunner Griffiths of Ystrad. I first met Jim at a boxing show in the Vanguard Yard at Merthyr, where there was a fight between Dave Peters, who was middle-weight champion of Wales, and Jack Palmer of Newcastle. Driscoll was then quite a youngster. He was fighting somebody – I forget whom – but I remember Driscoll was all over him until he broke his wrist and had to

Jim Driscoll (Cardiff), British Featherweight Champion

chuck it. I went to talk to him and he told me what hard luck it was that he'd broken his wrist and he told me that he'd come from Cardiff. Next time I saw him was in Cardiff boxing for some charity, and he agreed at once to box on the booth for me. I could see he'd improved a lot. There was a couple of very useful boys at Pricetown in the Ogmore Valley, which was the first place he boxed for me, but when I put 'em in front of Driscoll they found they didn't know the way to box.

He fought Harry Mansfield, of Bristol, a real good 'un, who was on the booths with me for a long time, and Mansfield beat him, but when they were matched again Jim licked him. Everybody knows about Jim's big fights, but I'll tell you one or two things that only I know about him, and they'll show what a wonderful sportsman and good-hearted little chap he was. There was a charity show at Ystrad for a man who had met with an accident in the pit and lost his wife as well, so he had nobody to look after the children. It was a terribly sad case. Jim was by this time well up the ladder and a famous man, but when they told him about it he turned up and boxed three men that night, and three good 'uns at that. Because he turned up we took £75 at the gates, Driscoll was told so and he was asked what his change was. What do you think he said? He told 'em he had come to help this family, not to make money, and he put his hand in his pocket and gave them five guineas. That was the kind of man he was.

They gave him a wonderful send off, and they sent him some little present as a kind of a memento and to make him understand how much they appreciated his kindness. Driscoll did a lot of his early boxing with me, and when he became famous he didn't forget me. That wouldn't be Jim's way. After he'd had his great fight with Joe Bowker at the National Sporting Club – he beat Bowker in 18 rounds – he turned up to appear for me at Porth on the following night. He fought Bowker on the Monday, and when I told the crowd he'd be on my platform on the Tuesday night they wouldn't believe it. But there he was right enough, and you should see the applause the Rhondda boys gave him. At that time he used to do his own business. He had practically no manager, and whenever I wanted him he'd be there. The public thought the world of him, and I've known him to take more roughing from men twice his size on the booth than I'd have thought any boxer could stand. When we were showing on the Salisbury ground, Ferndale, a big slingy chap from Blaenllechau came along and gave us a lot of trouble. He'd been doing a lot of fighting on the streets and in public houses, and had been giving the police some trouble. Perhaps I'd better not mention his name.

Night after night he'd come to the booth and give us a lot of buck, saying he'd never seen a good 'un on a booth yet. I told him we were there to give a boxing entertainment, and not fight with the public in a quarrelsome way, but he wouldn't keep quiet. I had Jim with me at the time and Jim said, "I'll see to him." I said "Be careful. He's very big for you and these mountain fighters can stand a lot of punishment. But believe me, mister, from the time they got out of their corners he never put a glove on Jim. There he was slashing away right and left with blows that you'd think would have stretched a man dead if they'd only landed, but Jim wasn't there to take 'em, and by and by he side-steps this fellow, catches him with the right, and it took us about a quarter of an hour to bring him round. Neither he nor the crowd exactly knew what had happened to him, for they never saw the punch. Next night another man named Enoch Collier came along and said that there was no man in Ferndale or the whole of the Rhondda Valley that could put him down.

Driscoll put him out in two minutes. Then a chap who was with Collier had a go, and Driscoll laid him out in two seconds. Jim made a special journey from some place far inland in America to keep a promise to box for the benefit of Nazareth House, Cardiff, and he had a great welcome there. I think that his funeral was the greatest that any fighting man ever had in the whole history of boxing. I went from Merthyr to attend it. Next, I'll tell you about his fight with Fred Welsh at St. Mary Hill fair – I had the offer of that fight and refused it – and I'll tell you something about Fred Welsh too.

Part 8

I didn't have much to do with Fred Welsh, but I remember him and Jim Driscoll fighting at St. Mary's Hill Fair. There were two boxing pavilions there, mine and another one belonging to a man named Gess. I was offered the fight but the conditions didn't suit me, and Fred Welsh wanted to stand at the door and take the money. I said "There's another boxing saloon across the way. Perhaps you can come to terms there." They went there, and Welsh and Driscoll fought a six-round draw. But to tell you the truth I didn't think it was a genuine fight. They were just making a show for the money.

But I remember long before that – it must be going on for 40 years ago – Fred Welsh and my youngest brother, Ernest Scarrott, having a fight when they were boys, and there was a boy called Gitto Gibbons in it as well. Our caravans were then in the Mill Field, Pontypridd. One day I saw my brother Ernest coming out of a stable with his eye blacked and his lip swollen, and after him came Gitto Gibbons, and he'd also been knocked out. After them came a third boy, and he was the smallest of the three and looked very shy. That boy was Fred Welsh. They'd been boxing, and I don't know where they had the boxing gloves from, for they didn't belong to me. I remember saying to my brother and Gitto Gibbons, "Have you let this boy give you two a thrashing?"

One day I went to Newport and I found everybody was talking about a boy named Johnny Basham. He appeared a delicate looking boy, but he could fight

Freddie Welsh (Pontypridd), World Lightweight Champion

anything in the streets. I fixed up my booth and the next thing I knew was Basham up on the stage against another boy and Johnny handled himself very useful. He'd then be about 16 or 17 years of age. I asked him if he'd box a chap named Templar, of Bristol, at the Pontypool fairground. He said "I'll fight him. Will you give me my train fare and a few bob in my pocket?" I said, "You can have thirty bob and your train fare."

Along he comes to the Pontypool fairground, and he brought a tidy gang from Newport with him. They both fought pretty clever, but this Templar was an experienced man and Basham was only a boy. Templar caught him with a hard punch in a breakaway and very near put him out. I said to Templar, "This boy has been fetched here to make an eight round contest, and he must be on his feet at the end of the eight rounds, or your services will not be wanted here any longer." Basham improved in the third round and seemed to be getting the best of it. In the fourth round he was more than holding his own, and in the seventh round he put paid to the Bristolian.

Everybody was surprised and made a great fuss of Basham, and Templar could hardly understand what had happened to him. Basham improved rapidly and very soon he was going great guns. About a year later I came again to Newport on to a fairground on the Rodney Parade kept by Edward Danter. Basham was now engaged by another boxing booth proprietor named Jack Gage. I brought to Newport a London boxer named Curley, who was extra clever, and Gage wanted to match Basham against him for £25 aside. I said, "I don't feel inclined to match Curley against Basham. He's not experienced enough and not good enough, but so far as a

Johnny Basham (Newport), British & European Welterweight Champion

small purse goes I'm prepared to offer it." The job was accepted for £5, and Basham put Curley out in seven rounds. Basham had more to thank Jack Gage than me for starting him in boxing.

Another well-known boxer who fought for me was Pat O'Keefe, the middleweight champion of England. He boxed for me at Cardiff. Talking about middleweights, I don't think that Frank Moody has had all the credit that's due to him from the Press or the public. His performances in America against the negro Tiger Flowers, then the best in the world at the weight and a slaughterer, was wonderful. Moody must have travelled thousands of miles from one part of the United States to another on his American tour. I remember Frank as a boy, running about with other schoolboys in Pontypridd, and I used to catch him and other boys boxing in and out of the booth at the Pontypridd fairground. But it was filling in turns and it suited the crowd before the big fights came on.

I noticed Frank one night boxing another boy, and I said to some of our people that was there, "This boy looks like becoming a champion." The first real thing I saw him do was to fight for a side-stake a boy called Kid Evans, of Trehafod, for £10. I was at Tonypandy at the time, and I remember giving them a purse because I knew the people they both belonged to. I had very little directly to do with Frank from that time on, but I remember getting him a job to fight one of the champions of the Rhymney Valley, Lunty Price, of Bargoed. That was in 1916 at a big theatre in Bargoed, and was for the purpose of raising money to send cigarettes to the boys in the trenches.

Frank Moody (Pontypridd), British & Empire Middleweight Boxing Champion

I was asked to find an opponent for Price, and I wrote to Pontypridd for Moody, who was then about 16 or 17 years of age. Frank said to me that he didn't think he was good enough for Lunty Price, but I said to him, "Look here, you don't know how far you can go yet, and in any case you've got nothing to lose." Moody put up a fine performance which delighted everybody, and he won on points. I predicted him to become a real champion and I told a lot of Pontypridd people so. The only thing I thought was that perhaps too much strain was put on him too early. I told Mr Teddy Lewis; him and me used to have a lot of debate together. "I'm afraid you're bringing him along too quick." Moody had a fine trainer in Llew Williams, who used to keep the Ruperra Hotel in Pontypridd. Mr. Teddy Lewis was a great man. He made champions and found champions work. As a manager of boxers, he was the best in the country and one of the straightest men in the game. He was also a great handicapper in track events, and his death was a big loss to boxing in South Wales and to sport in general.

Another boxer that I thought a lot of was Billy Fry, of Tylorstown. There was a wonderful fight between him and a man called Tom Coombs, also from Tylorstown, in my booth on the fairground by the Salisbury Hotel, Ferndale. It was for £25 aside and my purse of £25, and Fry won on a knock-out in the seventeenth round. I can tell you of two other good contests I put on at the same ground in Ferndale. One was between Ivor Day and Billy Eynon, of Merthyr, for £50 aside. I gave a purse of £50, and they chose Jack Smith, of Manchester, as the referee. He and the gloves came to £8. It was a very hard fight from start to finish, and they were backing Eynon to win up to the last round, but Jack Smith gave it as a draw. The very next fight I had on the same ground was also a good 'un. It was between Walt Price, Treorchy, and Jack Jones, Merthyr Vale, for £50 aside and my purse of £50. Jack Jones won on points. I opened a big place at the skating rink in Tonypandy before the war and I put on some good fights there. One of the best was between Joe Johns, of Merthyr, and Dai Roberts, of Caerau – Dai got killed in the war – for a purse of £80 – £50 for Roberts and £30 for Johns. They were about 10 stone and the match must have been for the championship of Wales at their weights. There was a crowd of about 4,000 and there was any amount of money on Roberts, but as the fight went on Joe Johns seemed to be always there when he was wanted and the result was a draw. One of the best fights I've ever seen.

Part 9

"Never let this boy of mine put on the boxing gloves." That was what Tom Thomas's father, who was a farmer living at Tonypandy, used to say to me. He and Tom used to come to the booth to look at the boxing when I was showing at Tonypandy. I used to answer "No sir, I won't," but when Tom got going there was no stopping him.

This was about 42 years ago when I first saw Tom Thomas and his father. The game pulled Tom like one of these here magnets, and by and by he would have it that he must have a go in front of my booth with my other boxers. He was then a fine looking youngster, but as he was green at the business we were careful who we put him on with. But he himself was anxious to tackle anybody and as time went on he grew very big and husky and strong, not extra tall, but very broad and thickset and muscular. I'll tell you where he had his first real test. He came with me when I took my booth to Pontycymmer. But that afternoon we all had a very tough time of it except Tom Thomas. I had with me Jim Driscoll, Harry Mansfield, Jim Courtney of Barry – and he could fight – and George Dixon, a negro from Boston, U.S.A. Along came a big mountain fighter from Blaengarw, and he kicked off as bold as brass by asking who was the best man on the booth. Tom Thomas was the biggest, but he was young. Tom was anxious to take on this man from Blaengarw but he was doubtful whether he could pull it off.

Tom Thomas (Penygraig), British Middleweight Boxing Champion

"I'm afraid this man is too good for me, Scarrott," he said to me, but I told him, "You've never seen him perform, you know nothing at all about him, and anyway, he can't kill you in a couple of rounds." It was agreed that they should box six rounds, and I remember it was Jim Driscoll who tied on the gloves for Tom, who was very nervous. This fellow looked so strong, and there was a lot of talk about what he had been doing in mountain fighting. But after the first round I had no doubt but that Tom could tank him and when he got back to his corner I said to him "You go right in after this chap, but be careful and use that right hand."

This fellow came at him like a bull, but Tom had learnt slipping and dodging from the others on the booth, and he side-stepped him, caught him on the chin as he floundered by, and laid him right out. I was pleased and so were all the boxers on my booth. I remember Harry Mansfield speaking to him and telling him it was about as good a punch as he'd ever seen in his life. Tom Thomas's father heard about this, but still he wasn't pleased with Tom going in for the fighting game. He came to me and said, "Scarrott, I told you not to encourage my boy to box."

I told him, "If you don't want that boy to fight you'll have to keep him away from boxing booths or keep him chained up or something. Believe me, his heart and soul is in the business." Old Mr. Thomas looked very serious at this and he asked me, "Do you think he's going to become any good and make a champion?" I called Jim Driscoll, Harry Mansfield and Dave Wallace, three of the best men in England at the time and they all told him Tom would become a real champion. But the old gent

Harry Mansfield (Bristol), one of Jack Scarrott's booth boxers

didn't appreciate the idea at all. We moved to the Vale of Glamorgan for the St. Mary-hill fair, then one of the roughest fairs in the country. All the bullies and all the ruffians from far and near were there.

In addition to a large pleasure fair it was also a very big horse and cattle fair. I warned Tom Thomas that we were going to a very rough place. A large number of farmers at the fair came to see Tom as he was a farmer's son, and by this time he was a splendid figure of an athlete. We hadn't long to wait before a big ruffian came up, and we offered him £5 for six rounds against Tom. A gentleman named Mordecai held the money. Tom didn't box up to form for the first two rounds and his opponent was laying into him and having the best of it. But in the third round he started to box smartly and to place his punches very nicely. He slowed his man with a punch in the stomach, followed that up with another punch to the same place, and in the fourth round he knocked him out. This pleased the farmers no end and hundreds collected round Tom, all talking in Welsh and congratulating him. After this Tom Thomas never looked back. He had learnt a lot from Jim Driscoll and Harry Mansfield. In fact I've never known a boxer learn so quick.

In about a week's time after the St. Mary-hill Fair we moved to Port Talbot. There he was tackled by a mountain fighter named Bullo Rees, a strong, big fellow, who took him on for £5 for six rounds. Rees just before that had fought 40 rounds on the mountain with Bill Lane, Cwmavon, and licked him. Rees started rushing tactics and kept up a very rugged, dashing style of fighting until some of the spectators were backing him to win. But it didn't come off. I was advising Tom and he had Driscoll and Mansfield in his corner as well. After a few rounds Driscoll and Mansfield told Tom to shoot in a punch on the breakaway, and true enough as Bullo Rees was getting away from a clinch Tom connects with the right and out he goes. The next night who should walk up but Billy Morgan of Swansea, the South Wales champion. He'd heard of Tom Thomas and had come after the money we were offering to any man who could stand up against him. Thomas made very short work of him and put him out in the second round. That was two of the best men in South Wales that Tom Thomas put paid to in two days.

All the promoters were after him now and were offering him big fights, and he won very quick victories over all the fighters who tackled him. Next we heard of him as the Welsh champion, and everybody knows how he beat Charlie Wilson in two rounds and became the middle-weight champion of England and holder of the Lonsdale belt. If he hadn't been cut off in his prime by rheumatic fever I do believe he'd have become a world champion.

Part 10

Brutality ! mister, that's what some people called it, when Jimmy Wilde started on my booth. I remember I had him boxing for me at Taff's Well when he was about 16 or 17 years of age. Some gentleman came along and said it was brutality to put such a delicate little boy to box in the booth. They got quite angry about it, and told me to take him away before somebody hurt him. I said to them, "Now don't you excited at all, gentlemen. There's no need to worry about this lad getting hurt. You wait until the boxing starts and you'll see who'll be doing the hurting."

Up comes a mountain fighter about 30 years of age and weighing about 12 stone who was supposed to be the cock of the walk in the Pentyrch, Tongwynlais and Taff's Well area. I said, "I'll give you £1 if you'll stand three rounds against this little nipper." The people started shouting "Shame" because this chap looked big enough to eat Jimmy, but in the second round Jimmy caught him with a right on the chin and laid him dead out. It took us nearly ten minutes to get him round. The next night another chap came along, and he was quite insulted when we suggested that he should have a go at Jimmy. He said he'd come to fight grown men, not boys. Jimmy put him out in 15 seconds, and honest, mister, I don't think he weighed 5st. at that time. He was the most marvellous boxer that ever put on the gloves, and I've never known a man to create such a sensation. Even about this time I'm talking about, when he was only 16 or 17, he was putting 'em all out. And there was no taking the count and

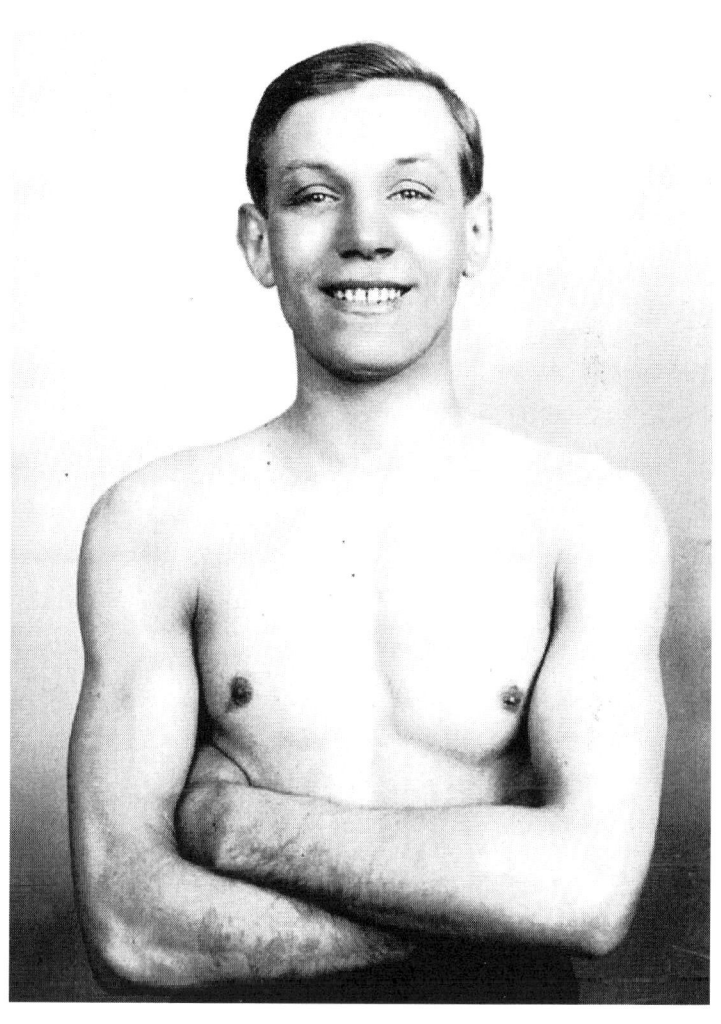

Jimmy Wilde (Quaker's Yard), World Flyweight Champion

getting up again. When he put 'em on the floor they remained there.

I first spotted him when I took my booth to Tylorstown about 34 years ago. He was then no bigger than a spider, but he was fighting from morning till night. I asked him once, "My boy, will you go to the back of the show and see that the other boys don't get in at the back?" By and by I saw crowds of people going round to the back of the booth. I went to see what was the matter, and there was Jimmy Wilde putting up a terrific fight against a gang of boys. After that we fetched him from the back to the front and put him in the boxing booth. You couldn't keep him off the platform, although the boxing gloves he had on were very nearly as big as him. I remember a wonderful fight between him and a bigger boy named Dai Chips. It was a fight between two boys, but two champions of the world could not have put up a better show. From that time on we put him on as the boy champion, and he used to lick boys older and twice his size. The best boy you could find did not stay long in front of Jimmy Wilde. When he was about 17 or 18 he came to box for me at Caerphilly, where there were a good many mountain fighters. I had a gang of good 'uns with me, but Jimmy Wilde was all the talk.

When I put him in front of the booth a man who was supposed to be a champion mountain fighter said" You ought to be ashamed to put a boy like him to fight. I can beat the best man you've got, and as for this boy (meaning Wilde) I could take hold of him and twist him in two." You should see his face when I told him that I'd give him £1 to stand up to Wilde for one minute. He wouldn't believe it. "It's bluff," he said, "you can't catch me like that, Scarrott." I said to him and his gang, "There's no catch about it. You can hold the money yourselves. Stand this boy a minute and the money is yours." Well, he took it on, and we charged sixpence instead of three pence for admission to the booth, as the fight was something out of the ordinary. As it happened we had a very good class of people among the spectators, and there were women among them, which was very unusual for boxing matches in those days. They were all talking about what a shame it was to put such a delicate looking boy against such a grown man. You never saw such a thunderstruck looking lot of people in your life when Jimmy got to work. After only five seconds, mister, Wilde caught this chap with two left hooks on the point of the chin. This chap made a rush, but Wilde pushed him to one side and caught him a beauty with the right – a clean knock-out. After the people got over their surprise they were clapping and hooraying and carrying on like anything.

It was also at Caerphilly that a couple of ruffians – and they were fairly big fellows – came along and they had plenty to say for themselves. They reckoned it was all rot about Jimmy Wilde being able to fight. I said, "I'll tell you what I'll do. He'll beat the pair of you inside four rounds, without stopping, and you shall hold the money." They accepted the offer, and this fight drew a large crowd among people like bank managers and business men, for the fame of Jimmy Wilde had spread throughout the town. Jimmy let the first fellow go until the second round, when he gave him a tap that you wouldn't have thought would hurt anybody, but it put him right out. No. 2 gets ready, and Jimmy went right for him. This chap aims a swipe at Wilde. Wilde sidesteps him – one punch – out! By the time 1916 came Wilde was world famous. I was showing on the Tredegar fairground, Pontypridd and it was there that I paid Jimmy Wilde £50 for four hours boxing.

That night Jimmy did a performance that I don't think will ever be equalled. He put out twenty three men, of all sorts and sizes, in four hours. The offer was £1 a minute to all comers, and without pulling the gloves off Wilde stopped 19 men, each within the minute. Three and a half hours out of the four hours that he had agreed to box were up at half-past nine. I then asked him if he could do with a rest, and he said, "I could," I told him to take half an hour's rest and come back to box again from ten o' clock to half past ten. We announced that he'd fight again three or four times after ten o'clock and that the same money – 1s. – would be charged for re-admission. Large crowds hung about waiting and among them were many of the biggest business people in Pontypridd, to see the last fights, and Wilde stopped another four men. That was the last time he ever boxed for me. He was a marvel and a mystery and I don't think we shall ever see his like again.

Part 11

Another boy I always thought very highly of was poor Percy Jones, of Porth, who became fly-weight champion of Great Britain. I knew his father very well and also his mother, and perhaps it was because they lived close to the fairground at Porth, where I used to show, that Percy took to boxing. Tom Thomas' father used to object to him boxing, as I've told you, but in the case of Percy Jones it was his mother who was very much against it. After Percy had started she often came to the booth to see if he was there or if his name was on the front of the booth.

I remember he was matched against a boy from Caerphilly, but his mother saw his name in front of the booth and she begged us not to let this fight take place. I hardly knew what to say. I sympathised with a mother's feelings but on the other hand I knew that Percy would make a real champion and I didn't want to stand in his way. His father was delighted with the way he was shaping, but he used to say "It's his mother." On this occasion, when the match between Percy and the Caerphilly boxer was due to come off, I said to his father "We'll smuggle this fight through." We took the board with his name on it down from the front of the booth. Later we put it back but kept somebody watching to take it down again if they saw his mother coming. Percy Jones was then only starting, and the betting was 20 to 1 that this Caerphilly boxer – I forget his name – would put him down.

Percy Jones (Porth), World Flyweight Champion with Jim Driscoll

But the fight proved one of the best ever seen in Porth, and although Percy Jones was quite a boy at the time he hit his opponent three punches in succession on the point of the chin in the twelfth round and the Caerphilly lad collapsed. It was a great pity Percy died so early. Everybody in South Wales boxing felt sorry and sympathised with his relatives.

I've met some rum coves during fifty years as a showman and in the boxing world, but one of the strangest I ever knew was an Irishman named Mike Riley, a man who might have made a fortune in the game if he could only look after himself. We met him, looking very rough and down and out, on the road between Hirwain and Brecon, and gave him a lift to Brecon Fair. There he asked me to put him on the booth to box. At first I told him to go to the next booth, which was short of volunteers. Eventually, at his request I put him on against a Boston (U.S.A) a negro named George Dixon, who was about the cleverest man we had. Dixon could box from all angles and had a very easy way of catching 'em as they came along.

I was about the most surprised man in Wales when I saw Riley make him look like a novice. Everything Dixon had been doing so cleverly against other men was hopeless against Riley, who made him miss right and left. We gave Riley a job on the booth right away and we went from Brecon to Abertillery, where there was a very rough gang about that time. I opened the booth at Abertillery with Mike Riley, George Dixon, Pat O'Keefe, Ginger Osborn, of Liverpool, Jimmy Dean, of Pontypridd, and Darkie Thomas and Llew Morgan, both from Neath. There was then a boxer in Abertillery named Bill

Griffiths, who had been training to fight someone for £100 aside, but the match had been called off. I believe Griffiths came from Tredegar. He was about 13st. 6lbs. Griffiths came to my booth and said he'd fight the best two men on it. He was then in first-class condition, being trained to a hair for the fight which had just been called off. I said to him – and he was a very surprised man to hear it – "Here's Mike Riley, whom I picked up as a tramp on the road. He shall fight you for any part of £100 if you'll fight in my place."

The fight took place a few days before Christmas at Rodney Parade, Newport, at Danter's World Fair, for a side stake of £50. A man named Plummer from the "Sporting Chronicle" was the referee and he and the gloves cost £10. Mike Riley was fighting a well-trained man, inches taller and stones heavier, over twenty rounds, but he put his man on the floor several times in the 18th and 19th rounds and won. Griffiths' own backers told him he should chuck in his hand after letting a much lighter man picked up off the road by Scarrott beat him. But listen while I tell you what happened to Mike Riley after that fight. I gave him the £50 purse, and he must have had pretty nearly another £50 from the people in the crowd, who went mad over him and carried him shoulder high. Believe it or not, in about a week he came back to me without a penny piece, and in the same condition as he was when I picked him up off the road. I said to him, "I've paid you £50 and offended some of my other boxers by picking you instead of them for the chance to win it, and here you are without a penny."

There was an old gentleman in Newport connected with shipping called Mr. Ball. I asked him when he had a boat going for Liverpool, and said there was one going next day. I asked him to give Mike Riley a passage home on it, and he did so. That was the last I saw of Riley, but he'd have made a champion if he'd only used his head. Another remarkable little chap that I had with me – and I daresay many of the old hands in South Wales would remember him – was a little Scotch fellow named Pedlar McMann. He was very small and not very clever, but he was a real pocket Hercules and very dangerous. Every chap about his own size with whom he put on the gloves "smelt the floor".

Once at Caerau a big chap came along and said, "Where's this Scotchman?" McMann replied in his Scotch accent, "I'm here, mon." This big fellow – he was from North Wales – then said he wanted to fight a man and not a boy, but the match was made, and there was such a rough crowd expected that I applied for three policemen to control them. There was any amount of money being laid on the big fellow, and I believe old Tom Scadan was the referee. At first McMann was hit all over the ring, but in the fourth round he laid his man out for nearly an hour.

Part 12

The strangest man and the most extraordinary looking man I ever clapped eyes on in all my life had nothing to do with shows and boxing, but he'd have made the fortune of any showman who could have got him to join his show. This was the famous Dr. Price of Llantrisant. He was a rum 'un and no mistake. A lot had been put in the papers about him, and most people know how he cremated his son, whom he called "Jesus Christ Price" in order to shock the chapel people, in a barrel at the top of the hill at Llantrisant.

There was a commotion among the people, who were furious about it, and they would have set about him on the hill had not a policeman, who was a very strong and determined fellow – he was Police-constable Phillip Francis – stood by with his truncheon and kept 'em back. That night the crowd came storming round his house while he was out, but his housekeeper, who was the mother of the boy he cremated, kept them at bay, standing at the door with a pistol in her hand. Cremation being against the law at the time, he was arrested, and I saw Dr. Price in Pontypridd after he was arrested with Superintendant Mathews who was a very nice man. There was tremendous excitement in Pontypridd about it. I had known Dr. Price well by sight long before that. Nobody ever saw a man dressed like him. He had on his head a fox-skin with the tail hanging down behind, a red waistcoat with white sleeves, green trousers with scallops on the bottoms, a shiny pair of boots and white stockings.

Doctor William Price cremates his child, Iesu Grist

He used to ride an old white horse, and sometimes he carried a torch in his hand. If a circus proprietor could only have got him to ride around in advance of the circus he'd have been worth a lot of money to him. I met him many a time while we were on the road. I remember seeing him at St. Fagan's, Black Cock, Whitchurch, Fairwater, Walnut Tree Junction, Llanharran, Llanharry, and Cowbridge. In addition to his strange dress he was a striking looking man, with a white beard down to his waist. I have known him to walk through Pontypridd with the little boy he cremated dressed up the same as himself, and didn't the crowd stare at him. He frightened us children to look at him. Indeed, I think practically the whole neighbourhood were afraid of him, although lots of people had wonderful faith in him as a doctor.

When Dr. Price was himself cremated, I went to Llantrisant to see it, and I've got to this day as souvenirs of him some cinders from the fire that cremated him. It must have been about 42 years ago, and there were thousands of people on the roads to Llantrisant that morning – farmers, miners, some on horseback, some on foot, and thousands of wagonettes, brakes, carts and all sorts of conveyances. There were lots of people from Cardiff there, and by the time I arrived the crowd was so great that I could hardly get near the spot. Talking about old times in the Pontypridd and Llantrisant districts reminds me of a funny incident that set everybody in Pontypridd laughing leastways it did all that were not teetotallers. There was in Pontypridd many years ago a mountain fighter named William Lee, but everybody called him "Mother" Lee, after his mother, a well-known old gypsy lady who was called Mother Lee before him.

A teetotal evangelist – I'm told his name was Tennyson Smith – came to Pontypridd to carry on a campaign to persuade the people to become teetotallers, and believe me, as things were in Pontypridd in those days he had his work cut out for him. This evangelist, to draw attention to his campaign, took a nine gallon cask of beer to the Berw Bridge in Pontypridd. What he intended doing was to put the cask on the parapet of the bridge, knock the top in, and pour all the beer into the River Taff in order to show the crowd what he thought of it. But unluckily for him the barrel slipped off the parapet into the river before he could open it.

Now "Mother" Lee was a very good swimmer and diver, as well as a fighter, and he used to dive off the Berw Bridge. In fact, he wanted to dive off the railways bridge close to it, only the police wouldn't let him because they were afraid it was too dangerous. Well, you may not believe me that "Mother" Lee lost no time in getting into the Taff to rescue that barrel, and he succeeded in doing it. Then he and his pals took the barrel to the famous old bridge at Pontypridd a little lower down, borrowed some pint pots from the Maltsters Arms, and they all had a good time around that barrel while the crowds of teetotallers stood by looking on and telling one another they didn't know what the world was coming to.

"Mother" Lee and I were boys together at Pontypridd, and we used to play pitch and toss a lot on the mountain and about the roads. There was also with us a young fellow named Dan Powell, and a fighter named Devons, who worked at the chain works and became a champion prize fighter. There was also in

Pontypridd at the time a man who was a bit of a prize fighter who was called Tiny Evans. Following an argument over a game of pitch and toss he and "Mother" Lee fought about 25 rounds on the mountain at Eglwysilan, I was seconding Lee, and I remember telling him, "He's only got two hands like you've got, and he can't lick you." They fought remarkably well, but the fight was stopped when there was an alarm that the police was coming and we all ran for it.

I remember another fight on the mountain at Eglwysilan which might have very serious consequences. It was between "Mother" Lee and a young fellow from Gwauncaergurwen named Dan Powell. It ended in a very bad knock-out for Powell and we couldn't bring him round. I said, "We'll make out he's had an accident. It won't do to say he's been fighting." We took him to a cottage at Abertridwr, told the people there that there had been an accident, and a doctor was fetched. The accident tale didn't wash with him. He said that Powell had been misused very badly, but we never said anything. We were mighty glad, I can tell you, when the doctor got him round, and we brought him back over the mountain past the rocking stone to Pontypridd. Powell was a fine and smart young fellow, and he put up some very good fights after that. He was matched to fight with Bungey Hill, but the fight fell through and Hill fought Sam Butcher instead for £50 aside. Butcher won. He is still living at Ynyshir. He had a brother called Ivor Butcher, who fought Alf Wight and Harry Mansfield. The Butchers were real mountain fighters. Next time I'll tell about a mountain fight I saw at Porth, when I was a very small lad, in which a man was stretched out on the mountain stone dead and the crowd ran away and left him lying there.

Part 13

We were encamped in the Britannia district of Porth, on the ground where Solomon Andrews built sheds for the horse trams, when I saw a man killed in a fight on the Porth Mountain. This was well over 50 years ago and I was quite a young lad. One Sunday morning I was on the mountain looking for our horses when I saw a crowd of men coming up the mountain. When they came near they asked me, "What do you want, my boy?" and I told them I was looking for some horses. They said, "Go on, then," and I went four hundred yards away. Then I saw them form a ring and I saw two men stripping off. So I went back and slipped in among the crowd.

It is difficult to believe it these days, but this fight in which a man was killed was for five shillings a-side! The men fought as a result of a quarrel they had got into the night before in a public house. I don't know their names, but one of them lived in Clifton's row, Porth. They fought for a considerable time and it was a very brutal fight. One man got very badly knocked about, and he was bashed into such as state that the seconds of the winning man said they were quite willing to stop the fight and let the loser keep the stake, but the loser's friends wouldn't have it. They would have that the fight must go on, although their man was staggering about and putting up a very poor show. The man who was winning wanted to stop, but his opponent's seconds got so fed up with them that they said to their man, "Go on, finish it!"

Then the man who had been winning all along steps up to the other and gives him one punch which puts him flat on his back and stone dead. That crowd panicked at once and ran away in all directions, some down towards the town and others here and there across the mountain. I was very young at the time and I was also very badly frightened. After I had run home I didn't tell my father and mother anything about it, but I kept on looking up towards the mountain where the dead man was lying. By and by I saw hundreds of people running up the side of the mountain to the spot, and hundreds watched him being brought back on a stretcher to his home in Clifton's row. I remember the men carrying the stretcher had difficulty in getting it through the door. I believe the man who fought and killed him got imprisonment for it.

One of the biggest shows I ever saw in Cardiff in the early days was in the old circus in Westgate Street, where the post office now stands. It was a benefit for Morgan Crowther, who had lost to Bill Baxter of London, on points after fighting 20 rounds at the N.S.C for the 9st. championship of England. It was a big blow to Crowther and his backers – I believe there were Newport and Cardiff men among them – lost very heavily. Many famous boxers helped at the benefit, and Dick Burge and myself were matching them. Among them were Archie Cook, the father of Gordon Cook, of Penygraig, Alf Kelly (Tonypandy) Ginger Jones, Patsey Cochlin, Illtyd Evans, Sam Butcher, a Bristol boxer named Skylines, Ben Jordan, and three Cardiff men back from the Army, brothers named Patsey Collins, Johnny Collins, and Driver Collins.

There was also a Bristol boxer named Harry Harry, and he was using very bad language in the dressing room. So I said to Dick Burge, "We'll soon get rid of him. Put him up next and put him up against Ben Jordan." Jordan was a light-weight champion of England and a very nicely spoken young man. As they left the dressing room we said to Jordan, "See him off." Jordan only hit him twice, and he was out until the show was over. It was a great night, and the contests, although they were no-decision bouts, were very keen. Archie Cook and Evans put up a needle fight that pleased everybody, but the great event was a four-round no decision bout between Morgan Crowther and Bill Baxter. It was such a wonderful contest that the crowd shouted for one more round, and if Crowther had fought Baxter at the N.S.C as he fought that night at Cardiff he'd have licked two of him.

Dick Burge finished up the night with an exhibition. He came from Cheltenham, and won the championship of England. I remember he won a 100 yards sprint and a pole jump at Liverpool in the morning and beat Harry Nicholas in 20 rounds on the same day. One of the greatest boxers that ever lived was old Bob Fitzsimmons, and I saw him give an exhibition at Pontypridd. He was 5ft 11 ¾ inches in height and weighed only 11st. 6lb., but I think he must have had about the most terrific punch of any boxer of any time. He came on to give an exhibition of punching the ball, and this is how he did it. He asked the crowd, "Which hand shall I hit it with?"

Some shouted 'the right" and some "the left." I forget which hand he used, but with one punch he sent that ball flying off its fastenings into the middle of the crowd. With his tall, lanky figure, respectable dress, and a bald head he looked more like a parson than a prize-fighter. I was among the crowd that saw him off at Pontypridd

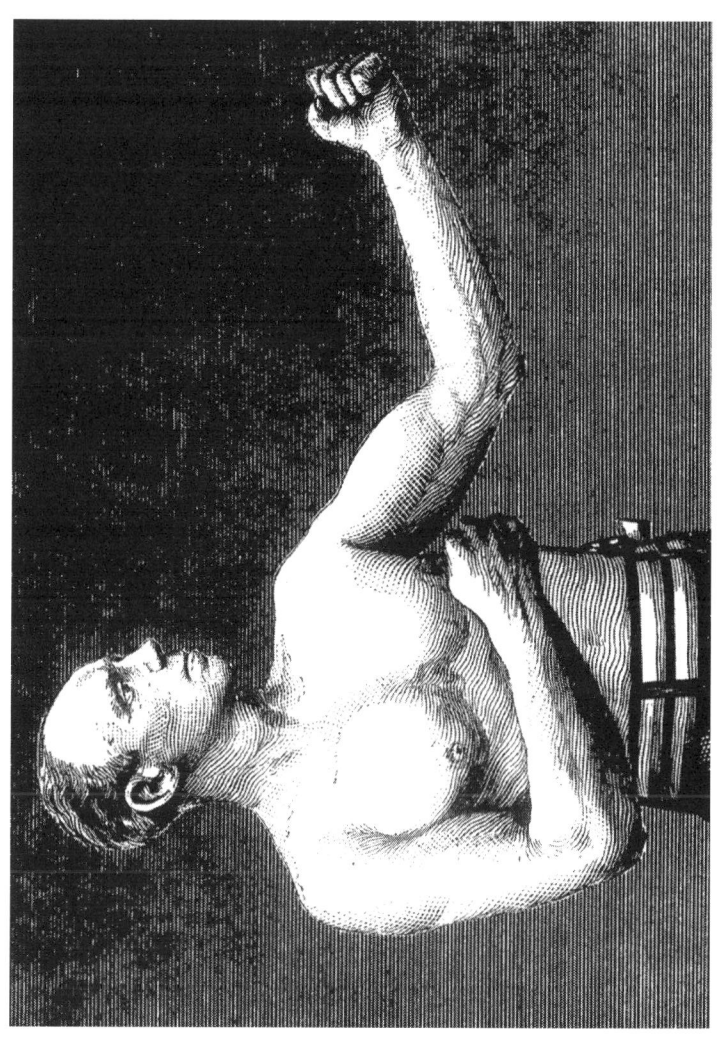

Bob Fitzsimmons, Middle, Light Heavy & Heavyweight Champion of the World

Station. One of the porters was struggling to lift one of his trunks, and Bob stepped across and lifted it with one hand. "Strength is what you want, my man," he said to the porter. Taking about Pontypridd reminds me of Jimmy Dean, who used to be known as "The Cast-iron Man." He had been in all kinds of work in Pontypridd, but he was always in the shows at the Butcher's Arms and he took up boxing. He was not a very clever boxer, but he could make it very awkward for them that could box. You couldn't kill him with a sledgehammer. You could tie him to a post and hammer him and then you couldn't kill him. I remember in the Butcher's Arms yard some roughs came along and they were after Jimmy Dean. He told 'em he'd fight 'em one at a time as many as they'd like to fetch. I also remember him hitting the referee by mistake and nearly knocking him over the ropes, which caused the crowd to laugh like anything.

Part 14

There was a man killed in the pit at Mardy, leaving a wife and eight children. Then the wife died, and a subscription was raised for the children. The men responsible for the fund came to John Scarrott. On hearing the tragic nature of the case he said "It is no use giving a paltry sum for these children. I will do something better." That "something better" was a benefit night at Scarrott's amusements, which realised over £100. It paid for the funeral expenses and clothed the children, and the balance was invested for them. During the war a fund established at Bargoed to give a suitable reception and presents to soldiers coming home on leave for the second time broke down. John Scarrott said "Turn these soldiers over to me." Benefits were arranged, and between £15 and £20 a week was raised for about 18 months.

At Tylorstown in 1916 Scarrott was asked to help the soldiers' and sailors' fund. He gave the organisers of the fund the use of his amusements for four days, which resulted in the fund being augmented by well over £100. Among the places in which John Scarrott has thrown open his fair for charity are Ystradmynach, Pontylottyn, Caerphilly, Fleur-de-Lys, Old Tredegar, Mountain Ash (where the fair was held in the great pavilion), Brynmawr, Abertillery, Blaina, and many other towns in the South Wales coalfield.

His late wife was also known far and wide among the show people of South Wales for her kindness to them in misfortune. Her maiden name was Priscilla Loveridge, and she was married to Mr. Scarrott at St. Catherine's Church Pontypridd, when he was 21 and she 20 years of age. She passed away four years ago. "She was very much against my starting in the boxing booth business at first," states Mr. Scarrott, "but later she became a great business woman, I lost a wonderful partner when I lost her."

Now for John Scarrott's final message to his readers. "I don't know whether you are tired of these yarns of mine, but, judging from what I hear in my travels up and down the valleys, a good many men have been very much interested to read them. "Well, it is no wonder that I have plenty of stories to tell after spending fifty years as a showman and boxing booth proprietor in the South Wales coalfield. "I don't think there were many places in the world like the Welsh mining valleys in the good old days. I have heard of the rush to the Klondike gold-fields and how towns sprang up like mushrooms in a night, and that there was a middlin' lively lot of customers there.

Very much the same kind of thing was happening in the Welsh mining valleys when I was travelling them in my young days. They came pouring into the valleys in thousands – the Rhondda Valley had 10,000 new men in ten years – and they were men of all sorts. There was work for everybody, and among the men that came in to get work in the pits were young farm labourers from West Wales and North Wales, Irishmen, Bristolians, old soldiers who had left the Army, you never saw such a mixture of humanity. Why you could get a respectable chapel deacon in the pit cutting coal alongside of a bloke that had just come out of gaol. And out of them all came some wonderful athletes. I've told you about the boxers –

but there were footballers and runners as well, and also some very remarkable singers.

They were remarkable times and they brought out some remarkable men, and there was I travelling up and down the coalfield with my booth in the thick of them. It's a great pity to see the valleys, where everybody used to have plenty of money to spend, gone as they are to-day. One more story before I finish, although I could tell you plenty more. I had my show in Holton-road, Barry, and I engaged an Italian strong man, who called himself 'Montano.' He used to do some remarkable weight lifting feats, such as lifting a 186 lb. dumb-bell with one hand, and offer £5 to anybody in the crowd who could lift the same weight in the same way. Also he used to offer £1 a minute to any wrestler who could stand up against him in any style of wrestling.

But his greatest and final feat was to have a cannon fitted on his shoulders and fired. I had never seen him doing this performance and I let him get on with it. He loaded the cannon with powder, some men lifted it on his shoulders and it was fired off. Mister, it fairly shook the town. All the paraffin lamps on my booth went out and there we were in darkness. People came running from all directions to see what was the matter. We men on the booth didn't know exactly where we stood. Men and women from the houses close by said the explosion had jarred their houses from top to bottom. An Inspector of police came up and asked me what I was doing.

I explained to him that I had engaged this Italian as a turn, but that as I had never seen him rehearse his act I didn't know what he was going to do. Had I known that the explosion of this cannon would be so terrific I would not have allowed him to do it. But there was no doubt about it, this Italian's weight-lifting and wrestling performances were very good. Well now, mister, let me say goodbye to all the readers of these tales. If they have enjoyed these yarns of mine as much as I've enjoyed telling them, I think they must be well pleased. I expect I shall have a good many discussions and arguments about them during the coming summer, but I shall be pleased to talk 'em over with anybody who comes along. A good many old friends of mine have been reading them, and I wish them all the best of luck.

THE END.

JACK SCARROTT'S PRIZE FIGHTERS

Lawrence Davies

Chapter 1

Fothergill Street

It is probably fair to say that a great number of people experiencing severe poverty in the area of Monmouthshire, South Wales during the late 1800's, could be found at Fothergill Street located in the town of Newport, near the English border. It was here that Jack Scarrett first saw the light of day on the 28th of March, 1870. Born into what might be termed humble beginnings, Jack's father, Levi Scarrett, seemingly had few material possessions. The Scarrett family was not unlike the other wanderers and unfortunates who numbered amongst the hundreds calling this run down, slum area of Newport, home.

Industrialisation had seen untold numbers flocking from the surrounding countryside, and from all corners of the United Kingdom. While all sought the possibility of a better life, most would only find the unceasing grind of an uncertain future in the town's factories, or jobs labouring in the ever expanding coal and iron industries,

Merchant Street (Newport), situated close to Fothergill Street

where men were quickly and easily replaced in the event that any dared complain about their lot. Well-heeled and well moneyed entrepreneurs seeking to make their mark and increase their fortunes descended upon the rich coal fields of South Wales in their droves. After the coal had been extracted and the iron ore had been smelted, Newport found itself at the forefront of efforts to capitalise on the regions vast mineral bounty. A teeming population of labourers and engineers had found employment assisting in the building of a canal network stretching from the valleys to the West to transport the coal and iron to the hulls of the ships waiting at dockside to carry it across the sea and onwards to the furthest edges of the world.

The rapid expansion of the town was a tale familiar in centres of industrial activity throughout Britain. At the start of the century Newport had consisted of just under a thousand occupants, although by the end, it would be home to nearly 70,000. With the relentless increase in industrialisation, the numbers drawn to the town expanded year on year. Many had sailed from as far afield as Ireland, forced from their native land by the desolation of the Great Famine, and arrived in South Wales seeking a better life and had found their way to Newport. Few, if any, would find anything remotely resembling a more stable existence. Competition from other workers drawn from all over the mainland ensured that most were forced to sell their labour for a minimal wage. At the dockyards, and on the canals and tram roads, most found tenuous employment as navvies, where injury was frequently commonplace, and occasionally fatal. As the few made vast fortunes, there can be no doubt that more often than not, they made their money at the expense of the many.

Clerks, underwriters, shipping agents, and associated trades would also find a bustling and booming town, where fortunes could be quickly made. It was a world away from the sedate pace of life that had been enjoyed by the people of Newport in 1800. Agriculture and salmon fishing had been the main occupations, with only limited work to be found on the occasional ships that put down anchor at the undeveloped wharves. This would be in stark contrast to the misery endured by the occupants of the town by the middle of the century. By the 1840's the general health of the townspeople would take centre stage as the main concern of the Town Council. Cholera, Typhus and Smallpox had decimated the population in recent years. Newport was bursting at the seams, and was struggling to find room to bury its dead, let alone house the constant stream of newcomers. Sewerage was inadequate, and polluted the drinking water, with human waste being discharged directly into the River Usk. The pumped water supply, where available, was often tainted with seepage from overcrowded graveyards. Large numbers of the population chose to use the dirty canal waters as their main source of water, which may have seemed the lesser evil amongst some of the more polluted water sources available to supply their daily needs.

Finally in 1849, the General Board of Health was petitioned to conduct an enquiry to determine which issues needed to be dealt with as priorities in order for the town to provide a better standard of living for its population. To this end, the Board of Health sent a representative, George Thomas Clark, to visit Newport in August of 1849 and report back to the Board of his findings. The scenes of extreme poverty that George Clark uncovered at the town were deeply disturbing, even at a time when the living conditions of workers supplying the labour requirements of the industrial age throughout Great Britain could be held up to question. The areas of Friar's Field and Fothergill Street itself fared particularly poorly in Clark's subsequent report, having been an area where the poorest of the poor could be found.

Today, nothing of these areas remain, although the worst of the slums of Newport's past were to be found in the busy streets where John Frost Square, the Kingsway Centre and the Central Library now stand. Many of the leading lights of Newport had long been accused of both exploitation and corruption, with some of the most deprived areas having proved that there was plenty of plenty of money to be made from human misfortune. One particular case in point was a building known locally as the 'Rookery' at the top of Stow Hill, which contained no less than 86 unfortunate ill-kept souls. Like so many buildings given over to worker's 'accommodation' it lacked even the most basic plumbing, and had just two privies discharging their waste into a nearby open ditch, into which the nearby Fever Hospital also sent its drainage. Despite many of the inhabitants of the Rookery also being young children, this did not seem to bother the builder and owner of this atrocious building, one town Councillor Townsend.

The lack of sufficient drainage had caused concerns as early as 1845, by which time it was impossible not to note that '…many of our highways are literally open drains' into which the filth from surrounding houses were washed, creating stagnant pools of decomposing matter, ringed with flies and rats. Fothergill Street was composed of just 21 houses, but was home to a few hundred destitute workers. Each house consisted of four or five separate rooms, with each having been let in turn to separate families. These were again further sub-let to any number of between 8 to 14 other people. The majority of Fothergill Street's occupants were Irish navvies, who slept in nothing more than beds made of shavings and rags in cruel heaps on the floor. The atmosphere in each room was unquestionably grim, often with fireplaces stopped, and windows closed to retain heat at the cost of ventilation, where the barely healthy were breathing the same dank and heavy air as the unquestionably sick. In some instances, wet clothes were hung to dry alongside those trying to rest their aching bodies in their 'nests' of rags for a short period of time before returning to their back breaking labour, and as one rose, another person would drop into their bed and take their place.

In these conditions, misery, disease and death stalked the houses as almost constant threats to the continuation of life. Inside one room five beds had been squeezed, with six men in each of them, three with their heads in one direction, and three with their heads in the other. Another room, where the atmosphere choked the lungs with dank thick air, was found to have 42 people sleeping in it, despite measuring just 12 feet by 14 feet. The cupboards were given over to the womenfolk or to the children as sleeping space. In one instance the mother of a tenant was found with three of her grandchildren sleeping in shifts in a small cupboard just 20 inches wide and 4 ½ feet long.

Even more shamefully, it was reported that even though the tenants were willing to pay an additional 2d. or 3d. a week for water, the landlord had refused to make the necessary outlay for pipework or fittings, despite having been offered the necessary materials by the Water Company at a much reduced rate. Even before the houses of Fothergill Street had been entered, the state of the street outside gave some indication of the depths of misery that might be experienced within. There were no drains, or gutters, with the result that slops and refuse were thrown directly into the street by the occupants. To compound the problem, a slaughter house has also been erected in the near vicinity, adding blood and animal waste to the pools of human waste gathering outside the houses by those unfortunate enough to be forced to live there.

Twenty years after Clark's report, little had changed, Fothergill Street and its 'abominable court' gave shelter to those who owned little or nothing, and where a bed or rags might be secured for a few coppers. There could be few more lowly places to call home, and no meaner place into which a new life could be brought. It can be assumed that there were either few alternative housing choices that Levi Scarrett could afford, or that the necessity to provide some form of shelter for his heavily pregnant wife had forced Levi to seek out the most readily available port, a bed of rags or shavings for Fiance Scarrett, formerly, Smith, in Fothergill Street. It wasn't until the 18th of April that Levi would make the journey to formally register the birth of his son, John, which he

Registration District	Newport								
Dosbarth Cofrestru									
1870. Birth in the Sub-district of Newport in the County of Monmouth									
Genedigaeth yn Is-ddosbarth				yn					
No. Rhif	When and where born	Name, if any	Sex	Name and surname of father	Name, surname and maiden surname of mother	Occupation of father	Signature, description and residence of informant	When registered	Signature of registrar	Name entered after registration
1	2	3	4	5	6	7	8	9	10	
247	Twenty Eighth March 1870 Fothergill Street Newport	John	Boy	Levi Scarrett	Fiance Scarrett formerly Smith	Hawker	X The Mark of Levi Scarrett Father Fothergill Street Newport	Eighteenth April 1870	W Devons Registrar	—

Jack Scarrott's Birth Certificate

did in the company of the registrar, W.D. Evans, by making his mark, a simple 'X' as he had not received any formal education, with Levi being unable to read or write his own name. His occupation was listed simply as 'Hawker' covering a tenuous existence that might entail peddling the sale of any number of easily transportable or self-crafted goods. It is plausible that Levi might have had some prior experience in crafting goods of his own, and was recorded on the 1891 census as having been a 'Basket maker'. Intriguingly, on the same document, Levi's birthplace is also recorded as having been 'Bedshire' in Gloucestershire, although no such place actually exists.

While it seems possible that the document may have been transcribed incorrectly, it appears likely that Levi, like so many others was drawn to make his way across the border from rural England into Wales, and met Fiancé Smith on his travels in search of a better life. Whatever the truth of it, finding themselves in such oppressive surroundings, it hardly proves surprising that given the general sense of hopelessness that settled on Fothergill Street, and the dangers that it presented to the health of their new baby John, at some point Levi and Fiance Scarrett decided that they had no option but to hit the road once more.

Chapter 2

Martin Fury vs. Jack Hearn

In the years that followed, Levi and his family appear to have travelled quite widely, a fact supported by their inclusion on the Census of 1891, when the 'Scarratt' family are documented as having lived in a canvas tent in the district of Ystradyfodwg, near the bustling market town of Pontypridd. By this time however, Levi, aged 40 is listed as having been living with a wife by the name of 'Sophia'. Due to the large number of travelling people sharing the same name, it is particularly hard to distinguish which of the extended family members of the Scarratt family are which, a problem compounded by the free ranging movements of the various members. This situation is further complicated by the multiple variations in the spelling of the family name, with the name having proved problematic for official document compilers, and newspaper men alike down the years. Skerrit, Skarrot, Skerret, Scarratt and most commonly, Scarrott, would all be used at various points in time. For the sake of clarity it makes most sense to use the most frequently used name, with 'Scarrott' being the name by which John appears to have been most commonly recorded under.

Whether or not Fiance and Sophia are actually the same woman is difficult to prove or to discount. There is an entry for a Fiance Scarrett (46 years old) in the death index of 1895 in the Cardiff area, although it is equally possible that Levi had left Fiance and taken up with another woman by the name of Sophia, and afterwards stated that they were married without ever having been formally wed. Despite these issues, the 1891 Census does give some intriguing insights into just how widely the ever growing Scarrott family would travel in order to make a living. By 1891 there were six members of the same Scarrott family sharing the two room Canvas tent, with Jack having long since packed his bags and struck out on his own to make his living as a booth boxer. Levi aged 40 is listed as the head of the household, with Sophia having been listed as his wife (also 40). Also sharing the cramped living space are Levi Jnr. (aged 18), Sophia (aged 14), Susan (aged 8) and Earnest (aged 5). The birthplaces of each child are different, and it would appear that in the years after having left Newport the family travelled widely throughout South Wales. Levi Jnr. was born in the booming 'iron' town of Merthyr Tydfil, Sophia was born in Newport, Susan was born in Neath, and Earnest was born in Pontypridd, which would appear to be the town that the family most often called home while Jack Scarrott was growing up.

That the family roamed far beyond these places while selling their wares can be established by the fact that it was not in Pontypridd that a young Jack Scarrott would witness his first bareknuckle fist fight, but amongst the

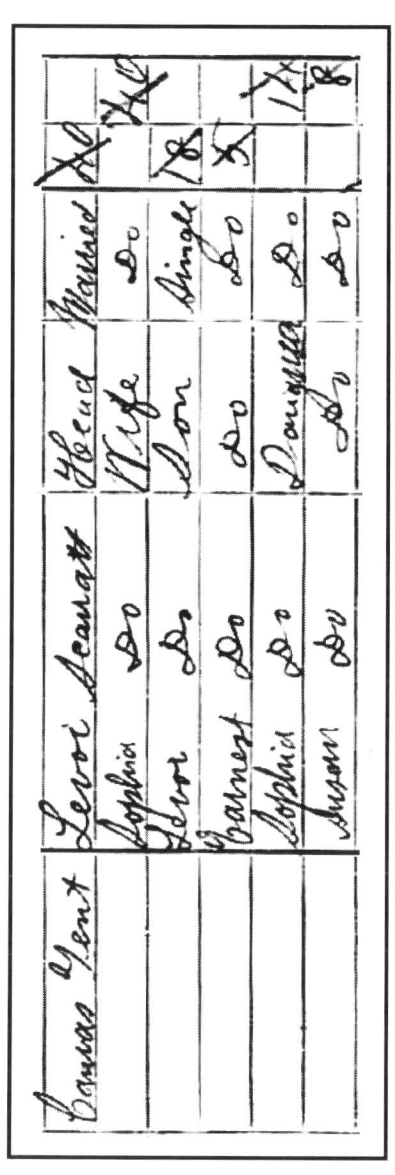

Section of 1891 Census showing the 'Scarratt' family

sand blown dunes in the area known as Black Pill, near the city frequently referred to as 'Copperopolis' after its vast copper smelting industry, but better known today as Swansea. It happened quite by chance as Jack was running errands for his mother, and witnessed a fight that he would remember with absolute clarity, even over half a century after the battle itself.

The fight between Martin Fury and Jack Hearn could quite conceivably have occurred when Jack was nine years old, although it is plausible that he may have been even younger. By the time William Hughes sat Jack Scarrott down to recall the main points of a long life spent in and around the boxing booths, Jack was sixty six years old, although he mistakenly believes that he was actually sixty nine years of age. While Jack proves himself to be a fantastic story-teller, his tales range back and fore between incidents witnessed, facts half-remembered and some stories that appear to be recounted second hand. Having never been taught to read or write, and having no way to record or remember exactly when an incident occurred other than his remarkable memory, age is an elastic concept for Jack. There is simply life before the booth, when he was a fledgling 'booth boxer', and then the time before that when he was merely a 'boy', sneaking under the canvas of a boxing booth to witness the 'champion' William Samuels in all his glory, or playing pitch and toss with his friends on the side of a mountain overlooking Pontypridd as a teenager. There is no true differentiation in age, there is only life prior to when Jack Scarrott became a booth boxer and before he could consider himself having become a man.

Regardless, we can infer that Jack was quite young when he first witnessed his first bareknuckle battle between Martin Fury and the gypsy known as Jack Hearn. Hearn was a fighting man who was familiar to all the gypsies. Certainly on the brief details recalled by Jack Scarrott, Hearn was an imposing figure, weighing in at roughly fifteen stone (210lb.), and had a formidably strong and rugged appearance, standing well above the average height of the time at approximately 5ft 10 inches tall. Fury would appear at first glance to have been an unlikely challenger, weighing in at about 11 stone 6lb. according to Jack's recollections, and therefore giving away about 50lb. in weight. Hearn also came with a big reputation, having said to have decimated the ranks of gypsy fighters that had previously dared to meet him in battle.

There are apparently no records to tell us anything more about Hearn, other than he is remembered as having fought and beaten all of the gypsy men that had come his way, and perhaps this in itself would recommend him as a likely victor against Martin Fury. As Jack recalls, the gypsies fought solely for the love of the battle itself, and there were few instances in which an outsider might venture onto a camp in order to get a gypsy to fight outside the circle of his own people, there being few opportunities to earn a purse for a battle outside the usual mountain fighting matches at this time. This love of a fight for fighting's sake was most pronounced in the gypsies or 'tinkers' that arrived in the wake of the Great Famine, with the new arrivals showing a characteristic enjoyment of bare-knuckle fighting. In 'Gypsies of Britain' by Brian Seymour Vesey-Fitzgerald

(1973) the Irish gypsy is very clearly remembered as having been of fighting stock;

'He is by nature a fighter, and he fights with a cold fury and a fixed desire to maim that is rather frightening. When the travelling Irish first invaded Wales and the Welsh border counties they came in rough contact with the Gypsies, and the Gypsies very definitely had the worst of it. So much so, in fact, that they would rather move camp than risk a fight, unless they were in greatly superior numbers.'

For this reason it is no surprise that the gypsy women feared that a battle between Hearn and Fury might result in either injury or fatality and the subsequent police interference that might force them to move on. Jack does not appear to think of himself as one of the gypsy camp people, although would appear to have set up camp with his family in the near vicinity, and for the most part lived a similar lifestyle of constant movement and travel, largely dictated by the calendar of the Welsh fairgrounds.

Martin Fury is just one of many intriguing characters of the early Welsh boxing ring that have largely slipped through the net of modern boxing history, although he was undoubtedly a very fierce individual and a more than capable fighter. Few credible tales that correspond exactly with the known timeline of his active days appear to have been properly recorded, other than in a few brief anecdotal accounts linked to other forgotten fighters of the age. In some instances he has been recorded as 'Black' Martin Fury, in the same way that Jack Scarrott is often remembered as 'Black' Jack Scarrott. It seems likely that this name stemmed from the wearing of a black leather waistcoat, an item of clothing adopted for practical reasons amongst gypsies, horse people and showmen alike. Where else could Jack safely deposit the coins collected for entry into his booth than into the deep pockets of his battered old waistcoat?

Strategically speaking, Martin Fury appears to have gained enough ring experience by this time to overcome the physical advantages of Jack Hearn. The fight between the two men roughly corresponds to many other recorded instances of surprise victory in the prize ring, where a clever fighter could often beat a 'better' man and secure victory by 'playing' for the face, using superior ring tactics to force an end to the contest. By using footwork and his speed in hitting to his advantage, Fury moved in and out of range, beating Hearn to the punch. While hitting for the bonier areas of the face was not without danger in risking damaging the knuckles and putting a fighter out of commission, it was a tactic that in this instance paid off for Martin Fury.

At this time, a fight along gypsy rules appears to have been conducted roughly along the same lines as it is conducted today, with the rounds being open ended, and only ending when one fighter actually went down, as a direct result of a punch or strike. Scarrott makes no reference to throws or falls, often used to secure victory in prize fights decided under the London Prize Ring rules, more frequently adopted on the other side of the border in England, and occasionally used in battles of 'championship' status in Wales. He does recall, however, that the whole battle lasted approximately an hour and a half, by which time Hearn must have presented a truly gruesome spectacle, judging by contemporary pictures that show a man's face terribly distorted and beaten after

Illustration from 1886 showing the facial injuries sustained following a bare knuckle fight of one hour forty five minutes duration

having been engaged in battle for such a length of time. In any case, the injuries sustained speak for themselves, with Fury's knuckles having damaged the soft tissue of the face of his opponent to the extent that Hearn was completely 'blinded', forcing the crowd of spectators to lance the area around the eyes to drain the coagulated blood from the swelling to enable Hearn to fight on, although ultimately he was blinded again and was unable to continue the contest.

As a spectacle for a young boy to witness there can be no doubt that in amongst the surging crowd of yelling spectators, Jack would have found it difficult, if not impossible to turn away from such a new and savage spectacle. What is perhaps more surprising is that there appears to be no sense of alarm or fear in Jack's account, and that he records the story of the battle with something almost approaching emotional detachment from the scene. Fury won through his superior 'science' to use the language of the time, and due to his tactical awareness of the best way to meet a man who was physically his master. It would prove to be a useful reminder for the future years that Jack Scarrott would spend at ringside that looks could be deceiving, and that very few of the champions of his boxing booth would be hulking fighters of formidable size and strength.

It seems surprising that Jack Scarrott would be able to recall the names of the two combatants over half a century later, but it is plausible that Jack Scarrott remained familiar with Martin Fury long after witnessing the battle against Jack Hearn. It is possible that he may have even discussed the battle itself in the years that followed with Martin Fury, or seen Fury engaged in other pugilistic contests, either in bareknuckle battles or within one of the travelling boxing booths. Like many others, Fury appears to have been a very mobile pugilist, and in later years could often be found around the area of Pontypridd, where Jack Scarrott would spend many of his formative years, and would later situate his boxing booth.

The wider Fury clan were also well known in the area, with a few members having been summoned to the local court in 1899, when police were called to the New Inn Hotel in Pontypridd in order to remove one Thomas Fury and Emily Bates from the premises. Thomas refused to leave and created a scene after abusing the other customers. Martin Fury was also charged with terrorizing the local people in nearby 'People's Park' where Martin had apparently roughed up a young boy, and afterwards lobbed a stone in the direction of Inspector Thomas, who had been called to the scene of the crime. Martin appears to have been unbothered by the arrival of the Inspector, or the threat of further policemen being called, having drunkenly announced to all and sundry that he 'did not care a damn for a thousand police'. His relation, Emily Bates was well known as a troublemaker to the police, with Superintendent Cole stating before the court that she had been convicted 43 times previously. In terms of sentencing following the offence, Bates got off most lightly, only being sent to jail for fourteen days. By contrast, Thomas Fury was sent down for 28 days, with Martin's reputation for trouble ensuring he received 21 days with hard labour.

There are a few other scattered references to be found to Martin Fury in the Welsh newspapers, but there is nothing that can give us any true insight into his ability as a pugilist beyond what Jack Scarrott tells us. For a time, intriguingly, he appears to have found occasional employment as a second and corner man in the boxing booths themselves, having been namechecked as a corner man in at least one account of a contest under the flapping canvas of John Stokes booth in the early 1890's. Perhaps an ongoing familiarity with Martin Fury in this context accounts for the reason that Jack Scarrott could recall Martin Fury's name and that of Jack Hearn, so long after both had faded into obscurity.

One pugilist that Jack Scarrott was certainly very well acquainted with was the self-styled 'Heavyweight Champion of Wales', William Samuels, who definitely was a man who once met, was very hard to forget. He would also long remember Samuels' battle with one 'Sam Lane' as having been one of the 'most remarkable' bare knuckle fights that he ever saw.

Chapter 3

William Samuels

There can be no more of a memorable or remarkable fighter in the whole of Jack Scarrott's recollections than the fearsome heavyweight champion of mountainside and booth, William Samuels. Such was Samuels' fame that it could be said that he didn't fully enter into the greatest moments of his recorded fighting career until he was himself well past the half a century mark. It is perhaps fair to say that Samuels had probably never done anything without having been quite sure the wider world would and certainly *should* hear of it.

Born in Swansea, there is little of the early days of Samuels' life that is not shrouded in mystery, although he would claim that he had been born in the Rising Sun Inn, and was reportedly born into a very well-known Carmarthenshire family. Samuels grandfather is recorded as having been a clergyman, although Samuels would state that his father had been a clergyman too, with his father having been remembered by the local newspapers as having been a '...mountebank and versatile entertainer of the million', and perhaps 'one of the best known men in Swansea' in his time. Whatever the truth of his background, one thing can be said about William Samuels, he was a one-off, and whoever came before Samuels in his family line is unlikely to have been as good as a self-publicist, entertainer or even half as good as preaching when occasion demanded it so much as old 'Billy Sam' himself.

As a young man he had built his built his reputation as a fighter in bare-knuckle bouts on the 'Burrows' a rough and desolate piece of land located behind Shackleford's copper and lead smelting works at Swansea. It was here that those in the know would gather at dawn to fight, with lookouts scattered here and there to watch for the 'beak', although any policemen would be ill advised to approach the battleground unless strengthened by sufficient numbers to guarantee their safety. Even Jack Scarrott, often critical of other 'showmen' could surely pay the great showman of Swansea no greater respect a number of decades after his death by stating;

'William Samuels...was a great fighter and a great showman. In fact, I think he may have been the greatest fighter of his time in the whole of the country.'

In later years, Samuels would claim that in the days of his youth as a young pugilist he had travelled from Swansea to Pembrokeshire when he was about eighteen years of age to witness the famous American pugilist John C. Heenan in action in a travelling circus. Young Billy received a lucky break when Heenan's sparring partner, Tom King was found to be too drunk to perform, and Billy reportedly stepped in as a partner to assist Heenan in demonstrating his skills before the crowds. Although the story appears to read a little like fiction, there might well be some truth in the old story. Certainly Heenan did visit Wales, in the company of 'Howes American Circus' in the early 1860's and is recorded as having performed at both Newport and Cardiff. It is entirely credible that Samuels may well have had the fortune to have crossed fists with Heenan in an exhibition before the crowds. In an interview with the veteran boxer in 1899, when Billy was said to be sixty one years of age, the showman would recall that he had met Heenan on the Mill Hills near Cartlett Kilns before a large crowd when both had been attached to Myer's Circus. It was after this time that Samuels became a professional boxer, and would ultimately become regarded as having been the champion boxer of Wales, a title that he claimed for the next thirty years.

On his return to Swansea, Samuels had cemented his growing reputation as a fighting man after a confrontation with Thomas Pearson in 1865, Pearson was a clog maker who ran a shop in the High Street, and well regarded on the underground bare knuckle Swansea scene, fighting under the alias of "Cloggy". Pearson, convinced of his pugilistic superiority to Samuels, had been quick to state that he would 'thrash' Samuels if the two should ever meet in battle. News of Cloggy's proud boastfulness had quickly reached the ears of William Samuels, who challenged Pearson after bumping into him in the High Street, asking 'You say you can beat me – can you do so now?' Clearly taken aback by the challenge, Pearson proved to be a less than willing opponent, replying 'I don't know, I don't want to try. I have had ten days for fighting, and I don't want to go down again.' Unimpressed by Pearson's response, Samuels gave Pearson a forceful slap across the face. Pearson walked away, further antagonising Samuels by suggesting that he intended on reporting the matter to the police, stating "that will do, you shall have ten days for that, same as I had".

It was enough to ignite Samuels growing rage, and he charged at Cloggy, and the two ended up scuffling in the street. William Samuels wound up in court shortly afterwards for assault, and freely admitted that he had struck the first blow after hearing of Pearson's disparaging remarks regarding his abilities as a pugilist and was fined 11 shillings including costs after a police statement had testified that to the fact that Samuels was of good character.

Although apparently the only claimant to being 'Heavyweight' champion of Wales at this time, William Samuels was not a particularly large man by modern standards. In Jack Scarrott's recollections of him, Samuels stood 5ft 9 inches tall, but was a very well built man for his weight, which was anywhere between twelve and thirteen stone. Perhaps the only photo now surviving of old 'Billy Sam' as he was popularly called reveals a haughty looking individual standing proud and erect and donning a curious outfit, part circus ring master, part pugilist, with long boots matched with outfit of a fighter from an earlier age, topped with the fighting 'colours' of the old rogue, wrapped about his waist.

From what is known of Samuels, he cut his teeth in the old style, having reportedly fought some forty or fifty battles with the 'raw 'uns' as bare knuckle matches were often termed. Samuels was undoubtedly as much of a showman as he was a fighter, with many of his best moments having been brightened sufficiently by Samuels' tendency towards proud boastfulness. From his younger days he had knocked about with members of the circus and fairground crowd, and was often in the company of members of the Taylor family, well known for acrobatic feats of daring on the Welsh fairground circuit. Afterwards a nephew, one Harry Taylor would go on to run the Ivor Athletic Club at Swansea where boxing matches were held, and where Billy Samuels could often be found in his later years at ringside offering his opinions on up and coming prospects, and occasionally even entering the ring to 'school' a youngster or two.

Aside from entering the ring, and demonstrating remarkable 'science' with gloves and noticeable agility, even past his fiftieth year, Samuels was well known for feats of strength, which is no doubt how he developed his noticeable upper body development and brawny arms. It seems unlikely that Samuels could have found a better female counterpart than his wife, Elizabeth. Elizabeth Samuels, on what is known, was a particularly formidable female foil to the old showman, having appeared on the booth front alongside Billy as a 'strong woman' with Jack Scarrott remembering that she often allowed Billy Samuels to break large stones placed on her chest with a sledge hammer. It was probably the influence of Elizabeth that would lead to Billy's decision to include demonstrations by female pugilists on his show, possibly the only boxing booth in South Wales that is recorded as having done so at this time.

Having been at the forefront of local acclaim as a strongman and a bare knuckle fighter who had turned to the gloves for so long, it seems unsurprising that the showman was very defensive of his home patch, and was very protective of his position as the pre-eminent supplier of boxing talent on any of the fairgrounds throughout South Wales, all of which he seemed to believe were his own personal 'turf'. Jack Scarrott appears to have been a fan of William Samuels from his childhood days, recounting how he had wanted to see Samuels' show when it had pitched up at Abercwmboi, featuring Samuels as the main attraction. With the show costing 3d. it proved too expensive for young Jack Scarrott, having a single penny in his possession, and like so many boys before, and so many after, he decided to try his luck by sliding in under the canvas round the back of the boxing booth.

Jack Scarrott found that his attempt to gain entry was more than worth the effort. On this occasion Samuels stepped up, and put a pretender on the boards inside three rounds. Foolishly, one of the local hard men hailing from Aberdare, one Dai Magee, was brazen enough to doubt whether Samuels was likely to be able to do the same to him, and stated as much. Samuels, for all his faults, never appeared to be a man to doubt his own worth in the face of a challenge, and invited the rabble rouser to 'Step up'. Probably on point of principle, Samuels made sure he levelled Magee inside a round. The effect on a young Jack Scarrott can only be imagined, and it seems plausible that Scarrott had found a hero to emulate as a future boxing booth proprietor. The boxing booth customers seemed less satisfied with the performance, perhaps, given Samuels' nature they would have preferred to have seen Magee take the old champ down a peg or two. Samuels was quick to answer the grumblings of the crowd, retorting from the ring that '…he didn't care for all of them, and that he'd lick the three best men in Glamorgan. Despite the 'hooting and booing' of the crowd that followed the statement, it does not appear as if any more of them dared to offer to stand against him.

William Samuels was not averse to pulling off the gloves and meeting a challenger on his own turf with bare knuckles if occasion demanded it. On one occasion, Jack Scarrott recalls that he travelled to the Deri mountain near Fochriw to meet Ivor 'Gwynn' with the knuckles for £5 a-side, despite having not a 'single supporter in the crowd'. With there being a minutes rest between each knockdown, Samuels met the challenge in typical style, resting Gwynn on his knee between rounds, and afterwards knocking him down and out in eight or ten rounds.

Samuels had run a boxing show long before Scarrott's time, and the booth is remembered as having pitched up very close to where Scarrott witnessed his very first bareknuckle contest between Martin Fury and Jack Hearn at Swansea's seafront as a child. One old timer would relate in the *Cambrian Leader* in 1918 that in the early day of the fairgrounds, and even before the grand later days when John Studt and his brothers had run some of the greatest and most expensive roundabouts ever seen in the United Kingdom, Samuels had built his booth up alongside, where his bruisers had flexed and bounced on the platform outside to entice the crowds to step inside and witness a contest first hand;

'I remember Studt used to bring his show down . . . we boys used to push his roundabout around and have rides for nothing . . . he had a horse to do it after, then a handle. Billy Samuels used to put his boxing booth near the Antelope . . . There was more 'n one row at the shows. I mind a chap who had the handcuffs put on one Good Friday, but he got away and a blacksmith sawed 'em off up in Sketty.'

Despite Jack's clear recollection of the events leading up to Samuels' memorable fight with 'Sam Lane', key aspects of the fight appear to have eluded Jack Scarrott. This is mainly due to the fact that Jack's memory of the event is one of a twelve year old boy, looking on from the margins. Sam Lane was not in fact called Sam Lane, nor was he a boxing booth proprietor, at least at the time of his battle against William Samuels in 1882. Sam Lane had been an alias adopted by another bare-knuckle fighter turned booth boxer by the name of Robert or 'Bob' Dunbar. Little is now remembered of Bob Dunbar, but suffice to say, after his days of glory in which he apparently claimed the lightweight championship of Wales for ten years, he would still be remembered even outside Wales as one of the greatest fighters that the country had produced. Dunbar had first 'come to the front' in Shrewsbury, having reportedly fought a stiff battle against one Jack Owen who he beat in just three minutes short of an hour with the knuckles, and a short while afterwards returned to his native South Wales to further his pugilistic career.

Naturally, as a bare knuckle fighter looking for a break and an easy way to make some money, Dunbar's thoughts would turn towards the boxing booths, and so he elected to take a paid engagement as the main performer on William Samuel's booth. Prior to this time Bob Dunbar had learned the best way to avoid the law was to fight under an alias to avoid prosecution for prize-fighting and adopted aliases including 'Young' Lane, 'Little' Bob Lane and Sam Lane. At times he was billed as having been from Scotland, or Birmingham although Newport was the town that Bob Dunbar called home, and is likely to have been where he first came to light – certainly Bob and his booth could be found there most often in the years that followed, although for a time he also set up shop at Ebbw Vale.

As a fierce young man, having been said to have been 'about 22' at the time of his meeting with Samuels, it seems natural that he would take offence to the aging showman bossing him about, with Samuels apparently pushing up forty at the time of the meeting. Jack Scarrott's memory about the particulars of the fight are correct, stating that the fight occurred on a field off the road on the Whitland – Carmarthen road, which was being used as a campground next to the Llanelly fairground where the fairground people had pitched their tents and hitched their horses. A disagreement that began in this humble setting would erupt into an explosive confrontation that neither Billy Samuels nor Robert Dunbar would be able to forget for many years afterwards.

Chapter 4

William Samuels vs. Bob Dunbar

John Graham Chambers was born in Llanelly on the 12th February 1843. He is remembered today for having drafted the Marquis of Queensbury Rules after having become friendly with the Marquis, John Shoto Douglas, whilst attending Cambridge University. The Marquis of Queensbury Rules introduced such standardised practise as a minutes rest between round, and the introduction of the three minute round. Ultimately this would pave the way forward for such pioneers in Welsh gloved boxing as William Samuels and Jack Scarrott to enable the bare knuckle art of the mountain fighters to adapt sufficiently to provide gloved 'boxing' entertainment on the fairground. Chambers was well known as a sportsman and rowed for his University in addition to having accompanied Captain Webb alongside Webb in a boat when Webb became the first man to have successfully swum across the English Channel to France. It seems likely that more than anyone John Graham Chambers would have been utterly disgusted with the spectacle that unfolded between William Samuels and Bob Dunbar on a muddy campground near his hometown on 2nd October, 1882.

If fault can be found with either Bob Dunbar or William Samuels, it would be fair to say that Samuels was mostly to blame for what followed. Trouble and disagreements had reportedly been brewing between the pugilists for some time prior to one event having pushed both over the edge. Dunbar sustained a fairly painful injury, having dislocated his knee after a particularly awkward fall off of one of Samuels's horses while Samuels's booth was travelling to Llanelly Fair. With such a serious injury hampering Dunbar's ability to move easily, Bob Dunbar was keen to break off his agreement to appear in Samuels' boxing booth. Samuels thought differently, even though Dunbar secured a medical certificate to prove the seriousness of his injury. Unfortunately , Samuels refused to pay the stricken boxer's £3 wages unless the young pugilist showed up for duty on the booth apron, as William Samuels believed that Dunbar's non-appearance as one of the main attractions would mean a downturn in his booth takings.

On Monday 2nd October, 1882 matters came to a head when Dunbar strode across the campsite and demanded that Billy pay up the money owed. It wasn't a request that Billy was likely to concede without dispute, and a verbal exchange quickly led to a darkening in Billy's temper, and made a physical exchange unavoidable. Despite Samuels advancing years, he had never been a man to doubt his own worth when it came to a battle with the naked fists, and while Bob certainly had youth on his side, he had picked a formidable opponent when he chose to engage the booth proprietor in a contest. Even fifty years after having first seen William Samuels perform on the boxing booths, Jack Scarrott's memory of William Samuels would remain completely undimmed, and he would conclude after many long years on the boxing booth that;

'For dangerous punching, Samuels was the greatest fighter I ever saw'

As the other fairground people gathered around Dunbar and Samuels, it transpired that not everyone shared Jack's viewpoint. If there could be anyone that led popular feeling on the fairground it was likely to be John Studt. John had certainly laid a few blows himself when occasion had demanded it, but was by and large a friendly giant, standing a massive 6ft 4 inches in his boots. John was the head of the famous Studt family, having taken control of the letting of pitches on many of the fairgrounds of South Wales, mainly due to his business acumen in developing the premier roundabout and amusements businesses to be found on the Welsh circuit. Indeed, it was John, supported by his brothers and their elderly German mother, who could be seen at work their lucrative roundabouts at the fairgrounds throughout South Wales even past her eightieth year that had almost singlehandedly developed the concept of the Welsh 'pleasure' fair. Without the Studt family, there would have been few top class entertainments and rides on offer alongside the ancient trade based fairs that their business had grown up alongside. It was the great roundabouts of the Studt family that had brought increased trade to the smaller stalls owners flocking and eager to pay over their fees to secure the best pitches where they might do a stronger trade. The numbers of smaller stalls and amusement concerns on the circuit had exploded following the expansion of the entertainments offered by the Studt family to the general public.

There was plenty of amusements on offer for those colliers willing or still able to part with a few coins after having made the obligatory pre-fair tour of the local public houses. Primitive test your strength contraptions nestled between freak shows, fat ladies, working colliery models, snake charmers and fledgling menagerie owners. There were card sharpers and novelty stalls jostling for business on the outskirts of the fair, where those foolish enough to put down their money found it quickly scooped up by the quick hands of those that had implored them to 'chase the lady'. The young men gathered outside the coconut shies and shooting galleries wanting to prove the keenness of their eye, and there were many haberdashery based concerns for the 'young missies' of South Wales, eager to purchase a bolt of new cloth for dress-making purposes, of lengths of ribbon to tie their hair and attract new admirers.

The Studt family had shared close ties with Samuels and his people for more years than anyone could remember, but John Studt was firmly of the opinion that William Samuel's day had passed, and remarked to his brother, Henry;

'This man will be too clever for Samuels'.

But Henry wasn't too sure, having seen William Samuels take on all comers on his booth down the years, and recognising that his stout old arms hadn't seemingly failed the old ring warrior yet.

'Samuels will be too strong for him' replied Henry.

Initially, at least, Henry's keen eye does not appear to have let him down. Samuel's fighting technique, long honed in countless bare-knuckle battles appeared the sounder strategy. In the days of knuckle fighting, where a match was open ended, and could, and often did go on for many rounds and hours, many combatants leaned towards a tendency to target the fleshier areas of the body. Jack Scarrott tells us that William Samuels was, '…never known to hit a man out with a punch on the jaw. It was always the pit of the stomach he went for, and that stomach punch of his put paid to everybody it landed on.'

The advantages of this strategy was that there was far less risk of damaging the knuckles, which, without the cushioning effect supplied by boxing gloves, were at far greater risk of being painfully damaged or broken through contact with the bonier areas of an opponent's anatomy. Targeting the face in the heat of battle was a dangerous affair, which might put a hand out of commission altogether, and proved to be a very risky strategy. For someone with a long term career with the knuckles like Samuels, to launch a sustained attack to the face a risky proposition. By barrelling into close range and attacking the stomach, Samuels would take a few blows but succeed in taking the battle to close range where ultimately his prodigious strength could come to his aid and lay his opponent low by landing a full arm shot to the stomach. This is what used to be termed a 'shot to the mark', or what would later be known as a 'solar plexus' punch following its adoption by World middle and heavyweight champion, Bob Fitzsimmons. It was only later, and into the gloved era that a man might be more frequently finished off and knocked unconscious by a punch to the jaw. It is some testament to the skill and raw power of Samuels that he appears to have been able to knock an opponent 'out' with a heavy stomach punch alone, with this punch having featured as the main weapon in his arsenal. This is exactly what appears to have happened to Bob Dunbar in short time. Although Bob favoured trying to land his punches on the face and boxed 'in and out' of range, Samuels launched himself into close range, enabling him to land his fearsome stomach punch '…with such terrible force that Lane (Dunbar) fell down dead out.'

At this moment, Samuels, who would have been in no doubt as to the potential seriousness of the situation then took it upon himself to nurse Dunbar back to consciousness by administering brandy, while 'rubbing' Dunbar back to the land of the living. Having started his pugilistic career in illegal mountain fights, and competitive fights on the turf at Swansea, Samuels had no doubt learned more than a trick or two in bringing a man round, as a bare-knuckle fighter, in many ways his liberty depended on it. Over the years there would be plenty of men who would end up behind bars serving a lengthy jail sentence for having accidentally finished off an opponent in a fight that had gone on too long.

It says plenty about the courage of Bob Dunbar that after having been brought round, his only thought was to resume the battle, believing that it was Samuels that had brought a 'lucky' punch into play and was eager to start again. Samuels had no doubt of his ability to level

Dunbar for a second time, and so both men stripped down for business.

It was at this point that Dunbar appears to have stepped up, and his strategy of boxing at long range and hitting for the face finally paid off. In the twenty five or twenty six rounds that followed, it was Dunbar that pushed Billy Samuels 'pretty near all over the field' and continued to punish him with impunity by 'playing for the face'. As a bare-knuckle man turned booth boxer, it seems plausible that Bob Dunbar, like so many other fighters, including William Samuels, was likely to have decided to 'pickle' or harden the skin around the knuckles to reduce the risk of damage to the hands. Many different solution or combinations were used by knuckle men and boxers alike down the years. Samuels reportedly used a solution of alum (a solution of potassium aluminium sulphate), and routinely 'worked' the flesh back from the knuckles to enable him to do more damage to his opponent. The great English bare-knuckle champion Jem Mace would recall that he used a mixture of whisky, copperas (iron sulphate), gunpowder, horse radish and other ingredients which turned his fists black.

In any case, whatever solution Bob used, if any, his knuckles held up, and he punished Samuels in exactly the same manner that Martin Fury battered Jack Hearn, or going back even further to perhaps one of the greatest prize fight of the age, that between the Brighton bricklayer turned English champion, Tom Sayers and his famous American opponent, the 'Benicia Boy' John C. Heenan, who was 'blinded' over the course of thirty seven rounds at Farnborough on the 17th April, 1860 at

Farnborough. This fight was the talk of the United Kingdom, if not the world, and was remembered in popular memory decades after the event. It is intriguing that Jack Scarrott seems to retain a great interest in this contest even though it had happened ten years before he was born. William Samuels would also state that despite the injuries of Heenan, he believed that John C. Heenan was on his way to finishing off Sayers when the fight was finally declared a draw. For Scarrott, the fight appears to have been one that interested him greatly, as the statement that Jack makes that he had visited Farnborough is the only indication throughout his entire memoirs that Jack Scarrott ever travelled into England at all other than having travelled across the border to see the fight held between Shoni Engineer of Treorchy and Jem Guidrell of Bristol in Gloucestershire. There appears to be no records or printed accounts of Scarrott's boxing booth having featured on the fairgrounds outside Wales.

Inevitably, having already 'levelled' Dunbar once, Samuels had no fear of defeat and was eager to resume the battle, despite having been 'blinded' by blows to his face. It is hard not to agree with Jack Scarrott, that even after receiving such a brutal battering that Samuels was '…all pluck from head to heel'. Samuels proved as much when he allowed himself to be lanced around both eyes to reduce the massive swelling around his eyes to enable him to fight on. Ultimately the decision to do so proved fruitless, with the swelling making it impossible for him to continue and finally, he reluctantly conceded defeat.

It is lucky that Jack Scarrott's own eye-witness account of the affair has survived as while there is a newspaper account of the fight, published in the *Llanelly*

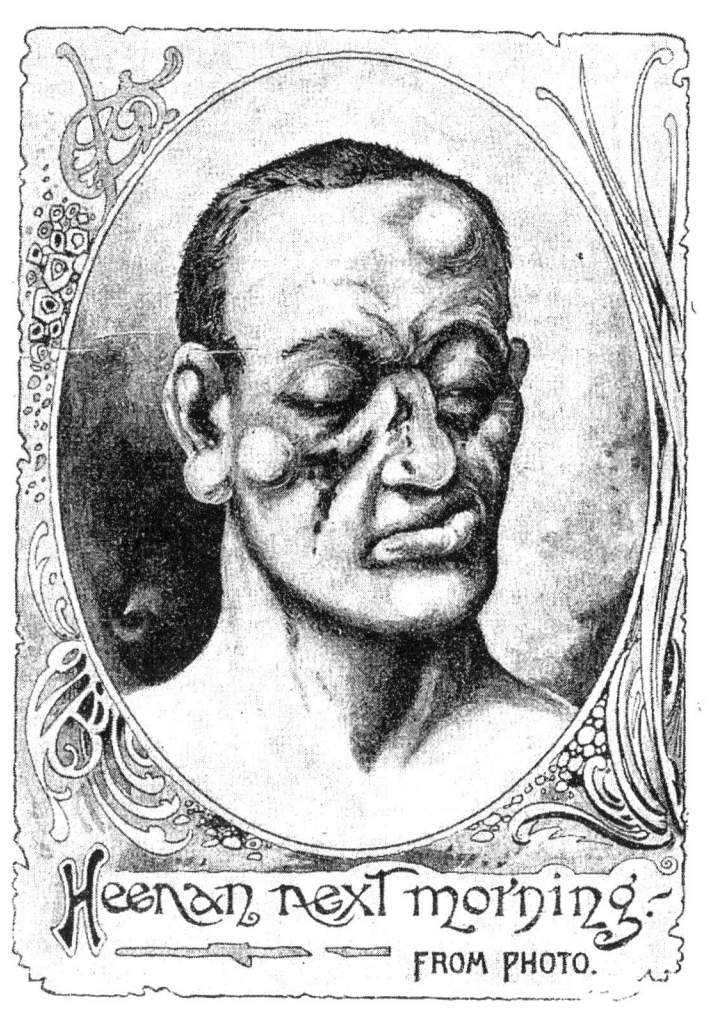

An illustration of the facial damage suffered by John C. Heenan in his fight with Tom Sayers in 1860

and County Guardian, a close examination of the piece shows it to be quite flawed in its coverage of the battle. The reason for this appears to be that the reporter of the fight appeared on the scene after the event and would seem to have reconstructed his account of the event from those statements given by the show people around the campsite.

The newspaper account makes no mention of the first knockout having been supplied by William Samuels, stating only that after the initial rounds, an 'armistice' took place that enabled Dunbar to strip and the fight to continue. The newspaper reporter believed that a further six rounds were fought, and not twenty five. The fact that the fight apparently took just thirty minutes gives some idea of the ferocity of the encounter, and perhaps Billy's gameness in his willingness to fight on after having received such serious facial injuries.

The state of Samuels by the end of the match is worth considering as an indicator of Dunbar's ability, with medical help having been sent for to bring leeches to the scene, so that some of the dreadful swelling to William Samuel's face could be brought down. It can only be wondered if Samuels might have been able to turn the tables had he met Dunbar in his youth, and not giving away over fifteen years to a tested fighter in the pink of youth. After the fight, Bob seems particularly 'flushed' with his victory, having decided to get more than a little drunk, and is said to have "…*strutted about cock of the walk", receiving with becoming modesty the congratulations of his admirers*'.

The misery of the situation was more than a man as proud as Samuels could bear. In short time, he quickly packed up his wagons and headed off in the direction of the town of Carmarthen, in preparation for another fair. The journey was halted long enough for Elizabeth Samuels to leap into action, having been emboldened by what had happened enough to decide to walk across the campground to one of the Studt family's living vans to challenge one of their servant girls to a fight following a recent disagreement, although nothing would come of the spat. It was just as well, the police would no doubt have come knocking, with their non-appearance on the fairground until after the battle was over being reportedly due to the fact that Llanelly's policemen had been shut up in the station going through their drills at the time of the fight.

It would not be the last meeting between the pair, although Scarrott believes that ultimately it would be William Samuels that had the last laugh, eventually forcing Dunbar clean off his patch (or patches) on the fairground(s) through constantly challenging to fight and not giving Dunbar a moment's peace, forcing the young upstart to seek his fortunes elsewhere. Afterwards the police at Carmarthen were shown to be a little quicker on the uptake than they had been at Llanelly, having stopped a match scheduled to come off on their patch, but it only altered the time table of the next occasion when Samuels and Dunbar would swap fists. Neither William Samuels or Bob Dunbar would ever be able to concede that their 'business' was ever truly finished, and even a decade afterwards both men would become enraged at the merest of suggestions that either one or the other had ever achieved the final or decisive victory.

Chapter 5
Shoni Engineer vs. Tom Books

Not too many years after the great battle between William Samuels and Bob Dunbar, Jack Scarrott's family settled their camp in-between fair times on the rolling green hills just outside of Pontypridd. For many years the settlement had merely been known as Newbridge with the town proving to be a popular spot for commerce and trade, following the expansion of the coal and iron industries. From nearby Merthyr trains rolled day and night, transporting iron ore and coal to Pontypridd and then onwards to Cardiff and Newport where they were loaded and shipped to destinations around the world.

Life beyond the fairground opportunities for money making must have proved increasingly hard for Levi, and was dependent on travelling to and from the towns and the villages and selling his wares door to door in order to fill the rumbling stomachs of his children. Although it is hard to document the movements of the family at this time it seems there was at least one additional child, by the name of Annie Marie 'Scarrett' who died in upsetting circumstances on Christmas Day 1884. Levi and his wife had travelled to nearby Mountain Ash in order to try and sell their wares on the 22nd December, leaving the camp for some unknown reason in the care of Jack's younger brother Levi, along with two other children, presumably Jack and Sophia. Intriguingly at this point, it is recorded that Jack's father, Levi was in possession of a travelling van, although a few years later they appear to be living in the two room tent noted in the 1891 census. While Levi was absent from the camp something went amiss, and Annie Marie strayed too close to an unguarded campfire and by the time Levi returned she was terribly burned. A doctor was called from nearby Mountain Ash, but the situation was desperate, and Annie Marie was taken to Cardiff Infirmary where she soon died from her injuries.

Jack and the other children were often left to themselves to take care of the camp area while their parents were forced out of necessity to tramp around the neighbouring towns in order to make their living. This appears to have left Jack with time on his hands to bother the local showmen that had set up home in and around the district. One can imagine that visiting the boxing booths owned and run by some of the early proprietors must have figured highly on his list of priorities. It is on one of Jack's outings that he came across the showman, Lloyd Roberts.

Little of Lloyd Roberts life is recorded in print, but it would appear that like many others he cut his teeth running the usual small fairground concerns that were cheaply produced from which a fledgling showman on the fringes of the fair might progress to better things.

Coconut shy's and Aunt Sally's – a variation on the theme where sticks were hurled at a model of an old crone's head – were ideal starter fare for a fairground man trying to make his way up the fairground ladder. After a time, he might even graduate to the 'swing boats' – large fixed seated swings, where a man with sufficient muscle power would push the 'boats' up into the air. In later times, a steam powered traction engine would take the man out of the equation. There was good money to be made with the swing boats, and even old Billy Samuels elected to continue running a set of swings and employ a few lackeys to staff it alongside his lucrative cocoa-nut stalls many years after he had moved into the boxing booth trade full-time.

Sadly Lloyd Roberts didn't seem to have been blessed with the same pioneering spirit as William Samuels, and it was at Treherbert that Jack Scarrott came across Roberts fretting over a problem on one of his first outings into the boxing booth trade. Roberts doesn't appear to have been much of a boxer personally, one of the few footnotes to his early life is that he was knocked out by the Cardiff booth boxer John O'Brien somewhere in West Wales early on in O'Brien's career. Nor does he appear to have had a great deal of personal initiative, having been stumped on how to raise £5 to purchase the necessary timber to construct a boxing booth to showcase a fight between 'Shoni Engineer' and Tom 'Books' of Pentre.

Of the two men, only 'Shoni Engineer' appears to have been remembered to any great degree. Shoni's real name was John Jones, and he came from Treorchy. He is remembered as a bareknuckle man of the mountain fighting variety, and judging by what limited accounts remain of his activities, he was thought to have been an exponent of great ability. His day job was as a blacksmith, and it might be imagined in a time where most physical work in and around the valleys (and fairgrounds) was supplied by true horse power, Shoni must have been exceedingly busy at the forge. There can be no doubt that he, like Bob Fitzsimmons, a much more famous pugilistic blacksmith, found that his employment packed dense muscle on his arms.

The majority of the career of Shoni Engineer, like most mountain fighters of the period, is recorded in a very patchy manner, although it is said that he was fighting on the hillsides 'almost from infancy'. In one of very few contemporary pen pictures of Shoni we are told that he was both '…sound and fit' in appearance, and was '…a good hale, strapping fellow, whose broad jaw, muscular physique and swinging length of arm' greatly impressed the onlooker. He stood at 5ft 10 inches tall, a reasonable height at a time when poor diet and poverty were rife. Jack Scarrott appears to have liked and admired Shoni, having stood alongside him on the booth platform in his brief days as a booth boxer, although Shoni appears to have had more to do with the world of the mountain fighter and presumably making money in side bets on bare knuckle matches than as a booth boxer proper. This said, he must have been a glove fighter of some ability, as he fought on the booth of Jimmy Day of Portsmouth who by all accounts was a fairly gifted boxer himself, having once beaten no less a name than Rees Mazey of Merthyr, who in turn once beat Redmond Coleman, also of Merthyr, well-known as a fearsome bare-knuckle fighter. Other members of Day's troupe included such names as Sam 'Butcher' Thomas of Ynyshir, Bill Lane of Cwmavon, and for a time, Jack Scarrott himself.

Curiously, Jack Scarrott rates Shoni Engineer's ability as a boxer at the very highest end of the scale, stating that 'Shoni Engineer was at that time the level best 10 stone 10 lb. man in England.', which would seem to be a particularly bold statement for someone who was never matched with so many fighters more familiar to boxing historians of the period. It has to be wondered whether Scarrott's friendship with Shoni might well have clouded his judgement, and made him think more highly of the boxer than perhaps Shoni deserved. Of Shoni's very early battles, almost nothing is now remembered, although it is said that in 1884 he met 'Brooks' (Books?) of the Rhondda valley who '...he easily defeated' in eleven rounds.

Tom 'Books' whose real name was Tom Davies has been recorded in print to an even lesser degree. He is said to have gained his unusual nickname through his father's occupation, that of a bookseller at Pentre. At the time the occupation of bookseller alone would have been unusual enough to recommend it as a nickname, with the vast majority receiving no further education beyond their limited school years. Most were shoved into the cut down pit trousers of an elder relative and shuttled to the bottom of a coal mine after a few precious years of schooling to spend their days digging in the dark in order to contribute to the family's upkeep.

According to Jack Scarrott, it was his own quick thinking and shrewdness that enabled Roberts to come up with a solution to provide the necessary £5. Having realised that Roberts owned a showman's van worth £30, Jack pointed him in the direction of a timber merchant at nearby Ystrad which would supply the timber if Roberts elected to leave his van behind as security. With a solution in hand, the first Lloyd Roberts boxing booth was built opposite Treherbert police station, which in retrospect does not seem to have been the best place to situate the booth, right under the noses of those employed to ensure the upkeep of law and order in the town.

Wind of the scheme reached the ears of the moral high ground of Trehebert pretty quickly, with the local preachers and deacons having decided to infiltrate the usual spectators that could be found making up the crowd. It must have been an event to remember, as Jack recalls it was quite probably the first boxing match ever to be held in the town. The duration of the contest must have given some cause for concern in any case, having been fixed for twenty rounds under Marquis of Queensbury rules. In some areas, police had decided to turn a blind eye to matches held in boxing booths, provided, of course, they appeared to be either showcasing pugilistic skill in the form of exhibitions or were holding matches that were fixed over a limited number of rounds, and did not appear to be fights where the men intended to 'injure' each other. As contradictory as the statement appears, with a fight by its nature consisting of two men trying to forcibly strike and damage each other, for the most part a fight limited to a few rounds appears to have settled public anguish enough for the booth proprietor to continue in his profession unmolested.

Despite any misgivings that Lloyd Roberts should have had, he elected to go through with the match anyway, although it came to an abrupt end after six or seven rounds after both men had been 'hammering away like blacksmiths'. The blame lay fairly and squarely with Books, who out of some frustration with Shoni dropped a glove off his fist in his own corner and then smashed Shoni on the jaw with a bare-fist. Possibly like many other bare fist fighters, Books decided he couldn't 'pluck a chicken' wearing gloves and decided to mix things up in the old style. Police stormed the ring and ended up charging everyone involved for the offence, from the combatants' right down to the seconds, the timekeeper and the referee. Despite having been found guilty and being fined very heavily, no further account of this event has been located in the newspapers of the time. This in itself is hardly surprising, so much boxing coverage in the Welsh newspapers is patchy at best, and stems from the concern regarding the growing popularity of boxing that was felt by the same chapel folk who could often be found lurking at ringside keeping a close eye on proceedings. For these men suppression of the sport through public condemnation was seen to be the usual route to salvation.

There would seem to be some rivalry and possible animosity between the fighters which would account for Books' unexplained behaviour in the match, as it is on record that both Shoni and Books met (presumably) prior to the boxing match at Treherbert. On 17th March 1884, at 10 am Shoni and Books met at Cefn-Ydfa House between Tondu and Maesteg, in a large ring of an estimated 4,000 interested spectators. Accounts are contradictory but the match had been made for either £20 or £25 stakes. A large proportion of the spectators, possibly seven hundred men in total, had travelled throughout the night from the Rhondda valley. They left a very easy trail for police to follow in their wake, having disturbed several publicans in the middle of the night to try and obtain beer and hard liquor to see them on their way to the scene of the battle. At one inn in Brynmenin they were refused admission and decided to put the windows through in an act of revenge. The match reputedly lasted either 25 or 28 rounds and left both combatants seriously bruised, with Shoni being floored in the final round of a 'punishing mill' and was unable to get up and toe the scratch in the centre of the ring and was therefore counted out. Both men were aided in escaping the clutches of the police, who arrived on the scene at the termination of the battle by the combined efforts of the crowd who closed upon the police, enabling the pugilists to escape.

Tom Books was reportedly a miner at the time of his bare-knuckle meeting with Shoni, and afterwards rose through the ranks to become an official at a colliery. He appears, like a few other ex-pugilists of the period to have decided to change his ways, and would in time become a deacon amongst the very same chapel folk who had infiltrated the crowd at Trehebert and publicly raised their objections so noisily. Shoni Engineer, on the other hand, was not for turning, and remained a committed outlaw and bare-knuckle man until the day he died.

Chapter 6

Shoni Engineer vs. Dublin Tom

John Jones of Treorchy, alias 'Shoni Engineer' was widely considered to have become the Welsh middleweight champion on January 1st 1887 after having demolished Pete 'Dublin Tom' Burns of Cardiff. Sadly, there appears to be no complete records of how many fights Shoni had between fighting Tom 'Books' Davies of Pentre in 1884 and meeting Pete Burns in 1887. Only one victory for John Jones of Treorchy appears to have reached the ears of the newspapermen, a fight against one Morris Tobin in 1885 when Shoni was said to be 21 years of age. Tobin might be considered a veteran by this time, having been ten years Shoni's senior at the time of the battle, and was employed as a coal trimmer at Cardiff. The fight occurred at the Fair Field at Treorchy and appears to have been a glove contest as opposed to a bare-knuckle meeting, with seven three minute rounds having been fought. Tobin was fairly well beaten, having been knocked down three times in the sixth round and then again in the seventh, with the contest having subsequently been awarded to Shoni Engineer.

It is not entirely clear whether Jack Scarrott actually claims to have been present when Shoni fought Pete Burns, but on the basis of his very brief statements regarding the fight, it would appear not, and in all probability heard of the fight second hand after Shoni Engineer's victory. Various key details seem to have been slightly misrepresented or at an odds with the details recorded in the press. The fight was certainly brought off in the district of Pencoed/Heol-Y-Cyw near Bridgend, but had originally been fixed to be held at Peterstone, between Cardiff and Newport. The match failed to come off, mainly as news of the proposed meet failed to reach the ears of Shoni Engineer himself, with the match having been fixed between the two rival bands of supporters. Pete Burns turned up at the appointed place for battle, but Shoni was a no-show, his followers having failed to catch him at home to alert him of the impending contest and as a result the £10 side stakes were duly coughed over by Shoni's people to Burns and his backers. Another match was arranged, and all parties would descend on the appointed battleground the following day.

With one eye fixed on the boundaries for possible discovery by the police, Pete Burns and Shoni Engineer donned their spiked fighting boots and got down to business watched by a select party of between just fifty and sixty spectators. Despite the cold morning air, the fight went on for a full hour and seven minutes. Shoni had it all his own way. Sadly, few battles of Pete 'Dublin Tom' Burns appear to have been recorded, although

Burns had other 'business' interests outside fighting, notably his shameful undercover 'shebeening' activities (the illegal sale of alcohol to neighbours from his home residence in Cardiff) which would eventually land him in the dock at Cardiff police court. Prior to having met Shoni Engineer, Burns was more honestly employed in a day job as a seafaring fireman, and was the older man of the two men, having been roughly 26 years of age. Burns was completely outclassed throughout the fight, which lasted forty seven rounds. Despite having been dominated throughout Burns reportedly '...took his licking gamely, rising up again and again after a knockdown blow, only to be once more sent to grass'. By the forty seventh round, Pete Burns was unable to continue. He had been badly punished and presented a 'shocking spectacle' and had to be led away by his downcast followers. Shoni's men by contrast must have been quite jubilant, having presumably recovered the money they had lost the day before, while Shoni left the scene of the battle quite happily, having '...received scarcely a mark'.

Shoni Engineer had been in the thick of the home-grown pugilistic talent for more than a few years, having regularly appeared on small halls and exhibition shows as well as on boxing booths travelling throughout South Wales, and his services as a trainer, second or corner man were frequently in great demand. It might be imagined that having assisted in the aborted Trehebert contest against Tom 'Books' Davies, Jack Scarrott was more than acquainted with a few members of the knuckle fighting fraternity even before he found himself in the booth boxing profession. As a boy he had already dodged a few policeman around Pontypridd when he was climbing up into the hills to indulge in a little gambling on a game of pitch-and-toss in the company of a few well-known local tearaways who shared Scarrott's growing interest in pugilism. Name checked companions of Jack Scarrott at this time include Dan Powell, William (better known as 'Mother') Lee, a 'fighter named Devons' who hailed from the world famous Brown Lenox and Co. Chainworks and would later become a 'champion prize fighter', and two other long forgotten Pontypridd pugilists by the name of 'Tiny' Evans and 'Bungey Hill'.

Little of these one-time friends of Jack Scarrott is recorded in the local press, although even as young men they appear to have taken a fairly active part in the local mountain fighting scene. Pontypridd was rapidly becoming a centre of commerce, with busy Taff Street having developed into a major destination for trade with shoppers flocking from the surrounding valleys to visit its many stores, and with the miners and ironworkers descending on the towns rough and ready public houses at the end of a shift at the coalface or furnace. Jack Scarrott would have been just one of many of Pontypridd's collection of young lads eager to push their noses up against the glass of the busy drinking establishments to find out what was going on inside amongst the congregations of older colliers and chain works employees, and the pit head champions and local prize-fighters that thronged the tightly packed bars. Many of these young men sought to emulate the prize-fighting activities of these older men about the town, whose tin ears and occasional black eyes marked them out as either occasional booth boxers or members of the mountain fighting fraternity. Some of these men would gravitate towards the town as a place where pugilism was slowly moving towards a fixed ring and boxing gloves from the bare knuckle fights fought on the mountains for the first time.

When writing about the days of his youth in Pontypridd, the world lightweight champion Freddie Welsh would say of the town, quoting his close personal friend, the 'Sage of Aurora' Elbert Hubbard, that "'…God made the country, man made the cities, but the devil made the small towns," and would recall that fighting had always featured as a part of his upbringing from his earliest days growing up there, stating that; '…though it is my birthplace, I have to confess that Pontypridd was one of his Satanic Majesties pet edifices. We were a tough collection, and had little to do but fight, at least that is about the only occupation we boys could find, or rather, the one we preferred to all others.' Freddie had a first-hand understanding regarding the pugilistic leanings of the Pontypridd men, as his own grandfather, Morgan Thomas had been a well-known local mountain fighter in his day. Most of the early gloved pugilists of Welsh's time would begin their careers in the travelling boxing booths, often having been 'inspired' by an older generation of booth owners who in some cases had either at one stage swapped fists in prize fights themselves, or could have been found gathered with other local 'sports' in dark corners of Welsh public houses whispering about a meet on the mountain the following morning between rival pugilists.

There can be no doubt that Pontypridd was a particularly tough town, having been known locally by the nickname of the 'Wild West'. With the local police force having had its work cut out in policing the town itself, it would prove even harder to spare the manpower to also effectively patrol the hillsides around. Whether in order to settle a grievance or to determine the pugilistic superiority of one local champion or another, mountain-fights were often scheduled to come off in one concealed 'bloody' spot or another, with nearby Llanwonno Mountain having proved to be a favourite spot amongst other popular locations hidden in the hills in which illegal mountain fights were brought off over the years.

On some occasions a hastily arranged prize-fight to settle a dispute was often decided upon on the spot, with multiple fatalities having resulted in the years that followed. In one fight on a Sunday afternoon in May of 1890, Trevor Roberts lost his life as a result of an impromptu fist fight arranged with one Lewis Price of Mountain Ash after a disagreement to decide who should pay for a pint of beer. The argument had started in the urinals at the White Thorn public house. With neither of the two men willing to pay for the pint, it was suggested by Roberts that they should fight the matter out. Both men agreed and left the inn to do battle on the road outside.

In the course of the fight, Lewis Price punched Roberts and knocked him to the ground, with his head coming into contact with a stone which fractured his skull. Roberts was carried unconscious to the public house some time later, where he gushed blood from his mouth and ears. Despite having received medical attention after doctors had been sent for, Roberts' condition worsened and he would die of his injuries later that evening. Sadly Roberts, an ex-quarryman had only travelled to live in the area from his home village of Groeslon near Carnarvon the previous January, after relocating to South Wales in search of the better pay on offer in the colliery districts. At Groeslon, Trevor Roberts left a widow and three children behind to mourn his untimely end, and all for the sake of the price of a pint of beer.

By 1890, and with prize-fighting having been so prevalent in the area, and with police time having been occupied so frequently in trying to bring the practitioners to court to account for their actions, it is perhaps surprising to note that there was at least one native ex prize-fighter from Pontypridd of some renown who was actively engaged in bringing the developing sport of boxing, or 'glove fighting' before paying audiences in a slightly more permanent setting. Jack Davis had achieved some fame after having unsuccessfully challenged Jem Smith in a bare-knuckle contest for the Heavyweight Championship of England on the 16th December, 1885 at East Grinstead and had been knocked out in the sixth round. Although prize-fighting would continue throughout the United Kingdom for many years afterwards the event would later be remembered as having been the last bare-knuckle fight to be held for the Heavyweight Championship on British soil. Despite the defeat, Jack Davis remained a popular figure in South Wales in the years that followed, having been billed to appear along with visiting London pugilist, Charles 'Toff' Wall for a six night engagement at 'Tayleure's Grand Circus' in Westgate Street, at Cardiff early in 1887.

Jack Scarrott would recall that in the days of his youth at Pontypridd he had been in the company of 'Mother'

**TAYLEURE'S GRAND CIRCUS,
WESTGATE-STREET, CARDIFF.**

POSITIVELY LAST WEEK OF THE SEASON.
NEW SCENES, NEW JOKES, and the Great CONGRESS of CIRCUS ARTISTES, in a Superb Display of NEW ACTS. WEDNESDAY, March 2, and DURING THE WEEK, Costly Engagement of

JACK DAVIS AND TOFF WALL,

THE CHAMPION PUGILISTS IN THE NOBLE ART OF SELF DEFENCE.
First time in Cardiff of

FRA DIAVOLO;
OR, THE BRIGANDS OF THE MOUNTAINS.

First time in Cardiff of those talented Young Equestrian, MASTER ROBERT AND MASTER ALFRED, As the British Foxhunters.
LAST GRAND DAY PERFORMANCE on SATURDAY NEXT, MARCH 5th.
Prices as usual. 72606

TAYLEURE'S GRAND CIRCUS
BOXING.
Mr. JACK DAVIES, Native of Pontypridd, and Ex-Champion of England, is Engaged, with TOFF WALL, the Middle-Weight Champion of the World, for SIX NIGHTS ONLY, and will be glad to see his Welsh Friends. 73732

An advertisement for an exhibition between Jack Davis and Charles 'Toff' Wall

Lee and Dan Powell when the two men had climbed up the hill to Pontypridd common and beyond the local landmark, known as the 'Rocking Stone' to meet each other in a mountain fight. In Scarrott's time the 'Rocking Stone' was well known as a meeting spot in the area, and although today the large round bottomed boulder no longer moves when a man climbs up upon it, as it once did, it can easily be seen why it served as such a useful and familiar point for the bare-knuckle men to meet and check to see if they were be followed by any members of the local police force before heading up onto the mountains beyond to settle their grievances. The location allowed a clear view of any approaching policemen from the direction of Pontypridd, situated on the opposite side of the valley, long before they had got within collaring range.

After arriving at a suitable spot, Mother Lee and Dan Powell got down to business, but were disturbed by the police before the fight could be drawn to a conclusion. It is interesting to note that 'Mother' Lee fell foul of the law on at least one recorded occasion in 1889 in the very same location, which bears remarkable similarities to the fight which Scarrott recalls between Mother Lee and Tiny Evans. On the day in question, watchful police sergeant Hallett of the Pontypridd police noted a less than cautious series of hopeful fight spectators wandering up Eglwysilan Mountain in groups of two and three. Fearing the worst, Hallett alerted his colleague, Police Constable Brown, and both men made their way up the mountain in the direction of Eglwysilan church, after having concealed their identities by changing into plain clothes. A ring had already been formed and two men,

'Mother' Lee and 'Tinus' (Tiny?) Hemmings (Evans?) were reportedly 'both stripped to the waist and fighting savagely' in a corner of a field just five hundred yards from the Church itself when spotted by sergeants Hallett and Brown. After the spectators had hastily bolted from the scene following their discovery, Hemmings was quickly scooped up by the police and deposited in the cells of Pontypridd station, while Mother Lee successfully evaded capture and wasn't apprehended until the following day at Taff's Well.

It is intriguing to note that while Dan Powell, Mother Lee, and other notable mountain fighters from the area appear to have been chiefly engaged in bare-knuckle fights, they would also play some part in the developing sport of boxing at Pontypridd, chiefly due to the efforts of Jack Davis. Following his retirement from competitive prize-fighting, Jack Davis would become the manager of a large entertainment venue at Pontypridd named Howard's Hall, where Davis would pioneer boxing as a sport in the town after having decided to hold glove fights on the premises in 1889. Davis' decision to do so would provide a venue for Jack Scarrott's bare-knuckle mountain fighting acquaintances to also test their pugilistic skills in lucrative boxing matches held under the Marquis of Queensbury rules.

Dan Powell and fellow Pontypriddian Thomas Lambert (better known as 'Bungy' or 'Bungey Hill') fought at the Hall on Monday 2nd December 1889, with 5 oz. gloves for £100. Powell had been trained by Illtyd Evans (also of Pontypridd), while 'Bungy' had looked after by one Shillington of Dudley. Jack Davis had engaged the services of Treorchy man, Shoni Engineer to serve as referee. Dan Powell was by far the heavier man and had the best of the contest from the outset. Despite having alleged that there had been a foul in the first round, and having been cut over the eye in the second round, Bungy's skills were seen to good effect and he fought with spirit. At one stage it seemed likely that Bungy might be able to secure victory after having landed multiple blows to Powell's chest, but would ultimately end up yielding to Powell's superior strength halfway through the sixth round.

Bungy had been known to the police as a prize fighter and occasional trainer to other bare knuckle men for some time prior to his meet with Powell, having been apprehended on his way to fight against Evan Morley, a fellow collier from Porth on the 2nd January 1888 for £10 a-side. The fight had originally been planned to come off at Gilfach Goch on Boxing Day, but was called off due to police interference. The fight was then re-scheduled to be held at Eglwysilan Common, although police apprehended Lambert and his backers after the men had been observed making their way to the battle ground from Llantwit Vardre where Bungy had been engaged in his training for the match. Lambert was afterwards bound over by Ystrad police Court to keep the peace. Morley was picked up a couple of days later at Pontypridd, and would also be held to account for his actions, and was bound over to the tune of £20 and sureties of £10 to keep the peace for six months.

Shoni Engineer would himself feature as a combatant in a glove contest held at the Hall the following year, when a large crowd gathered to witness a fight between the Treorchy blacksmith and Enoch Morrison of

Shrewsbury on the 5th May, 1890. Shoni had emerged victorious on a foul after five stubbornly fought rounds. Shortly afterwards Jack Davis would change the name of Howard's Hall to the 'Victoria Theatre', and while it became a popular venue for travelling music and dance hall acts to entertain the public at large, Davis also continued promoting matches between local fighters, in some cases assisting a few notorious bare-knuckle men in making the transition from the mountainside to the boxing ring. Early in July of 1890 Jack Raymond and Dai Phillips, better known as Dai 'Faggots' had performed at the Theatre, fighting an 11 round contest with 4 oz. gloves for a purse of £25. Both men had reportedly undergone severe training for the event with Raymond having been trained by 'Bungy' Lambert, with Phillips having been looked after by Jack Davis himself, and Dan Powell standing in as referee. Despite the fight having started promisingly, Jack Raymond knocked out Dai 'Faggots' in the second round, forcing his corner to 'throw up a sponge' to indicate their man's defeat.

At the start of August, patrons of the Victoria Theatre were treated to a match between James Jones, billed as 'the champion of Aberdare' and Stephen Rothwell of Abergavenny for a purse of £50 for a 12 round contest held under Marquis of Queensbury rules. The fight would prove to be a good one with 'some very severe hitting taking place' and was very 'stubbornly contested'. Despite the best efforts of Rothwell, the champion of Aberdare was seen to be the faster fighter, and was given the verdict by the referee.

By September of 1890, the Victoria Theatre had become so firmly established as a boxing venue that it was the scene of perhaps 'one of the finest fistic entertainments ever seen in South Wales' when Jack Davis elected to put on a benefit event for the popular featherweight champion, Morgan Crowther of Newport. Jack Davis' preparations give some insight as to how popular boxing entertainments at the Victoria Theatre had become, with Davis having had a portable 16 ft. ring built in the centre of the Hall specially for the occasion;

'The ordinary stage of the theatre was set apart for reserved seats, and in the centre of the hall had been placed a magnificent portable platform roped off as a prize ring. The platform, which was supported by eight posts, is 16 feet square. It stand three feet six inches from the ground, and is so constructed that it can be put up or taken down with the utmost dispatch.'

Jack Davis was reportedly very proud of the boxing ring, and believed it to have been 'one of the most unique stages in the country'. A number of sparring exhibitions preceded the main event, with Tommy Jones and Sam Gulliver of Cardiff having sparred three rounds, followed by a performance by J.H. Harris of Plymouth and Dan Powell in which both men were seen to exhibit 'fine form'. Crowd favourites John O'Brien of Cardiff and Shoni Engineer were also seen to good effect, their contest being '...well and determinedly fought throughout'. Sammy Hughes of Birmingham, another acquaintance of Jack Scarrott, met Garry Smith of Newport in a hard contest in which 'ugly clouts' were given by both sides. Hughes went for his opponent with the greatest gusto and proved to all that he was made of 'solid grit', ultimately taking the decision.

The sixth bout of the evening was between the old boxing booth proprietor and pugilist 'Professor' Charlie North and his son, who received one of the greatest receptions by the crowd. North was introduced by the Master of Ceremonies who reminded the audience of North's standing as one who had once 'held a high position' as a pugilist in his younger days and had afterwards 'produced some of the finest manipulators of the gloves in the country' on his boxing booth. Despite the warm introduction from the M.C., fortune had not smiled favourably on Charlie North in more recent times, having reportedly been 'flat broke' at the time of the exhibition. Despite this the booth proprietor was said to be philosophical about his situation, and was not seen to be downcast by his lot, coming up to the scratch to spar with his son smiling and happy. It was only after the spar that the aging pugilist would show the strain of his recent misfortunes when he '…addressed the audience in pathetic strains, and so worked upon their feelings that one susceptible individual in the audience humanely suggested that he should pass the hat round.' Jack Davis quite rightly vetoed the suggestion as the benefit had been organised to raise funds for Morgan Crowther, and not Charlie North, regardless of the old Professor's efforts to tug on the heartstrings of the audience.

Morgan Crowther had landed in hot water with the law earlier that year, following a fight with 'Chaffy' Hayman, billed as the 'lightweight champion of the West of England' a few months previously at Bath. The fight had been advertised as part of an assault-at-arms held at the Brock Street Hall, an event which was meant to showcase athletic ability and also featured displays with clubs and singe sticks. Police infiltrated the crowd after having received information that the sparring match between Crowther and Hayman was actually a competitive glove fight masquerading as an exhibition. After twenty minutes of light sparring their suspicions were confirmed when Crowther and Hayman set about each other with gusto, forcing police to send for assistance before entering the ring and drawing the fight to a close in the seventeenth round. The decision to do so had caused panic to spread through the crowd, with the doors of the Hall having been smashed by fleeing spectators eager to escape the long arm of the law. Both men had ended up getting arrested, with the matter ending up being scheduled to be heard at the next Gloucester Assizes, with Crowther and Hayman having been charged with causing a breach of the peace. With Crowther needing every available penny for his legal defence, he had jumped at the opportunity to appear at the theatre, and entered the ring at the conclusion of the evening and sparred for seven rounds with 4 oz. gloves against Hayman.

The event at the Victoria Hall was a great success, with Morgan Crowther having apparently been impressed by the quality of boxing on display, commenting to a reporter that there had been '…some good scientific boxing. The exhibition between Dan Powell and Harris is worth mentioning, while the fight between "Shoni Engineer" and O' Brien was an excellent one."

On the 6th of October, 1890, the Victoria Theatre would be the venue for another contest which attracted a great deal of interest in the town, with Thomas Lambert having been bold enough to enter the ring against the well regarded Ynyshir mountain fighter, Sam 'Butcher' Thomas for £25 a-side with 4 oz. gloves. A large and excited crowd gathered to see how 'Bungy' Lambert might fare against such formidable opposition. Sam, better known as a knuckle-fighter, had first pulled on the gloves after having been engaged to fight on William Samuels' boxing booth, where he had taken on allcomers and proved that he was a fighter worth watching. In the course of his travels, Sam had also benefitted from having indulged in a few rough and tumble bouts against such familiar opposition as John O'Brien, and 'Shoni Engineer' as well as having said to have tackled his close friend, the popular heavyweight Dai St. John of Resolven on occasion, despite having weighed just 10 stone in fighting condition.

Sam Thomas had started his glove fighting career a few years previously, after having met and beaten one 'Portobello' in a bare-knuckle contest. Sam had then defeated Hopkin Williams of Ferndale near Pontypridd with small gloves in two rounds for £5 a-side. David Davis of Mardy lasted a little longer, with Sam Butcher having taken seven rounds to beat him, in a match for £25 a-side, despite having broken his right arm in the second round. After this Sam would fight Enoch Morrison to a twelve round draw. Having gone the distance against Sam, Morrison was not seen to be particularly eager to enter the ring against him again, having chosen to forfeit £10 rather than fight a return match at 10st. 2lb.

Despite the hopes of those supporting the local man, Thomas 'Bungy' Lambert, the match was a sharp and decisive victory for Sam Butcher, who was seconded by Shoni Engineer who had also served as Sam's trainer, and one Harry Jones of Aberdare. Jack Raymond and Dan Powell stood in Bungy's corner, with Raymond having trained Lambert in preparation for the contest. In the first round both men made a good show of it, but in the second round, just as Bungy seemed to be gaining the advantage, Sam Butcher countered with some heavy body blows which were seen to turn the tables in his favour. The third round saw Sam bring all his strength into play and he succeeded in knocking Bungy out of time. The victory had been a decisive one, so much so that one Dan 'Power' (Powell?) of Pontypridd reportedly decided, like Enoch Morrison, to pay a forfeit two days later rather than meet Sam Butcher in the ring.

Sadly it would afterwards stand as one of the last major boxing contests to be held at the Victoria Hall, with the large crowds now patronising the venue having attracted the attention of a number of local churchmen who were quick to condemn Jack Davis' decision to hold glove fights on the premises. The ringleaders, Reverends Dr. Roberts and W.I. Morris rounded up a few likeminded members of the anti-boxing brigade and led a deputation to speak out against the contests before the Pontypridd Local Board of Health in October. Reverend Morris was particularly vocal in his condemnation of the contests held at the Hall, stating that they represented a demoralising effect on the population and were rapidly becoming a public nuisance. With the board having been entrusted with the control of local public halls, Morris and Roberts requested that the Board should endeavour to bring an end to the 'brutal exhibitions' by either

Jack Davis (Pontypridd), who fought for the Championship of England in 1885

refusing to renew the entertainment license of the hall altogether or by imposing further conditions on Jack Davis as the holder of the license, and inserting further clauses in order to prevent the continuation of the glove fights.

The Local Health Board was at first reluctant to interfere in the matter, believing that it was the duty of the police to ensure that the terms of the license had not been infringed. The Pontypridd police force had been under the impression that as long as the contests did not bear the hallmarks of a prize fight, with spectators gambling on the outcome, that they had no right to meddle with the boxing contests. With police time having already been stretched by the necessity to bring a halt to prize fights being held on the surrounding hillsides, they had little interest in increasing their work load by interfering with what appeared to be legitimately held glove fights. It transpired that the Chairman of the Board, Mr. D.J Leyshon was also the owner of the Victoria Hall and was quick to assure the Board members that he would do his best to induce Jack Davis to bring a halt to glove matches on the premises. Reverend Roberts seized his opportunity, and pointed out that the licence for the hall would soon expire, and so the Board agreed that they would bear the feelings of Roberts and his supporters in mind when the license of the Hall came up for review.

The pressure on Jack Davis to stop promoting boxing contests increased in November after the matter was brought before the quarterly meeting of the Local Government Committee of the Glamorgan County Council. The Clerk of the Peace would put further pressure on the Pontypridd Local Health Board after having been requested to write a letter asking them to consider their position when reviewing the renewal of the entertainment license. At the next meeting of the Local Health Board, Reverend Roberts again condemned the continuation of glove fighting on the premises, believing that despite the use of gloves, the contests held at the Hall had all the markings of prize-fights. His point of view was not upheld by the Pontypridd police themselves, with Superintendent Mathews having stated that he had not found that any of the men that had taken part in the contests had been seriously injured in any way. There had been no gambling on the outcome of the matches, which had been held solely for the entrance money. With the writing on the wall, Jack Davis appeared before the Board and said that he would stop holding contests on the premises should the Board of Health decide against his decision to do so. The matter was left in the balance until the Victoria Hall had been inspected. It was the beginning of the end, with the Board having visited the Hall early in December, 1890, and ultimately decided that there should be a clause inserted into the entertainment license for the theatre prohibiting its use as a venue for glove fighting altogether.

The efforts of the Reverend Roberts and his morally righteous followers to condemn the development of competitive glove boxing would have a limited effect in revising the attitudes of the fighting men of Pontypridd as regards the 'demoralising' nature of their sport. In many ways, the decision to force Jack Davis to stop holding matches at the Victoria Hall would have far greater repercussions than Roberts had evidently considered before vocalising his opposition to the boxing matches held at Pontypridd so publicly. For one thing, with contests having been held at one central location, and openly publicised throughout the town, Jack Davis had made the job of the police infinitely easier. Matches had been held under the watchful eye of an experienced referee, and conducted along the lines suggested by the Marquis of Queensbury rules using padded boxing gloves as opposed to bare-knuckles, with the result that there was far less risk of permanent damage or serious injury to the combatants.

Superintendent Mathews had stated as much on behalf of the Pontypridd police before the Local Board of Health. Keeping a close eye on the bare-knuckle throwbacks of Pontypridd had forced Mathews and his men out of bed before dawn to scour the hillsides on more occasions than he could probably remember. His job must have been made a lot easier with the majority of the local knuckle-men having had access to a legitimate boxing 'ring' and a place to congregate and watch a carefully controlled contest without the risk of appearing before the magistrate's court. Additionally with the men fighting for a set purse for their efforts within a boxing ring, and there having been an absence of gambling on the outcome of the contests, there was far less opportunity for the money men that had congregated around the mountain fighters to cleave off a handsome profit for themselves. For a while at least, the 'backers' and the motley crew that had attached themselves to the prize ring had been pushed into the background.

Potentially, the hope that Jack Davis had fostered in having tried to bring bare-knuckle mountain fighting out of the darkness, and establish the growing sport of competitive 'glove fighting' or boxing at Pontypridd could be seen as one that might serve to ultimately save lives, rather than one that would debase and corrupt the local population. Reverend Robert's narrow viewpoint could not take into account the fact that many lives had and would continue to be lost on the mountains following a prize fight where a man would often be forced out of his corner and up to the scratch despite having been punished beyond the point of return by 'friends' who would lose sight of the risk to his safety in their eagerness to secure their winnings.

The blinkered opposition of Reverend Roberts to boxing as a legitimate sport had tilted the balance, despite the obvious consideration that prize-fighting could only benefit from having been conducted under more closely controlled conditions, and under which the welfare of the opposing fighters could be monitored, with easier access to medical assistance in the event that a man was seen to be putting his health at risk.

Jack Davis had endeavoured to further develop the sport of boxing at Pontypridd, having witnessed the potential for fatal consequences in the unregulated prize ring first-hand in the final dark days of the London Prize Ring when he had battled towards competing for the Heavyweight Championship of England. Despite Davis' best efforts to further the progression of Welsh boxing as a sporting activity from the chaotic and dangerous world known by the mountain fighters, the future of the Victoria Hall as a boxing venue would fall victim to the viewpoint of a man who would find it difficult to think beyond the confines of his church and his books of scripture. Detached from the lot of his congregation, Roberts was unable to fully comprehend the way in which the harsh realities faced by his flock in their daily lives had perhaps left many of them hardened by their experiences, and had made prize fighting a reality of everyday life for many.

Like many churchmen of his day, Roberts would seemingly spend little time considering the frustrations and daily pressures of life amongst the working classes who toiled underground up to twelve hours daily, or sweating next to a roaring furnace, victims of an increasingly industrialised world where education was of little importance alongside industrial production. Opportunities beyond the darkness of the coal pit were limited, with the majority of young men having only benefited from the most basic education, most young boys having found themselves alongside their father or older brother in the local pit at fourteen. The sadness is that in most families the day that a child was condemned to a life down the pit was not a day of dread but one of celebration. With many households struggling to make ends meet, the necessity to put food on the table would mean that most families looked forward to the day when a child might be able to leave school and bring home a wage and help alleviate the pressure on the principal breadwinner.

Instead Roberts and his ilk were satisfied that their time was best spent delivering their time worn sermons intended to shame those members of their flock that dared to hang their heads on a Sunday morning nursing a black eye after having raised their fists at dawn on the mountain. Inevitably, with the decision to stop glove fighting at Pontypridd, men would once more return to the mountains to fight out their differences. In the years that would follow, many more would spill their blood on the rough turf above, with some having taken their final breaths lying on their backs, broken beyond repair. Their 'brutality' would no doubt make ideal material for the future sermons of Reverend Roberts, whose deep contemplation of the sinfulness of his fellow man would allow him ample scope to wax lyrically every Sunday. Roberts never once entertained the consideration that men have always fought, whether through pride, anger, vanity or folly. Nor would his close adherence to religious teaching allow him to explore the notion that if men were fighting with gloves in the ring, it was perhaps a better outcome than the possibility of them fighting and possibly dying of their injuries on a lonely mountain.

Chapter 7

Death on the Mountain

Long before the time of Jack Scarrott, the men of the South Wales valleys had taken to the hills above their towns and villages to decide who might be able to lay claim to be the 'champion' of the Valley, or maybe just their town or village. More often than not, just a few coins were laid on the outcome or a jug of beer. In the days when Jack was travelling throughout the valleys with his family, men were also climbing onto the hillsides above the town of Porth to decide who could be considered the 'best' man, or to settle a simmering grievance. One of the most shocking fight fatalities occurred on the morning of 1st August 1886, and was witnessed by Jack Scarrott in person when he was sixteen years of age.

John Jenkin James was the name of the unfortunate victim, who lost his life after a particularly brutal fight against one Evan Evans. Their argument had started in the unusually named New York Inn situated in America

Fach. A pub dispute between two other men had led to a quarrel between Jenkin James and another man by the name of Benjamin Jones that resulted in a dust up in a passageway. Evan Evans felt quite strongly that Jones had been wronged and after they had been turfed out of the bar, he told Benjamin Jones that he would happily beat up Jenkin James on his behalf. John Jenkin James left the pub shortly afterwards in the company of a couple of other drinkers and all made their way back towards Clifton Row where both the combatants lived. There was a further argument on the doorstep of Evan Evans, whose landlady, a truculent old lady by the name of Sarah Jones appeared on the doorstep and inflamed an already volatile situation after proclaiming that Evan Evans and her son would willingly fight anyone for 'any money'. This led to a further scuffle before it was agreed by all parties that John Jenkin James and Evan Evans would fight on the mountain for a mere five shillings aside. Having fallen out on previous occasions, both men appeared to be more than willing to resume their argument, and settle things once and for all with bare fists. Neither seemed to have guessed for a moment exactly how their foolish drunken bravado might end, with Jenkins stretched out in a wooden box.

Evan Evans and a companion headed home, while the other remaining parties dug in for the night and waited for the hour appointed for battle. It was at 4am on the Sunday morning that the two rival parties slipped out of the doors of their houses and walked up the steep incline to the mountains above, and it was here that they came across a sixteen year old Jack Scarrott wandering about on the mountainside looking for his father's horses, which

The fatal match in which Evan Evans killed John Jenkin James

had been allowed to stray and graze at their leisure. Having satisfied themselves that Jack was actually engaged in finding the missing horses, they turned their attention back to the matter at hand, with both sets of men eager to see their man do battle. None saw a quick witted Jack Scarrott double back and slip in amongst the crowd as they formed a makeshift ring.

Evan Evans appears to have been the better man from the outset, knocking John Jenkin James down with far greater frequency than James could achieve. Having shown his fighting superiority Evans appeared satisfied with his performance and wanted to bring the fight to an end. It was James that refused to concede that he had been beaten, telling the crowd that he '...would be carried home first' rather than give in. Even to Jack's youthful eye it appears that the truth of his statement was a dangerous omen, but the supporters of John Jenkin James were crying for blood, and wanted to see their man fight on. Jenkins was well beaten, and tumbled one way and then another, bashing his head against the stones in the dim light, making blood pour from both his nose and mouth. Although it was stated at the trial that Jenkins rested on a second's knee before falling over, it seems that one more punch from Evan Evans was responsible for knocking him senseless to the ground. Even fifty years later, Jack clearly recalls that Jenkin James own followers were yelling to Evans, 'Go on, finish it!' – at which point they sealed their own friends doom.

The key witness at the trial, one Joseph Holman, who was a collier living at No. 16 Clifton Row, would appear to have invented the story that Jenkins had 'tumbled' off a seconds knee into unconsciousness to avoid stating the horrible truth that Evan Evans, under pressure from James' own backers, had moved in and delivered a fatal blow to a man that had already suffered severe injuries. The fight went on for roughly one hour and fifteen minutes, with thirty two rounds having been fought on un-cleared rough turf in dim light. Holman claimed that Jenkins was immediately laid to rest on a 'cushion' of clothing quickly supplied by the gathered supporters, which also does not square with Jack Scarrott's impartial eyewitness account. The utter destruction of Jenkin James at the hand of Evan Evans led to nothing more than blind panic among the pack of men gathered on the mountain, and they scattered across and down the mountain in an effort to flee the scene as quickly as possible.

What isn't apparent is whether anyone actually checked to find out if John Jenkin James had actually died. No-one appears to have tended to him, or checked to see if there were any signs of life still left in his battered and broken body. There also appears to have been an uncorroborated amount of time between the final fall of James and the decision of the men to return to pick up the body. Possibly the main eye witness called at the inquest was forced to modify his story somewhat to cover the amount of time that passed before the body was recovered. It was stated that the body of Jenkin James was recovered from the scene of the fight between the hours of six and seven a.m., giving anything up to nearly a full hour after the time of the contest when James could have lain unattended on the side of a cold barren mountain.

The necessity for the spectators to claim to have attended to James is apparent if the other men concerned were to avoid the possibility that they (along with Evan Evans) were to be charged with manslaughter. Key aspects of Joseph Holman's testimony do appear to be suspect, and it seems likely that having lived in the same road as the combatants Holman would have come under intense pressure from the others involved to modify his story. Holman did claim that when James' body was recovered and taken to his house he was still alive, although the first of two doctors to be called to the house (Dr. Conway Joyce) stated categorically that by the time he arrived at the house, a little after 7 am, James' body was already stone cold.

A post-mortem revealed that James had been treated very roughly, having numerous bruises as well as two black eyes. Blood had been oozing outwards from under the scalp behind the left ear and there was significant clotting of blood on the left hemisphere of the brain. Holman had claimed that James had dashed his head on a stone in one of his final falls, which would appear to be a complete fabrication in order to disassociate Evans from his final smashing blow, but this was deemed unlikely to have occurred by Dr. Joyce who stated that there was no injury or external signs of damage comparable with a blow against a stone to the rear of James' head. In summing up the post mortem findings, Dr. Joyce said that it was his opinion that the fatal injury occurred in the last round, stating that the 'immediate result of that injury would be insensibility'. Dr. Joyce's remarks would cast further doubt on Joseph Holman's assertion that both men had decided to bring the fight to a halt and had actually shook hands prior to James toppling off his second's knee.

At the end of a difficult trial, Evan Evans seems to have been unable to accept his part in the demise of John Jenkin James, stating for the record that 'I am not guilty, it was a fair fight'. The seconds, William Henry Holman, and Griffith Evans were held accountable, along with Thomas Williams (the timekeeper) for their part in allowing the fight to continue far beyond an acceptable duration. It was also noted that they were not the only parties that could be blamed for having played a part in the James' death, with Sarah Jones, Evan Evans' landlady also having been held to blame for her part in furthering their disagreement. Ultimately, a man had died through the negligence of many, though the blame lay with a punch launched by Evan Evans, and a verdict of manslaughter was returned against Evan Evans after a short deliberation on the part of the jury. More is the shame for all involved, and as Jack Scarrott rightly remembers, that a man lost his life for a mere five shillings a-side and the sake of his own foolish pride.

Chapter 8

William Samuels vs. Toff Wall

Despite his advancing years, William Samuels was still having a particularly busy pugilistic career even though his days of youth had long since passed by 1886. Having passed his fortieth year a number of years previously, the old bare-knuckle champion showed no signs of slowing down, shown by his willingness to engage a particularly well-known English champion in battle. The hulking 'Jem Smith' was a familiar figure to the 'fancy' as the collective followers of the prize-ring were known, and after taking the Heavyweight Championship of England the previous year against Jack Davis of Pontypridd on the 16th December in 1885, Jem Smith was the man to beat. He presented a formidable obstacle to anyone who wanted to take a shot at the title. While his boxing abilities were somewhat crude, he was a man blessed with prodigious strength. His bulky frame gave Smith the appearance of a heavily trained bodybuilder of enormous power rather than the more athletic appearance of a classically trained boxer.

Despite having beaten Jack Davis, Smith was labouring under something of a cloud following a disgraceful fight with Alf Greenfield which had been fixed to come off at the town of Maisons Laffite in France. The match had ended in scenes of chaos after nearly an hour when Smith's followers had broken into the ring with knives drawn and proceeded to threaten anyone who dared suggest that their man was on his way to defeat with mortal injuries. The match was unsurprisingly declared a draw in the thirteenth round. On his return to England, Smith went down the usual exhibition route, choosing to increase his earnings with a lucrative music hall and theatre tour where he would often give displays of boxing in the company of his brother, Tom. It was while engaged at 'the old Panopticon Music-Hall' originally known as the Philharmonic Hall, a grand and cavernous building that still stands in Cardiff's St. Mary's Street, that a rather proud and haughty middle aged challenger made himself known, asking;

'Who is this man who is offering money to anyone who can stand up against him?'

The off-hand manner of the stranger caught the twenty three year old champion off-guard. 'Who are you?' asked Jem Smith.

'I am William Samuels, the champion of Wales and I'm here to have a go at you' replied the indignant Samuels. Smith seems rather taken aback by the boldness of the Welsh champion, and deciding that the challenge would be bad for business, Smith stated that a 'novice' by the name of "Toff' Wall would take his place the following night, and if Samuels remained standing after six rounds, he would win £10 and a gold watch. Samuels was more than willing to meet the challenge, and so the match was made.

Smith was particularly confident that Charles "Toff" Wall would do the job, having put up his entire £10 purse for his standing room only six night appearance at the old 'Phil' and with good reason, as his 'novice', "Toff" was one of the most universally feared domestic middleweights of his day. Sadly Samuels' challenge appears to have found the newspapermen of South Wales napping, with only limited coverage of the match appearing in print form beyond Jack Scarrott's recollections. The match turned out to be a walkover for Toff Wall, with the *Western Mail* stating that 'Tom Waugh' was easily the superior fighter, and was as;

'…neat and smart a boxer as ever held up his hands…Samuels tried all his old tactics, but he was nowhere with his more lithe and youthful opponent, who found out the weak points with which he had to deal, and made "mincemeat," as the saying goes, of the Merthyr man, before he knew where he was. Samuels, however sore he may be over his defeat, can console himself with reflecting upon his long career of successes, and with the knowledge that a man of forty-five cannot be expected to hold his own with another half his age, and with a reputation of being one of the best, if not the best, sparrer in the kingdom.'

Jack Scarrott's familiarity with the particulars of the match would indicate that the 'talk of Cardiff' reached as far as Pontypridd, where Jack presumably travelled from in order to pay over two shillings for one of the cheapest seats to see the hero of his youth on the stage of the grand old music hall. Inevitably, the old champion resumed his old 'rushing' style, trying to dash to close quarters to land his legendary stomach punch. Toff would appear to have been unwilling to tolerate Samuels's time-worn tactics, and apparently '…lifted him clean up, so he tamped on the boards like a football'. The match came to an abrupt end in the fourth round when Samuels was knocked over the ropes and into the band pit, if Jack Scarrott's memory is correct.

Inevitably, Samuels's greatest supporter was his wife, Elizabeth Samuels, who apparently went 'half off her head because Samuels was getting the worst of it' and greeted the cheering of the crowd with indignation, and started hitting out 'right and left at the men around her.' In the scenes of chaos that followed, the police rushed in and brought a halt to the proceedings.

At first, Samuels apparently took the defeat in good spirits, having afterwards decided that 'Toff' could provide him with a nice little earner if he could employ him to travel on his boxing booth. Samuels offered Toff £2 to meet all comers on his booth, which Toff, being a bit down on his luck at the time, willingly accepted, and both men went on to spar at the Philharmonic Hall for another six nights.

Nothing more was heard of the matter until eight years later, when London based sporting newspaper, the Mirror of Life decided to reprint key details from the career of Charles "Toff" Wall, and recounted a few details of Wall's meeting with the old showman. At the time, Samuels was doing exceedingly well for himself. He had not only founded a permanent booth in Swansea, the Gloucester School of Arms, but had also taken on the tenancy of the Kings Head public house in the High Street, where he lived 'in state' as the town's most pre-eminent bruiser. Most likely a subscription to the newspaper meant that a copy dropped on William Samuel's mat, with Samuels having been as interested in the ongoing doings of the prize-ring as ever.

It was with some measure of extreme irritation that William Samuels would read of his reported 'defeat' at the hands of "Toff" Wall, and shortly afterwards Samuels drafted a letter which subsequently wounds its way from Swansea to the postbag of the Mirror of Life offices, which was duly published along with an editor's note;

"Toff" Wall is rather modest than otherwise in narrating his exploits. The remarks which Mr. Samuels objects to were from a statement published at the time. However as audi alteram partem (hear the other side too) is our motto, we publish his letter – ED.

To the Editor of THE MIRROR OF LIFE

SIR – Seeing the untrue statement made by "Toff" Wall, who was supposed to be the middle-weight champion of the world, I here tell him that his statement is entirely without foundation.

The truth of the matter is, that "Toff" Wall was sent to come to Cardiff to meet me and defeat me in three rounds. He undertook the job, but failed. I never met him in any contest for a purse after his failure to knock me out. I was engaged by the manager of the Philharmonic Music Hall at Cardiff to spar Wall for six nights at £10 a night.

I was really engaged to spar Jem Smith, but he refused to spar me, saying that he had a boy who would spar me. "Toff" Wall was the boy.

I think the six nights that I sparred "Toff" Wall gave him every possible chance of smothering me, which he should have done, as I was then forty-seven years of age, at least twenty years older than him. I was never asked to fight in my life without accepting. I sparred at the Philharmonic at Cardiff with John L. Sullivan, receiving £10 for three three minute rounds.

I am very sorry for "Toff" Wall being in such poor circumstances; as for myself, I am just as popular around Wales as ever, although I received by "Toff" Wall's account such a smothering at Cardiff. If this smothering process had any truth attached to it surely it would decrease my popularity in Wales; but if you think it worth making inquiries you will find I am just as popular as ever, and able to spend in as many minutes what "Toff" Wall can earn in a week.

I have fought twenty-six prize fights with the knuckles and never been defeated, having met all classes. Hoping you will publish this in your valuable paper, I remain, yours truly

WM. SAMUELS.
(Retired Champion of Wales)
Gloster School of Arms, Swansea

The letter appears to have been a bit of an upsetting one for "Toff" to read, having believed that he had actually left Billy Samuels employment on fairly good terms, and the following week Charles 'Toff' Wall mailed in a letter to the Mirror of Life offices himself in reply;

To the Editor of THE MIRROR OF LIFE.

SIR, – I am very much surprised at Bill Samuels' letter. You know, Sir, that I brought you the account of my meeting with Samuels, and it was the same then as I told you the other evening. I will give you the facts as nearly as I can recollect again.

Jem Smith and his brother Tom were sparring together in Wales under their manager when Jem Smith, the then champion of England, was challenged by Bill Samuels, the champion of Wales. The manager did not think it would be good business for the champion of England to box a local champion like Samuels, and I received a telegram asking me to come down and box Samuels. I did not know Samuels's weight or size, but I went down to the music hall where the contest was to take place and saw the manager. "Oh, you are too small to box Samuels," he said "For God's sake, guv'nor, don't say that!" said I "I've come two hundred miles for the job, and I am stone broke. Don't say I can't box Bill Samuels now." The manager consented, and when we met I knocked Bill all over the shop, and I made such a mess of Samuels that the show was stopped. When we got in the dressing room Samuels gave me two pounds, and engaged me to box in his show, which many persons in Wales can testify that I did, going about with Bill Samuels to many places, and meeting all comers.

Trusting you will insert this, with many thanks, I remain yours truly,

CHARLES "TOFF" WALL.

From Jack Scarrott's point of view in the cheap seats, and the brief account printed in *The Western Mail*, 'Toff' Wall would appear to have been telling the truth, and William Samuels sense of pride would seem to have once again got the better of the aging warrior, although no-one could doubt his pluck in having dared to even try and stand up against such an opponent as the formidable 'Toff' Wall. Foolishly, his letter did enable one of his time honoured enemies to come out of the woodwork to shoot a few well-timed barbs in printed form to further enrage the old timer, one Bob Dunbar, previously known as 'Sam Lane', and currently engaged in running his own boxing booth at the Welsh town of Ebbw Vale;

Boxing Pavilion
Market Place, Ebbw Vale, Mon. S.Wales.

To the Editor of THE MIRROR OF LIFE

SIR, _ Kindly insert this rather lengthy reply to the boastful epistle from William Samuels, meaning to contradict your last week's statement pertaining to "Toff" Wall. I, R. Dunbar, not a self-styled champion, remember well when Mr. J. Fleming, the present boxing manager of the N.S.C, wired to Bill Richardson's. "Toff" and I went in to have a liquor; a telegram was handed to "Toff" that a letter would be there for him in the morning from Cardiff. "Toff" and I went again next morning for the letter. "Toff" said, "Read out, Bob." A glance at the letter caused me to burst out laughing. I said, "Can't for laughing. Spare my days, this is good! Why here's my old enemy waiting to have a go at you."

I then read the letter to "Toff," saw him to the station for Cardiff, and said, "Good luck, "Toff"!" knowing full well the drubbing in store for Samuels. If Samuels will look back at the register of his birth he will find he is now going on fifty-two; that would make him about forty-three when "Toff" shouldered him all about the ring. I question very much six nights at £10 per night, or £60 per week for one show of about nine minutes per night. With regard to Samuels's fighting abilities, his memory is a little at fault He has overlooked the second day of October, 1882, at Llanelly, when I (then known as "Young" Lane of Birmingham put him under the care of Drs. Buckley and Price in 33 mins; in all, fourteen rounds.

Perhaps this little bit from the Llanelly paper of October 5, 1882, will refresh his memory a little: "With regard to the punishment, let it be stated that Samuels paid his attention to Lane's bread-basket and sides, whilst Lane paid his attention to Samuels's mug, from which the cognac soon began to fly, and he gave signs of going into mourning by having his shutters put up." Has he ever heard the chorus of the song composed after the fight?

"Hurrah for Bob!" the people cried,
For Lor! To his surprise,
The champion's nose was damaged,
And black were both his eyes.

He has also ignored the fact that he, Wm. S. led a crowd of upwards of 200 people through the main streets of Carmarthen Town to attend him, closely followed by the protectors of the peace, who kindly guarded him in his caravan the remainder of the day, November 8, 1882. There are numerous little anecdotes that would tend to increase his boasted popularity. One I'll mention, that he has completely ignored the name of Bob Dunbar, alias "Young" Lane of Birmingham, from all his great battles. (Thanks.) I would not have refreshed his memory of these little events had he not cast a slur on an old friend, who is his superior in every respect and a man of sterling abilities. His letter might do very well for those who are not in the know, but I am only one of thousands who know better, and I take it as a piece of confounded impudence for him to try and gull the public. I may conclude by remarking that the one was a diamond of the first water, the other – paste. The bit of bogey with John L. was very good.

> *Trusting you will insert this in your valuable paper.*
> *I remain, yours truly,*
> *BOB DUNBAR.*
> *For ten years undisputed light-weight champion of Wales.*

While there is some undoubted truth in Toff's letter, the same can not necessarily be said of Bob Dunbar's. Certainly, Samuels remained an incredibly popular draw on home-turf (probably more so than Bob himself) and while this might be due to Samuel's headline grabbing antics, it must be said that the 'song' composed after the fight reads like something penned by Bob himself. While it is perhaps conceivable that someone may have penned a few lines to sell on printed song sheets, which were popular when sold on the fairgrounds for a few pennies at the time, it appears likely that it is something that had been conjured up by Dunbar.

There is also some evidence to suggest that it was actually Bob Dunbar that didn't fancy the idea of meeting William Samuels a second time. At Carmarthen, both would appear to have initially been willing parties in a re-match that was scheduled for the 15th November, 1882 – a day after the Carmarthen fair. Efforts by the interested crowd of spectators to witness a re-match were foiled by the police who successfully tracked fifty people to a field called Parkwaen. They were making their way towards a marsh near the gasworks, by the river side. Having rumbled the combatants at the scene, their supporters dispersed, having been unable to pitch the stakes for the ring. Having been given a stern warning by

Superintendent James, either Samuels or Dunbar was sufficiently rattled by the interruption to state that they should vote for the contest being "off" – not "brought off" in a battle, but "declared off". After receiving promises to the effect that the battle was no longer going to go ahead, the Superintendent allowed both men to leave the scene, and William Samuels and Bob Dunbar left the town the following morning with their ongoing dispute unresolved.

It wasn't quite the end of the affair, with Samuels and Dunbar ending up scrapping it out on the streets of Swansea, with Samuels having been the more eager to go somewhere quiet to settle matters in bare-knuckle style. On this occasion, Dunbar seems to have been more reticent to fight, although had proved quick enough as ever to run down Samuels' fighting abilities around the town to anyone that would listen prior to the meeting. Unfortunately their brief street battle was brought to an end by the interruption of Swansea police, who quickly collared Samuels. Bob Dunbar was quicker on his feet and made off in the confusion that followed. Despite Bob's apparent superiority, it was Samuels that afterwards made the offer to meet for a stand up prize-fight, reportedly offering Dunbar to fight, '…for as small a sum as he likes, or as large a sum as he can find, or to back himself for £50 to beat Lane if the latter will only stand for seven minutes each round.'

In would appear that Bob Dunbar thought better of the idea, and decided against another battle with the cantankerous old Swansea fighter, electing to up stumps and try his luck somewhere new. Undoubtedly, Bill Samuels probably thought he had the better end of the matter, as does Jack Scarrott. The old Swansea champ, William Samuels would continue 'ruling' on in his own town and farther afield as the champion 'of Wales', and would seek out further fame in new headline making stunts for many years afterwards.

Chapter 9
William Samuels vs. John L. Sullivan

The year of 1888 started particularly well for the mountain fighters and aspiring boxers to be found in and around the capital city of Cardiff, and it started with a bang early in January 1888 with the arrival of the great American heavyweight champion, John L. Sullivan. Sullivan had arrived at Liverpool on the 6th November, 1887, but his vast belt of hammered gold encrusted with diamonds did not accompany him on his journey to London, having been held by customs officers until his return journey to the US. Sullivan had been unwilling to part with the huge sum of £120 to be allowed to transport the belt onto British shores in order to show it off to the crowds that met him on his arrival.

The spectators who greeted his arrival at London's Euston station were even larger, with a full 5,000 strong crowd jostling and pushing to get a view of Sullivan as his train drew into the station. Before going on tour around the United Kingdom, a further 1,800 people scrambled to secure tickets to see the 'Boston Strongboy'

John L. Sullivan, the American Heavyweight Champion

in action against his sparring partner, Jack Ashton on the stage of St. James Hall in London.

On travelling from England and onwards to Ireland, Sullivan would only make one appearance in Wales, at Cardiff, where he had been engaged to appear for three nights at the Philharmonic Hall, and drew massive crowds that had been alerted to his presence on board before his train had left Newport. Sullivan, long used to gawkers and onlookers, reclined regally in his carriage 'with an air of weariness and indifference' and managed to maintain his dignified manner, and refused to take any notice of the people pushing their noses up against the train windows at the station to see the fistic hero of the hour. The only line of questioning that could begin to stir Sullivan from his lack of interest with the spectacle that presented itself was an enquiry from a roving newspaper reporter as to whether he had attributed any value to the 'championship' belt that has recently been given to his rival, Jake Kilrain by Richard K. Fox of the Police Gazette;

"No. As I said before, its real value is only about £30 and if I win it I intend to offer it for competition among the New York bootblacks."

Hot on Sullivan's heels was Charley Mitchell and Jake Kilrain himself, who were also scheduled to appear just down the road from the Philharmonic at Tayleure's Circus in Westgate Street, Cardiff. This was to be the first time that the main aspirants for the Heavyweight Championship of the World had all appeared at the same time in any town in the United Kingdom. Kilrain had proved a popular draw in Cardiff, mainly due to the elaborate tales that had been weaved around his fight with Jem Smith in December, to which Jack Scarrott appears to have been a willing listener. Truthfully, although a seemingly Herculean 106 rounds had been fought, they had not reflected well on Jem Smith. Smith had actually been knocked out in the very first round, before being brought round and brought up to scratch again to begin anew. In the later rounds Smith claimed that he had difficulty in seeing, as a result of this early 'flash' knockout although this can hardly have excused his conduct in the fifty first round when he had tried to gouge out Kilrain's eyes. With darkness rapidly falling by the hundred and sixth round, and with Smith falling to the grass at every available opportunity, there could have been no doubt that Jake Kilrain should have been given the victory. It was only the threat of assault by Smith's mob, who surrounded the referee that forced the contest to be called a 'draw'.

There were no seats to be had on the opening night at the Philharmonic Hall on the 3rd January, 1888, and when John L. Sullivan appeared with his sparring partner, Jack Ashton there was loud and enthusiastic cheering and they went on to spar four rounds before an excitable crowd. While lacking the dash that characterised his usual fighting style, there was no doubt that Sullivan still maintained all of his old power that had made Paddy Ryan once say of him that "…when Sullivan struck me, I thought that a telegraph pole had been shoved against me sideways."

Billy Samuels had somehow wrangled an invite to the event, and despite his age, he turned up at the Philharmonic Hall with the intention of seeing out three rounds of sparring with John L. Sullivan, the only man that would dare to do so throughout the champion's UK music hall tour. Many of the spectators came all the way from London, convinced that the flinty old showman might put on a show worth seeing. Local admirers of Samuels also turned out in number, hoping '...to see some real hitting, and trusted that Samuels might be good man enough to give Sullivan a chance to come out'. The net result was that the old hall was 'as thoroughly crowded, noisy and agitated as it could possibly be' and the air was reportedly 'full of Welsh enthusiasm'.

The account of the meeting from the US papers is worth recording in full, giving some idea of the gameness of the old Welsh champion in having dared to try and stand up before such a gigantic name in the history of boxing folklore;

'Samuels opened with a rush at Sullivan, who paid no attention to it until it was over, and then with a comparatively gentle tap sent the Welsh champion swiftly against the ropes. The Welshman came back and was sent away again. This went on throughout the round and the Welshmen were much delighted, for their knotty little man, though evidently in with the wrong snake, had proved himself plucky, and they, not understanding fighting, did not know how much trouble Sullivan was having to obey the injunction he had received not to knock his man out.

In the second round Samuels was allowed to disport himself considerably, Sullivan only stopping hits and scarcely pretending to strike out. This so delighted the little man's admirers that their exultation grew almost offensive. The great and only Bostonian began to regret his magnanimity, and whispered to his backer,

Phillips, that he must hit Samuels just once to take the conceit out of his friends.

Accordingly in the middle of the third round he let out his right arm, the one that works with such painful precision, and the round stopped short. William Samuels, champion of the Welsh hills, was doubled up in his corner. He got up by-and-by, shook hands with Sullivan and proved he was appreciative of the latter's kindness, and said that first and last blow showed him how many opportunities Sullivan had let go by. Samuels declined with emphasis the vociferous invitations of his friends to go on. Sullivan took his applause with calmness characteristic of true greatness.'

Despite his obvious schooling at the hands of the US champion, William Samuels was quick to applaud the fighting abilities of Sullivan, and would later tell an interviewer that he deemed Sullivan to be "the finest man that ever was in a ring, and the hardest hitter".

As ever, when put on the spot about the showing, which was one that could only be deemed to be one which showed Samuels as having been a game challenger, Samuels was prone to showing something of a selective memory of events if they were not showing him in the best possible light;

"The first punch he swung at me I ducked, and I could hear it whiz over my head. I believe it would have taken my head clean off if it had struck me. I dodged him all right through the three rounds until the very end, when he got me in a corner. He swung a punch at me and smashed the side wings in the hall. Then time was called, and I was glad, I can tell you."

Sullivan would later recall in his book, 'Reminiscences of a 19th Century Gladiator', that the only place he '...visited in Wales was Cardiff, where I gave an exhibition and met an ambitious boxer named Samuels, who, after the second round, cried "quits" and said he had had enough'. Sullivan's memory, which can be questioned at various points in the book, seems to be a little at fault, and caused Billy considerable irritation when approached on the subject by local press men. He continued to assert that Sullivan had given him £100 for having seen out the three rounds without finding it necessary to mention the punch that left him doubled up in his corner halfway through the third round, and was quick to denounce John L.'s statements as 'Sullivanic bounce'. It must be said that as Sullivan had refused to cough up to allow his belt to be allowed into the country to be seen by his many fans, it must appear to be highly unlikely that he would have even have considered giving £100 to a middle aged local 'champion' like Billy Samuels. As a result it is probably best to conclude that at the beginning of 1888, two master self-publicists and champion pugilists at different ends of the spectrum met another, with the lesser of the pair being a 'knotty' little Welsh chap that definitely won the hearts of his followers with a game display that he would recall with colourful touches and flourishes to the delight or irritation of many in the years to come.

Chapter 10
Shoni Engineer vs. Jem Guiderell

One fight in which Jack Scarrott definitely had a ringside seat was one where Shoni Engineer was matched to fight Jem Guiderell, a Bristol labourer, for £100 in May of 1888. Out of necessity the fight was held across the border in Gloucestershire at Berkeley after police interference made it impossible for the fight to come off on the East moors of Cardiff, a popular battle ground for bare-knuckle matches. Jack Scarrott for some reason records the match as having come off at Patchway, although newspaper reports give Berkeley as having been the actual venue for the contest. A couple of days prior to the match both men travelled to Gloucestershire for the weigh-in. Shoni weighed in at 10 stone 7 ½ pounds, while Guiderell weighed in at 2lb. less. Shoni was also seen to have a slight height advantage over the Bristol man, and at 5ft 10inches tall, stood 2 ½ inches taller than his opponent. Shoni was lucky enough to secure a quality trainer in Bill "Jockey" Saunders of Birmingham, while

Jem Guiderell was trained by Bill Briton, a fellow Bristollian, at his headquarters in Weston-super-Mare.

Due to the problems presented by the Cardiff police force, the fight crowd, with more than a few well known faces amongst its forty strong gang, descended on Berkeley. Although their errand was probably guessed, they found little opposition to their plans in the locality. The fight started at five minutes past six o'clock in the morning and appears to have been a long winded and punishing affair;

'From the very first the Cardiff man had all his own way. He scored first blood in the second round, knocking down his opponent with the same blow. Goytrell, (Guiderell) *however, stood up pluckily before his man, but though his efforts were great his science was considerably inferior to that of his opponent, and he suffered terribly in consequence. "Shoni" seemed at his best, and his blows fell with sledge-hammer force on the face and form of the Bristollian, who over and over again appeared unable to respond to the call of "Time." Odds on Shoni were freely laid by his supporters, but the backers of Goytrell readily accepted them, even though their man was being so badly handled. Seventy-eight rounds having been fought the result seemed a "dead snip" for the Cardiff man. Goytell's face was one mass of bruises, and his features altogether unrecognisable. The efforts of his seconds, however, were unceasing, and he, at the 78th round, again faced his man. The raw cold air of the morning had now taken hold of "Shoni," who was at this stage seized with shivers, and unable to do himself justice. Goytrell at once took advantage of his opponent's weakness, and at the 85th round "Shoni," overcome with the cold, was unable to respond, and the stakes and fight were awarded to Goytrell.'*

Curiously, the printed account makes no mention of the fight having been stopped by police, which is how Jack Scarrott remembers the contest ending. A *Western Mail* newspaperman was intrigued enough by the account of the battle to track Shoni down to a snug Cardiff bar where after a few short pleasantries, Shoni was put at his ease enough to give his account of the affair. By all accounts, the journalist found Shoni to be an affable sort of character;

'He was a man of about my own height, perhaps an inch shorter and a stone lighter. Vertically and horizontally upon his face, from the nose upwards, there were marks of a scrimmage. A billycock hat which he wore, slouched over the right eye, brought down its dark edge into contact with a broad white bandage, which completely covered that optic. The nose appeared to me to have been slightly spread abroad, possibly by Nature, possibly by previous encounters – a good hale, strapping fellow, whose broad jaw, muscular physique and swinging length of arm impressed one almost as much as his modesty and his almost over eager desire to give his opponent all the credit which was his due.

"I didn't see the fight, of course," said I; "but I was awfully astonished on reading the accounts to find out had lost it. How came that about, John?"

"Well, you see, sir," said John, "the fellow was as hard as…"

"Nails," I suggested.

"Yes, bricks; anything you like," was the reply.

"I'm certain I gave him as much as would have knocked out any three ordinary men, but he came up smiling each time for more."

"Is it true," said the landlord, "that you hit off a piece of his ear and the side of his nose in the second round?"

"No," replied John, with characteristic modesty.

"I gave him rather a bad slap with my left, and I thought I'd knocked him out, but he came up again, game as ever."

"Of course," said I, "the story of a Cardiff paper that you knocked his eye out is all moonshine."

"Just so," said John "I gave him a proper onener though, and the eye swelled a good deal, but that was all."

"I rather fancy he must have been very well seconded," I observed.

"You bet, said the landlord. "Why, Jack Davies, a man of sixteen or seventeen stone…

"Took him up in his arms, carried him to his corner, and nursed him like a child," said John. "I heard most of his second's tips, and we both did all we knew to get at each other. The umpire, who was as ignorant of prize fighting as my grandmother, told me once or twice that if I fell again he'd give the fight to my opponent."

"Never," replied John, "only after delivering one."

"And you know," our host put in, "that that, according to the rules of the London Prize Ring, is strictly allowable."

"I almost think I do," said I. "But what about those shivers, John?"

"Well," was the reply, "We fought in a place about as smooth as the floor of this room. There were bushes all round us pretty much as solid as these walls, only where I stood there was a great big hole through which the wind came howling at a fearful rate ."

"Did you toss for corners?" I queried.

"No, sir," replied John. "We took 'em by choice. About the fortieth round I felt the draught most awful, and cried to my seconds to put my coat on me. They were rather slow about it each time, and I got to shiver and shake so much at last that I was good for just nothing at all. My jaws kept rattling like a dice-box, and my legs knocked together as if I'd the ague; and there I was, quite unable to do anything."

"Who arranged the match for you?" said I.

"Did you know each other previously?"

"Never," replied John. "It was all done through one of the sporting papers."

"Are you willing to fight him again, John?" I asked.

"Nothing would please me better," was the reply. "I'd rather than £20 if I had a go at him tomorrow."

"Yes," said the landlord "and if you're going to say anything about it in the paper, you can tell Goytrell's friends that there's a couple of hundreds to be had on 'Shoni's' side any day they like to cover and pick it up. But I don't think they'll come up to the scratch again. They've already been challenged to another fight, but they've declined. Goytrell went straight off into the infirmary, and here is 'Shoni' now, right as a trivet, as you can see."

The resulting article did not go down particularly well on the other side of the border, with one of Guiderell's supporters proving eager to get their side of what had happened into print. An anonymous letter was sent to and printed in the *Western Mail* shortly afterwards;

THE RECENT PRIZE FIGHT NEAR BERKELEY
TO THE EDITOR OF THE "WESTERN MAIL"

SIR – Having read with interest in your valuable paper of Saturday the account of the interview with "Shoni Engineer" of Cardiff, relative to the fight between him and James Guiderell, of Bristol, I feel bound as one who was there, to contradict a few of "Shoni's" answers to your correspondent's questions. As to Jack Davis taking Guiderell up in his arms like a baby, there is no doubt that Jack Davis is a good second; but he did no such things as are imputed to him. He did, in conjunction with Billy Brittan, the other second, pick his man up in the ordinary way and take him to his corner. As to nursing him, I do not think he required much of that. You say "Shoni" said the referee was ignorant of prize-fighting, I must say that I have seen a few prize-fights in my time, and I never saw a fight where a referee acted with more tact and judgement in my life. As to being ignorant of prize-fighting, I might remind "Shoni" that he redoubtable and renowned Bill Knee, of Stroud, has acted before in the same capacity, and with success. Give credit where credit is due. "Shoni" also says that corners were not tossed for. That is emphatically wrong, for I myself saw corners tossed for between a Welshman and John Read, of Bristol. Read lost, and the Welshman selected for "Shoni" the corner with his back to the sun. Perhaps "Shoni" will answer to whom or when and where was a challenge made for a second match? I say nowhere. Where did "Shoni" get the information as to Guiderell being in the infirmary? I do not think he has so much as passed by one. I myself saw him at his own house on Friday night in company with Jack Davis, and again last night, and I think I use my judgement aright in saying that I think he is looking well. I hope "Shoni" will look over this little paragraph and answer it. By doing so he will oblige – I enclose my card and am, &c.,

ONE WHO WAS THERE
Bristol, May 28.

Although the differing viewpoints naturally suggest an understandably biased point of view from both parties, it is interesting that the unnamed writer of the letter sent to the Western Mail offices does not dispute any of the particulars that suggest that Shoni was definitely getting the better of Guiderell until the final stages of the fight. This being said, it does seem odd that Shoni Engineer should have chosen to fight in the manner that he did had he been such a superior fighter. If there was one tactic that was largely frowned upon in prize fighting circles, it was the old dodge of 'seeking the grass' and one which Shoni appears to have preferred, and while not outlawed by the rules of the London Prize Ring, it certainly was a method that might be viewed as slightly underhand. By throwing a punch and then throwing oneself down on the grass at the slightest blow, the crafty fighter could land blows to damage an opponent over time while avoiding any serious damage from return fire. In many instances, it could lead to an open ended fight of many 'falls' and punches of little or no consequence. It has to be wondered if Shoni really was the 'level best' 10 stone 10 lb man 'in England', as alleged by Jack Scarrott, he had to resort to such tactics to secure victory, particularly as Guiderell was a relative unknown in prize-fighting circles, having reportedly only entered the prize ring proper on just one previous occasion.

Chapter 11

Shoni Engineer vs. John O' Brien

A new holiday began in 1888 which would have far reaching repercussions on the local pugilistic scene in South Wales. After some difficulties with the industrialists, one of the miner's representatives and Member of Parliament finally won a much-needed, but unpaid holiday for the colliers on the first Monday of every month, which commonly became known as Mabon's day, after the nickname of its founder, William Abraham, known as 'Mabon'. Having toiled so hard on behalf of his people, Mabon was disappointed to discover that the founding of such an important landmark in worker's rights was quickly laid open to abuse by the very same colliers that he had fought so hard for. In fact, the majority of the men-folk found that the 'holiday' was most suited to the illegal activity of prize fighting on the mountains and 'bloody spots' of South Wales.

With an opening made for a day of less than respectable leisure activity, anyone not engaged in a

William Abraham M.P., known as 'Mabon'

prize-fight as a combatant or an interested member of the local 'fancy' could more often than not be found in the pub, and the valleys of Jack Scarrott's youth were well supplied with many options for the drinking man eager to satisfy a thirst for beer. There were small overcrowded bars in mean terraced buildings, with some having been converted by the growing members of the merchant classes into shops and stores. Some of the pubs had backrooms, where the early 'gymnasiums' were doing quiet business, as training quarters for the many men that had been drawn into pugilistic activities in their downtime, and where local 'Professors' of boxing, men like Patsy Perkins, and Bob Wiltshire could often be found, both at one time claimants of the keenly disputed Welsh lightweight title. Patsy Perkins had been the in-house boxing trainer at the Bird in Hand in Merthyr for a time, while Bob Wiltshire was well known to all and sundry around his native Cardiff as a bare-knuckle man. Billy Samuels' men, of which there were many, could also often be found knocking about in the area of the old Strand in Swansea, men like George Lucas, who would later work in Billy's 'Gloucester School of Arms', although had started as a knuckle man fighting on the 'burrows' like so many others including Billy's occasional referee, Chris 'Daddy' Yates.

It was unsurprising that at Pontypridd, a man looking for a good pugilistic pub of far grander scale might well look towards the Butchers Arms Hotel, situated right in the heart of old Pontypridd. The pub stood a stone's throw from the busy market, and was a cavernous building beloved by the hard-drinking and hard fighting crowd where anyone who might want to put their ear to the ground looking for a hot tip as to when the next mountain fight, or local championship was due to come off might pick up some useful information. There is some evidence to suggest that the pub landlord, an otherwise respectable individual in the town was often knowingly engaged in assisting some of the local prize-fighting fraternity with their development as glove fighters, if not the actual prize-fights themselves. Sam 'Butcher' Thomas is recorded as having pitched up at the building after his battle against David Davies in 1889, although it is to be wondered whether the fight came off in one of the many back-rooms of the public house itself.

Jack Scarrott would remember that when a fight was brewing at the bar, the pub landlord, old Edgar Treharne, would often appear and tell the customers to draw the blinds before moving the furniture out of the way to let them settle their differences in the bar itself and let the arguing parties fight a few surreptitious rounds at the bar side before getting back to the bartending business. On numerous occasions, pavilions or 'boxing saloons' were allowed to pitch up in the Butcher's Arms Yards behind the building. On one occasion the world famous heavyweight Peter Jackson, known as the 'Black Prince' appeared there in the early 1890's at a boxing exhibition, and would have been, in the opinion of many, a natural choice for world championship honours had it not been for John L. Sullivan's refusal to meet black challengers in the ring. Local man Jimmy (Frederick) Dean also fought at the Butcher's Arms yards on numerous occasions. Jack Scarrott remembers Jimmy Dean fondly, having taken him on as a booth boxer at one point in time, and while Dean is not remembered as a skilled boxer, he was well known as having been a very 'hard' man, fighting under his nick-name the 'Cast-Iron Man';

'You couldn't kill him with a sledgehammer. You could tie him to a post and hammer him, and then you couldn't kill him'

It sounds as though Jimmy Dean was something of a troublemaker, as more than a few local boys appear to have tried to finish him off, although Dean viewed the majority with disdain and would offer to fight them one after another. On another occasion, the one time champion of Shrewsbury, Enoch Morrison could also be found as a performer on one of the many boxing pavilions to set up behind the building. In addition to increased pub takings, and prize-fighting occurring on the turf of the green hills above the towns, there was plenty of scope for the clever booth owner to maximise his profits on Mabon's day as well. With the average miner eager to find some diversion from the hardships of his life, the booths of Tolley, Stokes, and the like are often to be found amongst the reports of boxing booths having been invaded by the police on Mabon's day. At times the booth could be used as a cover for a genuine championship fight, albeit with knuckles covered by the thinnest possible gloves. Usually the format was to put on a few good natured short exhibitions to establish whether the coast was clear and the booth audience was free of undercover policemen before starting a contest more resembling a genuine fight.

Shoni Engineer must have been in his element around the booths in these days, having been something of a local boxing and prize-fighting celebrity. Shoni's reputation had been bolstered by his victory over Pete

Burns, and his defeat of Morris Tobin. For this reason he was more than willing to meet any challengers for the Welsh title, and had no fear of a new fighter on the scene, John O'Brien, who was well known for fighting against all and sundry around the back alleys of the Roath area of Cardiff. Serious money, £100, lay on the outcome of the fight and people were starting to notice O'Brien after he had reportedly knocked out the showman Lloyd Roberts on a tour of West Wales.

The fight came off on May 1st 1889, but not without the usual difficulties, having been originally planned to come off the previous day at Brecon. Unfortunately the police got wind of the scheme, so the battle moved to the Marshfield area outside Cardiff on the Monmouthshire side of the county boundary. By starting the fight so close to a grey area of police jurisdiction it enabled the men to flee in one direction or the other in the event they were disturbed, and hopefully avoid prosecution. The change of venue proved to be a lucky break, with police having been thrown off their trail altogether. Odds favoured Shoni Engineer at 6 to 4, while John O'Brien stood as a largely untested opponent. Shoni had also undergone considerable training for the contest at Carmarthen prior to making his way to Brecon.

Unfortunately, Shoni lost the toss for corners, a fairly important consideration as the sun had risen for some time and put its slanting rays directly into his face, which appeared to cause him some difficulty. The foothold on the turf was also pretty poor, and it seemed likely that victory might well favour the better man at holding his ground in grappling. The fight having been fought under London prize ring rules, any manner of throw was deemed allowable within the confines of the 24ft portable ring. In all, nineteen round were fought with the spectators being surprised to find that Shoni's crown was well and truly toppled in just twenty three minutes, having reportedly been a particularly poor performance on the part of Shoni Engineer;

Round 1 – *Shoni shot out with the left, and O'Brien countered, also with the left. The men then got to close quarters. Shoni got in a blow on O'Brien's nose and drew first blood. The men then got to close quarters and Shoni went down.*

Round 2 – *Shoni passed his opponent's guard, and got in one blow, buts its force was spent, Shoni again fell.*

Round 3 and 4 – *No fighting at all. Shoni, who was evidently funking a bit, falling.*

Round 5 – *Better work was put in. Shoni stood up well, but O'Brien getting in a swinging blow with the left, knocked his opponent down.*

Round 6 to 10 – *Shoni kept at his old tactics. O'Brien would lead off, only for his opponent to seek grass. Shoni would have given in had his backers allowed.*

Round 11 – *Best round of all. Shoni pulled himself together and stood up well, and seemed to get slightly the better of the bout.*

Round 12 – *More grass seeking on the part of Shoni.*

Round 13 – *O'Brien again led off, and got in two or three blows before Shoni fell.*

Rounds 14 to 18 – *The same old game, though Shoni got in a few blows. In the sixteenth round he was knocked down. The* *only body blow in the fight was got in by O'Brien close to the mark.*

Round 19 – *Shoni led off, and O'Brien countered. They then got to close quarters. O'Brien slinging round his right, got on the point (the jaw) and Shoni went down. Shoni did not respond to the call of "Time" and the stakes were awarded to O'Brien. The eleventh round was the only bit of real fighting in the whole affair.*

After the fight ended, the Superintendent of the Newport police showed up in the company of a group of his men, but was too late to catch John O'Brien and Shoni Engineer who had scurried away from the battleground before the police arrived on the scene.

Jack Scarrott was very obviously not in attendance and almost certainly heard about the battle and forgot the details or was wrongly informed as to the outcome. Jack Scarrott wrongly recounts that the match came off at Heol-y-cyw near Bridgend, and that Shoni was beaten in six rounds and not nineteen. Additionally, he also make a number of mistakes regarding the particulars of John O'Brien's boxing record, although in fairness it must be stated that Scarrott had limited contact with John O'Brien other than having briefly appeared on the booth alongside the Cardiff man, in the period when Jack was appearing on the boxing booths as a booth boxer himself. At that time, Jack Scarrott can't possibly have imagined where the decision to do so would one day lead.

Chapter 12

Boxing Booth Days

Booth boxing was a hard life, and not one for the faint of heart, or indeed, anyone with a fear of injury. For those few that would rise up from the pools of local glove-fighting talent there were many more who simply didn't make the grade. It might be imagined that the majority hailed from the coal pit and from the foundry. It was the coal and iron industries that had brought the majority from the countryside to the densely populated towns of South Wales in the nineteenth century. Most found a hard way of life, where life was cheap, wages were often not much more than a pittance, and few men would grow to adulthood without experiencing the terrors of hurtling down a mineshaft to spend their working lives toiling in the darkness before their fifteenth year.

In many instances, it would be in the pit that young men experienced their first fights, having had a falling out that could only seemingly be resolved through swapping fists by oil-lamp many miles underground in a trench cut out to the rough dimension of a ring which was 'fit for purpose'. If it was not a dispute that could be easily settled down below, it was one that sent men quietly under cover of darkness up a nearby mountain at dawn, ready to resume the battle in the light of the rising sun. The mountain fighters became feared throughout the valleys, known for their hardness and brutality, and astonishing tales of the toughness of their spirit, forged with pick and hammer would filter down to the townsfolk. Some were quickly and easily recognisable, either for their injuries, which Jack Scarrott deemed '…enough to freeze the heart out of a bull terrier. Broken noses, black eyes, cauliflower ears, (with) lumps knocked off 'em'. Others had the stained faces and hands of those that took prize-fighting seriously enough to brine the face and pickle the knuckles. As the years rolled by, many saw the gloved booth boxing brigade as a softer breed, and targeted the more well-known names as soon as they heard they were at a nearby fair or indeed at any patch of rough land where a boxing booth showman might pitch up on his regular travels from town to town.

The hardness of these men can only be imagined in a world that has changed almost beyond recognition. In Jack Scarrott's day, it was not unusual for a fighting man to finish a hard day's work at the pit, and afterwards travel on foot up the sides of a steep sided lonely mountain range to a pre-designated spot in order to attempt to beat another man in a contest that might last hours for a few coins, or just a jug of beer with his cronies. For such men, the thought of walking fifty miles to a county fair to get boasting rights for having knocked out a fighter recorded in the press as having been a 'coming' man was no hurdle to stop their pursuit of local pugilistic fame.

Supposedly 'no mean exponent' with the gloves himself in his days of youth, Jack Scarrott freely admits that the glove fighters of his time had their work cut out for them, and that the booth boxers were often afraid of meeting the mountain fighters in battle. Jack certainly appears to have mixed in with some good company. He recounts that he was employed by at least two booth proprietors, and featured on the booths of both Harry and John Stokes and Jimmy Day of Portsmouth. Stokes was perhaps the more familiar of the two booth owners, and appears to have toured fairly widely throughout South Wales, having been recorded as setting up his booth at Barry as well as in the Rhondda valley. Many of the early booth men were boxers in their hey-day as well as being early boxing entrepreneurs, with John Stokes and Jimmy Day having been well known as capable boxers. Rising through the ranks and becoming a booth proprietor did not automatically guarantee an easier life, John Stokes could probably testify as much, having narrowly avoided being knifed by some of his patrons on one memorable occasion at Barry that was reported in the local press. It was while Harry Stokes was stationed at Treorchy fair that Jack Scarrott would remember that an outsider by the name of Fred Gray of London had nearly got lynched by the crowd.

Fred Gray would appear to have been one Frederick George McGrath (Gray) and was possibly born in 1862. It is thought that he married into the travelling life, and supposedly joined a boxing booth before having later gravitated towards the far safer occupation of roundabout owner. According to Jack Scarrott's recollections, he was something of an amateur swordsman, and routinely gave exhibitions of boxing with his wife. Swordsmanship of a sort to draw the crowds was a common practise for the early booth owner, as a novel means of attracting crowds to the front of the boxing booth. In one variation, a small boy would be asked to hold an apple out in his hand and the booth owner would swipe at the apple to cleave it in two, leaving the hand unmarked. The stunt was often little more than a showman's trick, with the blade only sufficiently sharp enough to roughly split the apple at one point. By drawing the blade, the hand would be left undamaged by the blunter edge towards the tip of the sword. Other minor fencing tricks could also be performed with practise, enabling the showman to pull in the punters.

As an obvious outsider at Treorchy fair, Fred Gray would seem to have completely misjudged the local fondness for boxing, and was in fear of his own safety after refusing to box the local mountain fighters who were already lingering amongst the crowd. The spectators seemed decidedly unimpressed by his decision to consent to only box with his own wife;

'Never mind about boxing with a woman" they shouted, "we've got plenty of men in the Treorchy for you to box with."

Desperately seeking a solution that wouldn't result in being turned on his head, Fred Gray sought help from Harry Stokes. We can assume that this was one of the occasions on which Billy Samuels, who was quite a progressive individual, hadn't turned up for the fair with any of his lady boxers making up the troupe to box Gray's wife. Stokes and Samuels joined forces, and loaned Gray their booth boxers (for a fee) and Jack, amongst their number, must have performed fairly well, as Jack Scarrott remembers that 'Stokes and Samuels made a good profit out of that fair.'

Jack Scarrott would seem to have spent some time working the booth apron front with Stokes, as he recounts that he also appeared on the booth when it was besieged by a 'tremendous number of big, strong, rugged fellows' when the whole troupe received a hiding at Brecon fair, and Stokes was forced to close the booth down. Jack remembers getting the worst beating of all, and also recalls the other members of the boxing booth as being Harry Stokes, Jack Eynon, 'Tug' Wilson of Leicester and Bob Griffin of Birmingham. Time has unfortunately eroded the memory of these men, with Tug Wilson being the only member of the troupe who is now easily recalled.

Tug's real name was Joe Collins and was a boxer of long experience, having originally started out in the prize-fighting days of the 1860's. The tale of Tug Wilson is an interesting one, having first come to the attention of the prize fighting world in his youth as a promising fighter. Tug afterwards appears to have faded into obscurity for over a decade before resuming his prize fighting career. He was then 'rediscovered' by Richard K. Fox of the U.S. periodical the Police Gazette, who had previously awarded Jake Kilrain his own version of a 'champion's belt' in a bid to enrage John L. Sullivan, his great enemy. Believing that in Tug Wilson he might well have found a diamond of the old school, Fox engaged

Tug to travel to America to meet Sullivan in a four round contest. A serious financial package sealed the deal, with Tug being offered $1,000 plus half the gate receipts at Madison Square Garden as well as his own expenses having been paid in full. Tug didn't need to be asked twice. A fairly ugly man, somewhat chunky and with a chubby downtrodden face, Tug Wilson seemed an unlikely challenger for Sullivan's crown, and it must be wondered whether Fox had even seen a picture of Tug before having decided to make such a lucrative offer.

When the match started, John L. Sullivan quickly realised he was in with one of the slipperiest characters the ring has ever known. Tug, far from wanting to engage the gigantic Bostonian in a genuine fight, took off backwards for all he was worth. Showing a firm understanding of Shoni Engineer style gamesmanship, Tug also made sure to drop like a rock every time Sullivan launched any type of blow. He dodged and flopped until Sullivan, who thought the match would probably be a walkover and hadn't bothered training prior to the event, had exhausted himself, partly through his own rapidly boiling anger, as well as through his physical exertions. Tug saw out the last round laughing, pleased as punch with his pay-day and holding Sullivan in a limpet-like clinch. It must have proved the most lucrative hugging match in Tug's entire career. True to form for most one-time big pay day pugilists, the money apparently didn't last. Tug was afterwards back to touring with the boxing booths with one eye out for a decent short exhibition match and a quick pay-packet for minimal effort, having later found himself short term employment when at the veteran stage after having been

Tug Wilson Lasts Four Rounds.

The Tug Wilson vs. John L. Sullivan contest

engaged for exhibition matches by the bareknuckle champion, Jem Mace.

Jem Mace seems to have been greatly taken with Tug, who he would afterwards remember as "…a very clever boxer, indeed, a prize fighter of the old school'. Although even Mace in hindsight had to conclude that as regards the match with John L. Sullivan, it was not '…so much a boxing match, as a carpet crawling contest' and that 'Had 'Tug' stood up to John L. Sullivan fair and square, he would have been knocked out in no time.'

John Stokes apparently found himself up against it on a number of occasions, with Jack Scarrott recalling that one day at the Abergavenny Races, the troupe found themselves up against stiff competition, with a rough gang having descended on the boxing booths occupying the ground. At least two booths had been in operation, that of John Stokes, and the 'Irishman' old Charlie North. Scarrott by this stage was experienced enough to have been wary of meeting some of the tougher gypsy men, whose own champions were eager to have a go at some of the boxers on the booth. It does some credit to Jack's shrewd knowledge of the crowds now appearing in front of the boxing booth each night to recognise that they were in trouble and of the necessity to reach out and engage some stronger opposition to feature on the booth front for Stokes. Not long after floating the proposition with Stokes, Jack Scarrott found himself tramping ten miles through the night to Talywain, which was the home place of two fearsome brothers, Arthur and William Butcher.

Both men were apparently delighted with the suggestion that they may like to take the place of the booth men, 'as if I had come to invite them to a feast'. Stokes seems to have had a few tricks up his own sleeve, having padded out the booth with a few 'dummies' – show hands with little actual boxing experience, and pitted them against each other merely to 'make a show'. The ruse appears to have worked, with the gypsies descending on the boxing booth even before it had opened, scenting fresh meat. A gypsy named Sam Price was bold enough to step up and challenge Arthur Butcher, and the battle that followed between Butcher and Sam Price was seen to be a grand battle, with the gypsy being knocked over the ropes and through the side of the tent. Sam Price proved to be a tough customer, and was straight back on his feet and climbing back into the ring and willing to fight on. Rapidly learning how to read a fight, Jack Scarrott remembers that while the gypsy was a strong fighter, Arthur Butcher wasn't a man to be underestimated, and by boxing him at distance, proved himself to be the better fighter. A couple of shots to the stomach finished Sam Price off, to the degree that 'he was not properly right until the next day.' It probably comes as no surprise, still having William Butcher as back-up, that Stokes 'didn't have a great lot of trouble' with the spectators afterwards.

Jack Scarrott was learning the ways of a boxing booth from the ground up, not only the day-to-day training and pecking order of the booth boxers themselves, but was also witnessing how well the various boxing booths were being run, and had gained an understanding of what separated the good booth owners from the poor. Along the way it was also getting easier to see which boxers might have the quality to raise themselves over the rest of the herd, and Jack was getting a regular insight into how to separate the true fighting men from the pretenders. In addition, Jack Scarrott was learning the most important lessons for anyone wanting to climb the ladder in the boxing booth trade, how to turn a bad situation to your advantage, and to make a decent house and a good return along the way. He was also learning the value of 'showmanship' although on this front it was doubtful if anyone could compete with the skill and flair of William Samuels of Swansea.

Chapter 13

William Samuels in the Lion's Den

After having landed such a fantastic public relations event as his three round showing with John L. Sullivan at the Philharmonic Hall, William Samuels was busy at work running the Kings Head in Swansea. He would hit upon a novel method of securing his status as the pre-eminent showman and pugilist of South Wales just a few months later. A couple of months before, Bob Wiltshire, who had at one point claimed the lightweight Welsh title, and would later be known more familiarly as the father-in-law of 'Peerless' Jim Driscoll, had achieved a feat of some daring when a travelling menagerie, or animal show, Bostock and Wombwell's, had pitched up at Penarth Road in Cardiff. At the time Bob Wiltshire had become the landlord of a well-known Cardiff hotel and bar, the Blue Bell Inn on St. Mary's Street, Cardiff, and would also later run the Cambrian on the corner of Caroline Street. In response to a bet, Wiltshire had agreed to enter a cage full of lions in the company of the female lion tamer, Madame Salva, though it was widely viewed as a foolhardy act rather than an act of bravery as claimed.

Several thousand people arrived at the appointed time, wondering whether Bob Wiltshire would even put in an appearance as it was widely rumoured that his intention was to pull out and not risk his safety through entering the cage. It had been stated that something in the region of £300 – £400 had been bet on the outcome, and had created a great deal of public interest in whether Wiltshire had the nerve to go through with it. After a brief introduction before the vast crowd, Bob had entered the cage but had wisely elected to stay far back behind the protective form of the lion tamer, and behind a guard he had passed twice before the lions and lionesses that were gathered within. After emerging from the cage, Wiltshire had been loudly cheered as the hero of the hour, and was presented with an ebony walking cane as a memento of the event. It was a good day for Bob Wiltshire, who was cheered a second time after leaving the arena by the large crowds that had gathered outside, who had wondered if the well-known boxer would go through with the stunt at all.

Samuels was not unacquainted with Bostock and Wombwell's animal show, having toured alongside the menagerie with his collection of his bruisers in years past, and knew the manager, Mr. Frank Bostock personally. Having read of the public adulation that had met Bob Wiltshire after having successfully emerged from the show unscathed, Samuels appears to have been inspired into hatching a far more audacious headline grabbing feat.

On hearing that Bostock and Wombwell's menagerie would shortly be visiting the town of Swansea, Samuels hatched upon a plan to prove that he was undoubtedly still punching above the weight of an upstart like Bob Wiltshire, and decided to prove that there was no man in South Wales who would dare stare directly into the face of a danger guaranteed to strike terror into the hearts of lesser men. Samuels would enter the lion's den, with no fear for his own personal safety, and he would do so alone, without the protection of a lion tamer to guard him. He would emerge unharmed, or pay the price and put his fate squarely before the claws of a 'fully grown forest-bred' lion and a dozen lionesses that had previously been noted for their savagery.

This would not be a 'stunt' or a showman's turn, but a life-risking venture guaranteed to show once and for all that Samuels feared no man or beast. Wombwell's menagerie was perhaps one of the biggest draws to be found on any fairground in the United Kingdom. It had grown from a small concern of just a few smaller animals, mostly snakes and non-threatening animals, into a vast and serious money making enterprise. In time it had expanded to include elephants, zebras, hyenas, monkeys, and larger reptiles, as well of course, as Wombwell's famous lions and big cats. There is much evidence that tells of the ferocity of the pack of lions, having caused serious injury to a few members of the public foolish enough to stray too near the bars of their enclosure, with at least one foppish gent having wandered too close for comfort to impress the crowds and fallen fowl of a swiping claw that had brought him into mauling range. Additionally, even the lion's 'tamers' themselves, armed with lashes, had misjudged their wildness on occasion, with one having been reportedly seriously injured by both tooth and claw. At a time when few people had seen the large and often fierce animals of the new world, a menagerie of note was a spectacle that everybody flocked to see, whether rich or poor, and Wombwell's was a sell-out show virtually everywhere it went.

The event was a guaranteed earner for the circus, and although there is no account as to whether Samuels received a share of the profits, it certainly made for good publicity in the town of Swansea. William Samuels was deemed to have 'given tangible proof of his pluck and daring' on various occasions, but he had never attempted 'a feat surrounded by so many dangers' as the one that he would now face. The inside and outside of the tent was ringed with Samuels' fellow townsfolk and admirers, eager to see the grand showman risk his all to prove his bravery even in the face of certain death. For some time prior to the event Samuels prowled the long length of the platform erected in front of the menagerie. He had lost none of his flair for showmanship, having pulled on his showman's boots for the event, and reportedly appeared in the same sash and outfit that he had worn when he had sparred with John L. Sullivan at Cardiff and had a blue rosette affixed to his breast. Few people other than the lion tamers themselves ever entered the lion's cage itself, and they were well paid for the dangers of their job. Many of the local townsfolk believed that on this occasion Billy had probably bitten off more than he could chew, and approached the pugilist to shake him by the hand, believing it to be the last time that they might see him, and said their "goodbyes". Samuels appears to have enjoyed the sense of occasion and 'invariably returned an encouraging and characteristic reply' in turn.

Despite the old warrior's confidence that he would emerge from the cage unscathed, large odds were being offered up to five minutes before entering the cage that William Samuels would fail to make good on his promise, and there were a few takers convinced that Samuels' nerve would finally fail him. At the time announced for Samuels to come into the tent and walk into the cage unaccompanied by the lion tamer, Madame Salva, there was no sign of Billy to be seen. Shortly after 9 pm one of the lion tamer's assistants fixed a lamp to the caravan which contained seven large lions. Finally, at five minutes past the allotted time, Mr. Frank Bostock made an appearance, accompanied by William Samuels, and both were given a warm reception. Mr. Bostock then announced that Samuels was to perform a feat of daring only once before attempted in the history of the menagerie dating back to 1805. Samuels had been urged to enter the cage of the lions with the lion tamer to protect him, but had refused to enter the cage at all, unless he was allowed to do so alone. Bostock then stated that Samuels '…was a Welshman, and a well-known Welshman to boot, and he trusted that the audience would recognise his truly British pluck by a large measure of applause'.

The announcement was met with loud cheering, and it was evident that there was 'a feeling of considerable anxiety and alarm' on the part of the crowd, many of whom feared that they would soon see the last of the proud champion of Wales. Samuels, however, seemed to show no feelings of uneasiness, and grasping only a trusty stout cudgel in his hand, boldly entered the cage. The lions appeared uneasy by the intrusion of the pugilist, and it appeared as though Samuels would receive a far warmer reception than he had initially bargained for. It was then that Samuels, 'possessed apparently with nerves of steel', and showing 'marvellous coolness' walked undaunted to the far end of the cage where the lions were 'awaiting only the slightest encouragement to spring on the intruder, and held his cudgel threateningly before the nose of the fiercest. Growls of rage greeted this act; but Samuels, in no way discomposed, walked among the animals, and made them fly right and left before him. This he did several times, and on one occasion acted so rashly that grave fears were entertained for his safety by those in charge of the exhibition.'

Samuels was seen to 'walk round the cage three times, and no mishap happened until the animals passed him for the third time, when by some means or other Samuels' left arm got slightly grazed by the claws or teeth of the animals.' Despite the threat to his continued safety, Samuels remained undaunted by the injury and kept the animals at bay the whole of the time he remained in the cage, and refused to let the animals make the slightest movement towards him, 'only when occasion really demanded it'.

While William Samuels walked around the cage at his leisure, a red light remained burning, and several of the menagerie men waited outside the cage armed with red hot irons waiting to spring to Samuels' defence in the event the lions sought to injure the intruder walking unaccompanied within their domain. It was then that

'Samuels again obtained the mastery over his savage companions, and showed his fearlessness of them by firing a loaded (*blank firing*) pistol at their faces.'

William Samuels maintained his courage to the last, and then went to the gate of the den and remained in a dangerous position while Mr. Bostock congratulated him on his display of daring, and was presented with a 'unique' and 'massive' chain made of spade and crown motif, and an illuminated certificate as mementoes of the event. After Samuels finally left the cage, the band struck up a rousing rendition of "See the Conquering Hero Comes". Once the cheering had subsided Samuels made light of his act, showing his usual flair for the occasion, stating;

"It was suggested by Mr. Frank Bostock that I should go into the cage unaccompanied, but I told him I would go into it alone or not at all. I was not in the least frightened. I am going into the cage again just now; I shall never be killed. I was never afraid of anything in my life, besides, you can only die once."

Samuels was afterwards 'borne in triumph out of the menagerie and through the streets' and was 'followed by a large crowd who cheered him vociferously' on his way to his home, to the Kings Arms in the High Street. No doubt many of the throng which surrounded Samuels had also learned that the same lions had attacked the experienced lion tamer, Madame Salva, at St. Clears a few weeks previously. Samuels had secured his status as not only the foremost man of the knuckles of his generation in Wales, but as a man who knew no fear. It was thought that;

'Mr Samuels has accomplished a feat which but few would care to attempt, and has succeeded in entering a den of wild and strange animals without material injury. He is now looked upon as a hero. If the lions had mauled and mangled him the public would have regarded his action as a piece of foolhardiness.'

The bold nature of Samuels' risky act would long after seal his reputation as someone of bottomless courage. The story would catch the eye of newspaper editors across the Atlantic, with the news of the feat having been reprinted in the New York Times amongst other newspapers. The story was also covered in the periodical *Frank Leslie's Popular Monthly* in a piece entitled 'Animals and Their Trainers' , with it being noted that it was probably a 'foolhardy feat' but also '…one which shows how essential are mere coolness and nerve when dealing with these beasts.'

Whether foolhardy or daring, Samuels seems content to have let the newspapers decide, he had proved his mettle, and more importantly had once more outstripped yet another pugilist who had dared to step on Samuels' home turf and had forgotten there was only one Heavyweight crown, with Billy Samuels having been determined to let no-one forget who was wearing it. He was wearing a commemorative chain to prove as much, and was cooling his heels in the back parlour of the Kings Head in Swansea, and probably enjoying a well-earned cigar.

Chapter 14

Shoni Engineer vs. William Samuels

Jack Scarrott was still plying his trade as a booth boxer in 1890 when he was twenty years old, and had joined the booth of Jimmy Day of Portsmouth, who was himself a good boxer. Jimmy Day would seem to have had a chequered career as a booth proprietor, having also served time as a small scale menagerie owner, and would seem to have started out with the usual coconut shies and cheaply built and maintained fairground entertainments. By the time Jack Scarrott was working on Jimmy Day's booth, he would have had a fairly solid team of boxers around him, consisting of Sam 'Butcher' (Thomas) of Ynyshir, Bill Lane of Cwmavon, and Shoni Engineer, and so Jimmy Day elected to take his booth on the road to Neath Fair, which had featured as a highlight in the Welsh fairground circuit since before living memory. By 1890, Neath fair was one of the grandest affairs imaginable. It still maintained a picturesque aspect in the days before the rise of the great thump of the steam engines, which were later used to power the grander rides, and brought all and sundry from far and wide.

Many of the men had made an especial effort, having faked a minor injury, or perhaps overstated the severity of another to enable them to avoid the walk to the pits at the call of the steam whistle to go to work. Those that downed tools quickly made their way by whatever means necessary towards the diversions and distractions afforded by the great fair. Some made a particular effort to scrub themselves up, donning new overcoats from the local clothing club, or wearing their best Sunday suits, and calling into the local pubs for a few straighteners before joining the excited crowds already gathering on the Corporation field. There were opportunities for the women to return home with a few luxuries to brighten up their homes, a new shawl perhaps, or a good pair of brass candlesticks for the mantle, or maybe a set of handkerchiefs made out of the finest Irish linen. The younger generation milled round the coconut shies, hoping for a few coconuts of milk to guzzle after the return home.

With the darkness of the pit forgotten for a time, the noise of the pick and shovel was replaced with the sounds of carefree laughter, and accompanied by the dreadful sounds of one organ playing louder over the sounds of its many neighbours. A man could pick up a few song sheets for a few pennies to learn one of the new popular tunes being sung to enable him to impress his friends in the singing parlours of his local pub on his return home, or demonstrate the strength of an arm grown strong through hard daily use in the pit or foundry by dropping a hammer on a 'try your strength' machine. Then there was always the overspill, the card-men, long practised and able to quickly part a man from his money in games of chance and sleight of hand. If a man still had money in his pocket, he invariably kept his hands firmly in his pockets. If his arms swung free, you could be fairly certain that he had already spent his money, or, more likely, that the slender fingers of a pocket-dipper had helped himself to the lot. For the local fighter there was also the opportunity to take on a 'professional', a booth boxer, taking his place amongst the rest of the troupe, arms folded, with thumbs pushing out his biceps, casting his practised eye over the crowd, staring some down, and keeping a close watch on those that dared to return his steely gaze.

At the fair of 1890, the local hard men were spoilt for choice. There was at least two booths in attendance, that of Jimmy Day, and the one belonging to crowd favourite, Billy Samuels. True to form, Billy was decidedly unimpressed by the boxers on display on Jimmy Day's booth. Before long, despite being allegedly about fifty years old by this stage, Billy delighted himself by repeatedly insulting Day's men, and with the fair going on for the best part of a week, Day's troupe soon tired of his verbal abuse. It was Jack Scarrott that hit upon the idea of getting fellow boxing booth troupe member Shoni Engineer to accept Samuels' continual challenges, as Shoni had for a time served as one of Billy Samuels' willing pupils and knew his style.

With two such well-known fighters on the bill, there were droves of people eager to see the outcome of a glove contest between the two men and it was deemed necessary for the fight to come off in John Scott's Circus.

As the match had reportedly been made for £50, and the victor was also going to carry off the ticket receipts for the night, a fairly considerable amount of money lay on the outcome, and appears to have persuaded Samuels to come out of retirement once more.

The previous year, despite now being firmly entrenched at the King's Head, Billy had been tempted out of retirement to meet a youthful challenger at Barnstaple Fair in Devon, one Tom Vincent of Plymouth, who was reportedly about twenty five years old at the time of the encounter, and is remembered by Jack Scarrott as having been the West of England champion. The match came off in Hurford's Pavilion, with a half crown being charged for attendance, as interest in the match ran high. At the time William Samuels was said to be fifty one years old, and had fellow boxing booth owners William Tolley and Frank Gess in his corner. Despite having been the shorter and older man, it was Samuels that hurtled into battle, although on this occasion, Samuels found that youth would eventually be served;

'Samuels had the best of the encounter for the first four rounds; after the ninth round the severe body blows of the younger man began to tell upon Samuels, who was, however, showing most science. Cries were raised in favour of a draw, but Samuels desired to continue the match. In the fourteenth round the Welsh champion failed to come up to time and he gave out. Samuels, who had never been beaten before, laboured under the disadvantage of having a slightly sprained hand. The contest lasted over an hour.'

It seems it was after this defeat, in which Samuels, despite his advanced years made an exceptional showing against a far younger opponent, finally decided to retire once and for all. It was keeping with his bottomless pride that he still continued to offer far younger opponents a match with the gloves for many years afterwards. He definitely appears to have had no fear of meeting Shoni Engineer in a glove match. Once more, the showman's vote appears to have been firmly behind Samuels, with Jack Gage, a Pontypool showman and Lloyd Roberts appearing in Samuels' corner as well as a Liverpool fighter by the name of Fitzpatrick, presumably one of Samuels' booth boxers. The match was confined to three rounds and was held under Marquis of Queensbury rules.

Although remembered a 'wonderful fight which ended in a draw' by Jack Scarrott, this does not appear to have been the case. As Shoni was a fellow booth boxer on Jimmy Day's booth, Jack was perhaps reticent to speak ill of someone that he was obviously quite fond of, additionally, as the fight had happened forty six years previously, Scarrott probably correctly guessed that the decision had been more or less forgotten. It must be said that there appears to have been some reluctance on Shoni's part to meet the old fighter, having apparently only wanted to meet Samuels in a contest consisting of two minute rounds. The fight proved to be more than Shoni bargained for, with Samuels putting on a show stopping performance and decisively beating Shoni Engineer;

FIRST ROUND

'The first round was started very quietly, but after a little sparring Samuel landed his opponent a supriser. Recovering, Shoni was knocked down, and then for a few seconds, both men sparred for wind. Again, however, Shoni was bowled over, and when on one knee Samuel sent him over once more. This last blow the "Engineer's" friends claimed as a foul, but the umpires were against them.'

SECOND ROUND

'In the second round the old champion had matters pretty much his own way, "Shoni's" attempts to get at him being very feeble. After being felled twice, the younger man showed signals of distress, but pluckily faced his opponent again, only however to be knocked clean over the ropes. Pulling himself together, Shoni Engineer resumed his place in the centre of the ring, but, missing an opening, Samuel for the second time hit him over the ropes, thus terminating the round.'

THIRD ROUND

'Shoni Engineer had little wind left in him when he faced the Swanseaite in the last round, but he was not yet beaten, and hit out manfully, though rather ineffectively. He was again knocked down twice in succession in this round, and then the men came to close quarters, and there was a lot of hugging. When they had broken away, Samuel hit his opponent where and when he liked, so that the umpires at the conclusion of the round had no trouble in deciding the match. The victory was popular with the spectators, who heartily cheered Samuel as he retired from the ring.'

His defeat at the hands of William Samuels did not go down well with Shoni Engineer, who immediatcly stated to the local newspaper reporters that he was unconvinced by his beating at Samuels hand that he was not the better man at 'sparring' and afterwards challenged Samuels to enter the ring again in a contest for a further £25. Possibly Shoni's people believed that it would be a case of throwing good money after bad, as there was little support for the re-match. When word of the challenge met Billy Samuels's ears, Samuels was reported as having stated that he was more than willing to meet Shoni for the appointed sum, asking only for the *Sporting Life* to be made the stakeholder and referee, but nothing appears to have come of the challenge. William Samuels made his way back to the King's Head on Swansea High Street in semi-retirement, and Shoni Engineer returned to Treorchy, having been well schooled by the old booth proprietor.

Chapter 15

Scarrott's Boxing Booth

1890 was a big year in Jack Scarrott's life, for one thing, he had met a girl by the name of Priscilla Loveridge from Cardiff, who evidently saw some promise in the twenty year old booth boxer, and they decided to get married. Jack Scarrott unsurprisingly chose his new adopted town of Pontypridd as the place to get hitched, and Jack and Priscilla tied the knot on December 15th, 1890 at St. Catherine's Church.

By this stage Jack was apparently already considering how he might make a living after having decided to make the leap into marital life. With Jack's knowledge of fighters and of life on a boxing booth, it probably seemed a natural step to take the time worn route from boxing on the booth to running a booth of his own. The decision to do so might well have been inspired by one's of Jack's experiences of having mixed in with some very well-known names, at a benefit appearance held at the Westgate Street circus for the Newport fighter, Morgan

Crowther, who had lost a hard 20 round battle to Londoner, Bill Baxter at the National Sporting Club in London. Much liked by the local fight crowd, they turned up in droves at the Westgate Street circus in Cardiff to try and raise funds for Crowther, who had been escaping from the clutches of the police for years as a young bare knuckle prize-fighter before going on to earn a solid reputation as a glove fighter. Well known mountain fighter, Archie Cook, as well as Illtyd Evans of Pontypridd and Sam Butcher of Ynyshir all turned out for the event, as well as the 'Collins' brothers, with a few prominent names from across the border, notably Ben Jordan and Dick Burge, the one-time lightweight champion of England, who later went on to make his mark as a promoter while running 'The Ring' in Blackfriars in London also having made an appearance.

Jack appears to have had a great time of it, and it might be imagined that he made up his mind to run his own booth shortly after this event. In any case, it was around this period that Jack took delivery of some timber and canvas of his own, and rolled up his sleeves, building his first booth at the Mill Field in Pontypridd. On balance it was probably a fairly humble affair, with Jack recounting that the first time that he opened his booth was at nearby Robertstown in Ynysybwl. Jack doesn't appear to have had the money to engage the local 'champion' fighters, Ianto Cwmavon and Twm Parry, and instead took on a couple of young gypsy fighters from a nearby gypsy encampment. They were completely unprepared for the challenges from the mountain fighters who were eager to strip another booth boxer of their pride, and received a fairly sound beating inside the booth tent for the princely sum of just eighteen pence each. Jack Scarrott very nearly had his own ears boxed as a result by an old gypsy lady when walking back from Ynysybwl on Sunday morning, so annoyed was the old woman by the punishment that had been handed out to some of her 'boys'.

With the founding of the Queensbury rules, many bareknuckle prize-ring men found that there was a route forwards through glove-fighting that was previously completely closed to them as a legitimate (albeit grey) means of making a living. Provided that the contests were of restricted length, and conducted using sufficiently large gloves to allay any fears that what was being witnessed was actually a thinly disguised prize fight in 'skin' gloves, they were largely allowed to continue in business unmolested.

There are few remaining indications of exactly where the booth was pitched in these years, although the census of 1901 reveals that Jack was most likely travelling the Welsh fair 'circuit' and in-between, pitching up on the outskirts of towns in fields or on rough patches of land whenever available. In 1901, when Jack Scarrott was listed as an 'amusement caterer', the family were living in a caravan in the Pontypridd district, with one of their neighbours (also in a 'living' van) being Jacob Studt of bioscope fame. By this time the marriage had produced four children, Hannah Marie, aged 8 (probably named after Jack's unfortunate sister Anna Marie, who had died in his youth) was born in Pontypridd, Priscilla, aged 7 was also born in Pontypridd, Phoebe (8) was born in Aberavon, and finally, John Jnr. was born in Llanelly (Llanelli) aged just one year old.

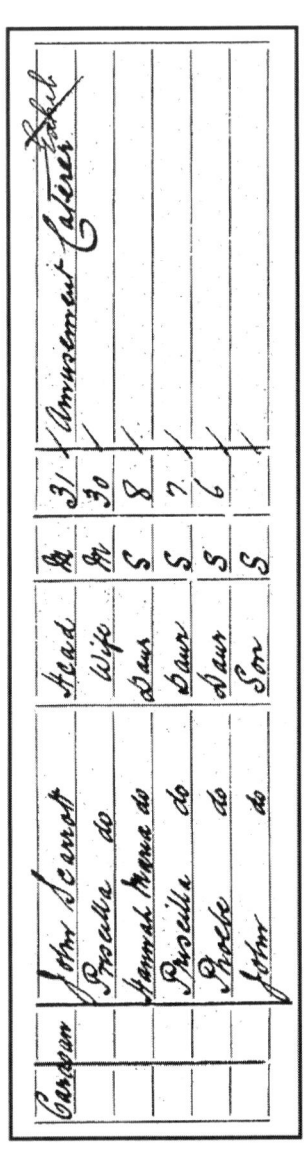

1901 Census showing the 'Scarratt' family

Intriguingly, in the early years of the booth, Jack was already taking his booth from Pontypridd to as far afield as Neath, having definitely set up his booth at Neath fair prior to 1894. This fact is borne out by the recollections of Wil John Edwards of Aberdare, in his book 'From the Valley I Came'. Edwards would recall that his brother, 'Twm' (Thomas) Edwards, himself a well-known knuckle fighter and frequenter of boxing booths had beaten one of 'Scarrett's' booth boxers on one of its visits to the famous fair, and had afterwards fallen foul of one of the many pickpockets who targeted the visitors. It would appear that Jack still had some lessons to learn as a booth proprietor;

'Twm won two sovereigns for standing up for two rounds against a professional boxer in a boxing booth and offered two more rounds at the same price, but Scarrett, the booth owner refused. Twm put the sovereigns in his trousers pocket and regaled himself for a little while at the coconut-shy, only to find that the sovereigns had gone when he had finished with the coconuts.'

Twm was greatly annoyed by the theft, remarking "You can't blow your bloody nose at that fair without losing your money." This event would have to have occurred prior to 1894, as on May 17th 1894, Twm was involved with a tragedy that would long haunt the developing sport of boxing in South Wales after he unwittingly killed his opponent David Rees in a boxing contest in a booth run by future lightweight champion, Patsy Perkins, which was surreptitiously located in a converted slaughterhouse in Aberdare. The death of the unfortunate man was deemed to be not entirely Twm's fault, as the fatal blow was struck when the man was knocked from the ring onto the unpadded stone floor and he lost his life through heavy contact with the flagstones. Everybody involved was put on trial including Perkins and corner man Dai St John, but it was Twm Edwards that ended up serving a short term in prison for manslaughter while the trial was ongoing. His brother, Wil, took a hot dinner to the police station every day for a week, but Wil's opinion of his elder brother sunk to a 'low ebb' when Twm said that he had got used to prison fare and, '…safe home again and free from the law, he spoke critically of those lovely hot dinners in grumbling tones, and expressed a preference for bread and cheese and pickles'. Shaken by the event, it drew a close to Twm Edward's boxing activities outside his employment at the local coal pit and he did not enter a ring, whether on the mountainside or in a boxing booth again.

Jack Scarrott, was learning the trade taking the money on the door himself for the first time, and naturally appears to have made more than a few mistakes along the way. One mistakes appears to have been to allow the rougher element access to the booth. On one occasion when Jack had set up his boxing booth at Ferndale, a free-for-all fight nearly finished off the booth once and for all. Having sent a cap around for a collection on behalf of an old mountain fighter, someone saw an opportunity and 'liberated' a shilling out of the cap. In the blink of an eye, men were striking out left and right, and apparently not knowing who they were hitting or why.

A mountain fighter named Dai 'Brawd' had been the first to step up, ham-fisted and ready to go, after hitting one of the booth employees. He had then stupidly threatened to do the same to Shoni Engineer when the

Treorchy man had dared ask what Brawd thought he was doing, and a mass fight had broken out, which levelled the booth and left the men inside fighting in the dark under the deflated canvas. The chaotic event recounted by Jack must have happened prior to 1894, as Shoni Engineer died in January of that year.

It seems plausible that Jack Scarrott had few, if any regular fighters at this time, with the vast majority having merely been taken on as prospective future champions of the booth in its movements from town to town.

While the fighters featuring on Jack's booth were probably ones of fairly humble origins, drawn from the rank and file fighting men of whatever district he was visiting, Jack Scarrott was learning the ins and outs of the trade. No doubt he was losing a little money at one fair, but gaining a decent return on a better contest in another town further down the way. More importantly he was working the door of his own booth. As events would show, Jack certainly had the most important set of ingredients for any boxing booth proprietor covered, the eye for a potential fighting man that could put on a show worth seeing, and the ability to 'put one over' on the paying public.

Chapter 16

Doctor William Price

On January 23rd 1893, the well-known Doctor and 'Druid', Dr William Price died at the advanced age of 92. His final act was to take a sip of champagne before quietly passing away at his home in Llantrisant. Doctor Price had already prepared for his subsequent cremation, having ordered a 61 foot tall white pole topped with a crescent moon attached to the top to mark the spot where he wished for the ceremony to take place on the nearby hills. If the details of his cremation seem unusual, they would no doubt have appeared quite normal within the context of Dr. Price's rather remarkable life.

Price had become apprenticed to a physician at Caerphilly before having travelled to London to study at the Royal College of Surgeons before returning to Wales to practise medicine. Dr. Price would find that his skills as a doctor and his reputation as a healer meant that he was greatly in demand on his return, even if his beliefs were thought to be rather unorthodox by the standards of the time. Price believed in vegetarianism, the importance of fresh air and exercise, and believed that smoking was unhealthy and dangerous. He also shocked his contemporaries with his radical views on nudity and free love. More than anything, what made Dr. Price stand out as a true eccentric for the townspeople of his hometown of Llantrisant was his adoption of the beliefs of the Neo-Druidic movement, a modern re-interpretation of the beliefs of the ancient Druids of Wales, eventually crowning himself 'Arch-druid' or leader of the Druidic movement in Wales.

He afterwards adopted the most peculiar dress, having numerous outfits made for him that would make him a familiar and unforgettable sight on his frequent wanders round the local area. Dr. Price wore a startling choice of clothing, consisting of a green coat matched with a red tartan shawl, with buttons specially minted featuring images of goats, which it appears was the physical form that Price believed he had occupied in a previous life. On his head he wore a fox skin with the brush stitched to the upper part of the pelt with the tail and legs draped over his shoulders. His hair grew over his shoulders, which he would often plait, and he let his long black beard grow down to his waist. In later years his hair and his beard would turn a snowy white, giving the doctor a most dignified, if unusual appearance. At his waist hung a sword, which he supposedly used in the course of his druidic ceremonies, many of which were undertaken around the Rocking stone near Pontypridd, which he deemed to be of particular Druidic significance.

It was here that Dr. William Price would marry his twenty two year old housekeeper, Gwenllian Llewelyn,

Doctor William Price of Llantrisant

on his eighty-first birthday in a druidic marital rite. Despite his advanced years, Dr. Price was seen to be as full of vitality as ever, and their union would produce a son on 8th August 1883, who Price believed would be instrumental in resurrecting the lost secrets of the Druids. Due to the importance of the child in bringing about an ancient prophecy, William Price named him 'Iesu Grist' or 'Jesus Christ' in Welsh, although it seems plausible that Price decided to do so as an act of mockery towards the chapel folk who had looked upon his adoption of Druidic beliefs with such derision. Sadly the baby was not destined to live for long, and on the 10th January 1884, Iesu Grist Price died in his cradle at Llantrisant. It was William Price's decision to personally cremate the remains of his baby that would lead to one of the greatest scandals that the town of Llantrisant had ever seen.

On the 14th January 1884, two colliers were walking home from church one evening and saw smoke rising from a field, and climbed a hill to witness Dr. William Price engaged in a ritual of his own composition. He was clad in a white robe with his hair and beard streaming behind him, and chanted a lament in Welsh for the death of his child. Soon the colliers were joined by crowds of several hundred chapel people who had left church only to be met by a sight that many deemed blasphemous, with Dr. Price having set light to the body of his dead child with a cask of paraffin oil, while chanting in Welsh with his arms outstretched and face looking up at the heavens.

Police Sergeant William Hoyle and Police Constable Phillip Francis were the first on the scene. Hoyle took command, kicking the barrel of paraffin hard enough to turn it over and for the burning corpse to roll out. Had the police not been there, it seemed likely that Dr. Price himself would have been burned by the mob, intent on punishing the Doctor for his foul deed. Phillip Francis was quick to pull his truncheon and threatened to strike any man that dared touch Price, and it was only through his quick reactions that Price was able to be taken to Llantrisant police station and then on to Pontypridd the following day.

Events would take a more violent turn on Doctor Price's release on bail, with Price having been pelted with stones upon his return to Llantrisant, forcing him to seek sanctuary from a gathering mob at the Bear Inn. On the same night, the infuriated townspeople had laid siege to his house while his wife Gwenllian was inside, hurling stones and smashing a window in their eagerness to gain entry. While in mortal danger from the anger of the mob, Gwenllian locked the doors and took up position behind the front door with two loaded pistols, and threatened to shoot the first person who forced entry while the townspeople hammered on the door. It was only by this means that she managed to keep the anger of the mob at bay until the police arrived.

It was afterwards felt that the decision to cremate the body in such a public setting and in such a dramatic manner at a time when the local church going public would be leaving their places of worship pointed towards Price's personal desire for fame and notoriety. It seems likely that a desire to upset those who had held his curious appearance and beliefs up for ridicule might well have influenced the Doctor. At the subsequent trial hearing, it was established that the act of cremation itself was not illegal, although the manner in which any cremation was undertaken in future should be done in such a way as not to cause offence to others, and Price was subsequently discharged. The case would lead to Price becoming something of a national celebrity, with the Doctor having afterwards fully embraced the cause of cremation, and would often use the hillside to cremate the corpses of his dead cattle.

Jack Scarrott would incorrectly remember that Price had actually cremated a 'little boy', but in fact the boy that he would remember following William Price around Pontypridd dressed up in the same curious fox-skin headdress and matching outfit was actually Dr. Price's second son, who he would name Iesu Grist II. Price was reportedly delighted at the birth of the child, who he believed would follow the same path that he had hoped would be taken by his cremated child and play a central role in restoring the glories of the Druidic order. Remarkably, by the time Iesu Grist II came into being, Dr Price had passed the grand age of eighty four.

Price would live on to the ripe old age of ninety-two, with the cause of his death being recorded as 'senile decay' and he remained a striking looking man to his last;

'Down to the time of his death his features retained striking characteristics, and old age had invested them with much dignity. His two eyes resembled those of a hawk, his nose was slightly aquiline in shape and his forehead was broad and lofty. He kept all his beard and it grew in shape something similar to a goatee and reaching down to his breast. It was striking and perfectly white. His hair, also white as snow was likewise allowed to grow

The family of Doctor William Price

long, and it was plaited in long strands, and looped up about the lower part of his head.'

Thousands of tickets were printed for the cremation of Doctor Price, which was to be held at Llantrisant in the same location in which he had cremated his son, Iesu Grist, with requests coming in from far and wide for tickets to attend the event days before the cremation was due to occur. Arrangements had to be made to try and keep the non-ticket holding masses that descended on the town away from the ceremony, with a guard having been put on the coal that was delivered in order to burn the corpse to stop people from claiming pieces of it as souvenirs. On the day of the funeral procession, an estimated 20,000 people made their way to the town by every means possible. The corpse of William Price had been prepared at his home at Llantrisant prior to having been laid to rest in a specially made iron casket with holes in the side to allow the flames to enter and reduce his body to ashes. The mother of Price's children, Gwenllian was dressed in traditional Welsh costume, as was his daughter, Penelopen, while Iesu Grist II was dressed in his foxskin hat and the outfit that had become so familiar to those that had seen the Doctor over the course of his long life.

The cremation created something of a celebratory atmosphere in the town, with the pubs having run out of ale, and commemorative items produced to mark the event were sold in great numbers. The iron coffin was then placed in a specially made furnace, and paraffin was poured on the coffin to get the fire started. Local police Superintendent Evan Jones was tasked with keeping the crowd peaceful throughout the ceremony, along with 35 police officers, and managed to ensure that the gathering remained respectful for the duration of the ceremony. Even with the ceremony over, and the casket having been shattered by the heat, the people kept coming. Many of those who had been unable to secure a ticket for the event had turned up afterwards, including a twenty two year old Jack Scarrott, eager to secure a souvenir or keepsake of the Doctor. Up to six thousand people remained by the funeral fire, eagerly picking up cinders to serve as 'relics of the extraordinary ceremony'.

A ton of coal had been left unused in the course of the cremation and was afterwards carried off by the residents of the town, either as souvenirs or to keep their own fireplaces stocked. For years afterwards people combed the field to find pieces of the remains of Dr. Price. One member of Pontypridd Council would relate that he had done a roaring trade in selling sheep teeth for half a crown each by pretending that they had been the teeth of the deceased Doctor in the years that followed. Dr. Price would remain the town's most famous occupant, long after the curious events of his long and strange life had passed from memory and into local legend. Today a statue of Dr. William Price can be seen in the centre of the town, wearing the curious outfit that had once served him so well in terrifying a young Jack Scarrott and the other children of Llantrisant and Pontypridd.

Chapter 17

Dangerous Jack and the Japanese Strangler

If there was an 'art' to being a boxing booth owner, it was making sure that you put on a good show, or put on the best show you could with the talent available to you. In the days before boxing regulations and boards of control, anyone could try and run a boxing booth, and as long as you had a tent and a board to advertise your show, you were in business. By the 1890's every sizable fair had a boxing booth, there was Patsy Perkins, Bob Dunbar's, Bill Moore, Taylor's, Lloyd Roberts, Jimmy Day, Felix Scott, Hughes, Tolley's, Sullivan's, Jack Gage and Frank Gess' boxing booth, and a great deal of others. William Samuels was also busy at work, duelling with his ex-booth boxer, 'Professor' Patsy Perkins for control of the lucrative Swansea fight scene, and also still running a permanent boxing booth in the heart of the city in the area of the Strand, a situation remembered by one of his youthful patrons, the journalist and boxing writer, Trevor C. Wignall;

'In my town there was a region known as the Strand, a poor and noisome district that was carefully avoided even by the social workers when they set out to do some slumming. It was there, two or three times a year that the showman we knew as Billy Sam erected his marquee. I was one of his regular customers, when I could find the fee for admission, and could dodge my father sufficiently to be certain that I would not be found if he wandered abroad is search of his erring son.'

Every booth tried a different means of pulling in the crowds. Some, like Harry Hughes, back in the early days, were fond of blowing on a trumpet, or performing various apple/potato slicing tricks to pull in the punters, others ran side businesses to pull the crowds around their shows. A loud costume topped off with an oversize top hat usually completed the usual outfit. Even into the 1890's old Billy Samuels could still be seen puffing on one of his cigars outside his fairground boxing show, pulling in the punters from his own swing boats and cocoa nut stalls set up alongside. Unlike "Billy Sam's" the vast majority employed a rolling stock of booth boxers, taken from whatever local talent was available, or men that could be picked up on the road. This troupe could comprise any number of up and coming accomplished local scrappers, taking the platform for the first time, in between local 'hardmen' well known for their battles on the mountainside, or at the pit-head or dock-side, and old timers, perhaps with enough knowledge to take on the raw novice, or veterans, men of the 'Tug Wilson school of hard knocks', with enough skill to ride out a short contest or exhibition. Haunting the local boxing booths with frequency, Fleet Street journalist Trevor C. Wignall saw more than a few of them round his hometown of Swansea in the 1890's and would recall that these early booth boxers;

"...fought for coppers or shillings. They battled with an energy and a please-the-customer zeal that some their better known successors of my observance would have done better to emulate. Not many of the booths of my tender years carried staff of boxers. One or two youths or veterans who could be relied on to dampen the ardour of sailors on leave or the local plug-ugly was the usual procedure, for it was understood that wherever the tent was pitched there would be lads who would give up anything and everything for the privilege of being engaged for a short season. Practically all the old-time champions were the graduates of smelly booths. It was under the naphtha gleams that I first saw Jimmy Wilde, the human match-stick and Jim Driscoll, the finest exponent of scientific boxing...The employment, or apprenticeship, was not the kind to recommend to the aesthete of the nineties, and there was no money in it, but I never met a booth-owner who complained of a shortage of applicants. The routine was largely what it still is, and what it was when it was first introduced.

On a platform that was part of the tent would stand a fleshy, heavily moustached individual, with rings on his fingers, a watch chain like a cable across his expansive middle, and perhaps tiny gleaming circles of gold in his ears. His duty was to catch the attention of the wandering crowds, which he invariably did by splitting the air with his bellows. His right hand was reserved for gesturing, and in his left he carried a well-worn and rather gruesome pair of large boxing gloves.

Once he had stopped the traffic he would go into a short lecture on the glories of the game, which usually brought in the revered names of Jem Mace or even Tom Sayers. Then he would wave the right hand, and in response the troupe would materialise, all clad in trunks and singlets, and respectable enough in appearance to engage in a display in an academy for the daughters of aristocrats. (It was much later that the booth-pug displayed his manly form by omitting the thin, armless shirt). Finally the man with the moustache would invite the gapers to step up and have a do, nominating as he did the featherweights and heavy-weights they would have to meet. There were financial rewards, of course, and these were generally up in the higher brackets of golden sovereigns-the only notes any of us ever heard about, and "heard" is the operative word, were fivers-but it is perhaps superfluous to remark that the "quids" were very infrequently clutched."

Beyond the usual offerings on the booth, even before the boxing boom that had brought such exotic pugilistic visitors to Britain as Frank Craig, the 'Harlem Coffee Cooler', and such notables as Bobby Dobbs and Peter Jackson, the best bet in increasing interest often lay in having a black pugilist turn out on the booth apron amongst the other more familiar home-grown boxers. Jack Scarrott would appear to have been one of the first to be able to see the financial value in a having a black 'champion' feature amongst the regular boxers to be found on his booth, even if in the first instance the fighter concerned might have been a fake who would not actually 'know a boxing glove from a turnip'.

Having come across a powerfully built black stranger on the road from Tonyrefail to Gilfach Goch, Jack engaged the powerful stranger to help his horses, who were struggling to make headway while pulling his caravan. Not speaking a word of English, Scarrott wondered whether he might have found his way on a

Trevor C. Wignall, the famous Swansea boxing writer

boat to the seaport of Cardiff and either got lost, or had decided to jump ship. At Gilfach Goch, Jack soon found a job that the stranger could handle, and a vital consideration for any booth man. He gave the stranger the job of guarding the back of the booth, to stop curious boys from sneaking in under the canvas. Jack himself had sneakily entered the booth of William Samuels many years before as a young boy to witness the bout between Dai Magee and Samuels. Finding that the 'tremendously strong' nameless black man was taking a great deal of interest in the fighting that was going on in the booth, Jack decided it was worth trying him out with a pair of boxing gloves. He chose to ignore the concerns of his wife, Priscilla, telling her, "Woman, there's a fortune in him."

It was at Pontycymmer that Jack first had him appear on the booth, and the manner in which he did so strongly suggests the simple minded ignorance the bulk of the public had with regard to anyone that had travelled from the new world, whether dressed as a man or some variety of beast. Any new spectacle with a colourful back story could easily 'pull the wool' over the eyes of the average man, having limited knowledge of matters beyond their own geographically limited constraints. Hitting upon the notion of 'Dangerous Jack' being as savage and wild as any of the lions to be found in Wombwell's menagerie, Jack hung up an old bone taken from a horse carcass and hung it on the booth front, his showman's patter undoubtedly causing something of a stir;

"Like a lion or a tiger, he won't eat civilised food. It's no good offering him tea and buns. Raw meat is the only food he'll eat,

and he prefers horseflesh. You see that bone? He's just gnawed eight or ten pounds of raw horseflesh off that for his dinner. We'll do our best to see fairplay, but I warn you that as soon as you put 'em up in front of him he'll be for you like a mad bull, and he knows no rules or regulations."

Although 'Dangerous Jack' was 'hitting and slashing away' in a style all of his own, he was remarkably successful, having 'put six so-called champions out in one week.' One miner by the name of Dai 'Rush' from Caerau Colliery looked like he might be able to cause Jack problems, but Jack's great strength came into play and assisted him in finishing Dai Rush off. Jack also recalls that 'Dangerous Jack' beat a boxer from Porth called Tom Scadan who was reputed to be a good boxer. It seems curious that as Jack Scarrott relates that he didn't know where his black champion had been brought from, he states quite conclusively that after a year, "Dangerous Jack" found a ship and went back to 'where he came from'.

One event that would suggest that Scarrott may have 'discovered' Dangerous Jack roughly around the mid to late 1890's is a report of a Mabon's Day fight that was scheduled to come off at the Drill Hall in Pentre in 1897 between David James ('Dai Rush') and Benjamin Lloyd ('Soulless' Ben) for £25 a-side under Marquis of Queensbury rules. It seems that the fight had strayed into the 'grey area' which suggested that a prize-fight was taking place and not a friendly glove contest, although the reasons why are not entirely clear. In some instances where police were unsure of the rules of boxing, the combatants appear to have been taken in because one was suffering too much punishment at the hands of another, and the stronger man might be seen to be guilty of an assault. Alarm bells would appear to have been raised by the hardness of the blows directed specifically by Benjamin Lloyd against David James, although it also seems probable that the light 4 oz. gloves used may have also have raised eyebrows. 'Soulless' Ben appear to have got the better of 'Dai Rush' and finally knocked 'Rush' to the boards with heavy blows in the seventh round. Through apparent lack of knowledge as to exactly what constituted the difference between a glove fight and a prize fight, bail was afterwards set for £20 each.

Having developed a great way to 'sell' a fighter as green at the business as 'Dangerous Jack', Scarrott would become practised at the art of selling dummies to the public that crowded into his booth every Saturday night. One variation on the theme was the one that he would later apply to 'Yuko Sako from Yokohama' who was another promising young booth boxing star in the making that Jack Scarrott picked up on the road between Crumlin and Pontypridd. Yuko Sako proved a popular draw, as he could sing and dance and play the mouth organ to help pull in a crowd. Noticing a slight oriental appearance to the boy, it was Jack that had the idea of shaving his head, except for a single top-lock, painting him 'yellow' and naming him 'Yuko'. Although this might sound like a highly unlikely ruse, unlikely to fool even the most naïve onlooker, it seems more plausible that Jack might have gotten away with the scheme inside the charged atmosphere and confines of a canvas topped booth, dimly lit by oil lamps or naphtha flares, and with liberal helpings of theatrical makeup. Yuko Sako definitely featured as one of Jack's regular champions at a

BOXING

News South Wales

Another Surprise Packet.

After Lunty Price (Gilfach) accounted for the happy Jap, Yuko Sacchi, at Bargoed, it was only natural that Mr. Jack Sharratt should look out for another champion, and he picked up a surprise packet in Arthur Poplis (Aberbargoed).

later stage, as a report in London based newspaper 'Boxing' in 1911 confirms, with one 'Yukio Sacchi' having reportedly fallen out of favour with Scarrott after having been beaten by Lunty Price of Bargoed.

Jack Scarrott was having to make do with the talent that he found, or dress a fighter up as someone that appeared to be more credible than he actually was. After spending a lifetime around the dupes, fakes and slanted games of the fairground, where few games truly favoured the chances of the punter actually winning a prize, Jack was merely making his inside knowledge of the fairground game pay for him. There was nothing that could truly prepare the boxing spectator for that rare gem, a boxer in the form of an apparent runt, and one that initially even the faintest heart might think of challenging. It would be some time before Jack would stumble across a boy named Jimmy Wilde, who would put all his previous 'champions' to shame.

Chapter 18
Bob Fitzsimmons

The Cardiff newspapers in 1896 had not been so enthralled by the knowledge of the imminent arrival of a visiting pugilist since 1888, when John L. Sullivan had come to town. The announcement that Bob Fitzsimmons was intending to pass through the town on his tour of Great Britain was met with great excitement throughout Cardiff at the start of July. Fitzsimmons had been crowned both World Middleweight champion and also Heavyweight champion of the World, following his defeat of Peter Maher earlier in the year.

Ordinarily, newspaper reports on boxing would be limited to a few lines on the outcome of illicitly held prize-fights that had reached the ears of the local newspaper reporters, but a boxing superstar as well-known as Bob Fitzsimmons meant that anything to do with the impending visit of the Cornish born ex-blacksmith made for good copy.

Fitzsimmons had been scheduled to appear as part of a display of pugilistic prowess known as an assault-at-arms event, in which a large number of familiar local boxers were engaged to show off their skills including Newport's 'Little Collier' Morgan Crowther, as well as Bob Wiltshire, Fred Isensee and Mike Sullivan, amongst others. That the visit of the Heavyweight World Champion would also occur at the same time as the Cardiff Fine Arts, Industrial and Maritime Exhibition of 1896 also guaranteed good crowds. The scale of the exhibition was vast, and included jungle scenes featuring living animals, the more familiar lions and tigers of the travelling menageries, but also crocodiles and alligators. At night the exhibition, which featured the only electrically controlled pleasure railway in the world, was lit by 10,000 fairy lights and was deemed the "greatest undertaking of its kind ever attempted in the Principality or the West of England."

Bob Fitzsimmons would not appear at the Exhibition, but at the Roseberry Hall, situated alongside the entrance to the grand event. It was thought that large crowds could be expected at the hall, with the modest sum of sixpence allowing the boxing fans to secure one of the cheaper seats. The only hindrance to a bumper crowd was the fact that Peter Jackson was also in town, and could also be seen displaying his boxing prowess at the Panopticon theatre. Martin Julian, Fitzsimmon's manager, arrived in advance of Fitzsimmons and was found to be a godsend for the local press having been talkative and approachable about 'everything in general and nothing in particular'. Julian had been well received by the local fight fans, and after being asked about his reception was quick to sing the praises about the welcome he had received in Wales, stating that the Welsh were a '…sporting little nation, sure, and I have never been treated better by the boys in any place that I have been so far. Of course, I have done well in England too, especially in London. They have made Bob and I members of the National Sporting Club, and treated us royally. I must thank the number of good sportsmen I have met in South Wales for their kindnesses and the hustling fun they have provided me with since I have been here."

When talk turned to the imminent arrival of Fitzsimmons himself, nothing could stop Julian from revealing his satisfaction at the recent performance of his man, in the way that 'only an American can'. Lolling back in his chair, with thumbs stuck in the armholes of his waistcoat, Julian threw his feet up on the table in front of him, and rolled his cigar to and fro in his mouth with eminent satisfaction before beginning;

"I'll not say a lot, for you will only say its Yankee guff. You may take it from me, however, he's the best man living. I think that if you remember the fact that he is both the middleweight and heavyweight champion, and look at his performances, you'll all be inclined to admit that for yourselves. And don't you forget that he's a Cornishman born and bred. It's a hard struggle for me to admit that, but there is no choking off the fact, and Bob will be found just as hard to choke off in a fight as will the proverbial Cornish bug."

Martin Julian had witnessed Fitzsimmons boxing prowess long enough to be a descent judge of his skills, having taken over the ex-blacksmith's business interests after he had beaten 'Nonpareil' Jack Dempsey for the middleweight crown in January of 1891 at New Orleans, and was quick to state that 'Fitz' had '…beat all of them – Peter Maher twice, Jem Hall, J Choynski, Hickey and others, whilst he has knocked hundreds out in three rounds'. Fitzsimmons was to be accompanied by his sparring partner Dan Hickey, who also came with a big reputation, and whom Julian was prepared to back in a contest against any middleweight in the world, bar Fitzsimmons himself. Also featuring as part of the entertainment was Ernest Roeber, billed as the champion Greco-Roman wrestler of the world, with £10 on offer to any man that could last against Roeber while avoiding being thrown for fifteen minutes.

The opening night, on Monday 13th July, 1896 was a massive success, with between two and three thousand people having assembled at the Roseberry Hall eager to see Bob Fitzsimmons with their own eyes. Two small local boys from Canton, 'Chick' and 'Prist', the 'two Canton midgets' started the proceedings with a few short exhibitions before Mike Sullivan and Bob Wiltshire took to the stage. Wiltshire, who some years previously had been an aspirant to the Welsh lightweight title showed all his old cleverness, but was seen to be out of condition. The last round proved to be the best of the encounter, and the popular local sportsman, Harry Wheeler, who had taken on the duties as referee seemed averse to calling 'time' on the contest.

The crowds were then entertained by the wrestling demonstration by Ernest Roeber, who had seen a challenger step up to try and claim the £10 offered by Martin Julian through succeeding to last fifteen minutes against the famous wrestler without being pinned.

Tedory George Costaky better known as 'Greek' George, was a big local draw, and believed that he might succeed where so many had failed in avoiding being pinned by Roeber. The first six minutes proved to be 'very even' with Roeber getting George into trouble, and with Greek George showing just as much skill in cleverly getting out of Roeber's holds. In the last couple of minutes, excitement reached fever pitch, with George having been pinned on one shoulder and then the other within a couple of inches of the boards. By the final minute, it appears as though Roeber would triumph, having got a three-quarter nelson on Greek George and was on his way to victory when the call of 'time' saved him.

The ball punching exhibition by Bob Fitzsimmons was without a doubt the show-stopping performance of the night, and that 'without being seen' it was unlikely that any 'conception can be formed' of the demonstration of his skills;

"Attached to a two-foot rope was a big football. This Fitzsimmons "punched" in every conceivable fashion-left, right with elbows, muscles; in fact, in all positions-first, at the rate of perhaps, 60 blows a minute, working up from this faster than the eye could count to, perhaps 200 blows per minute, winding it all up with a big smashing blow that snapped the rope and sent the ball flying across the hall – a really wonderful performance."

After this startling display of both precision punching and raw power, Fitzsimmons then engaged his sparring partner, Dan Hickey, to show off his boxing skills in an exhibition spar. Both men pulled their punches, with there being no doubt that there was a big 'reserve force' in the blows of the champion, and that Hickey was a clever sparring partner that could hit, and 'hit hard'.

Fitzsimmons earned himself a great number of new fans while at Cardiff, having also paid a visit to the blacksmith shop of Mr. Humphrey at the Tunnel, off Queen Street. While visiting the shop, Fitzsimmons showed off his abilities as a blacksmith by making two 'presentation horseshoes' which was something that boxer often did while travelling to give to friends and acquaintances he had met while on the road. The employees at the blacksmith shop would afterwards speak highly of Fitzsimmons boxing skill, and were quick to point out that the pugilist had also broken a trade 'record' by running a mile and making twenty four horseshoes within an hour.

With the performance of Fitzsimmons having been so well received at Cardiff, it was debated whether another showing would be in order, either at Merthyr or at Pontypridd, following the final show at the Roseberry Hall on the Tuesday evening. Pontypridd was chosen as the place for Bob to appear before he travelled onwards to Birmingham.

It was here that Jack Scarrott would see Bob Fitzsimmons once again snap the mounting ropes of his ball punching apparatus and send the ball sailing over the heads of the crowd. As usual, Bob's unlikely appearance as a prize-fighter would bemuse Jack Scarrott, as it would all the boxing writers of the age. Although Fitzsimmon's upper body had developed along the lines of a tall and well-muscled but lanky 'Hercules' due in part to his previous occupation as a blacksmith, his lower body development lagged behind, with his slender shanks causing 'Fitz' a great deal of embarrassment. So acute was this lop-sided development in Fitzsimmon's own eyes that the champion often elected to cover up his legs with thick woollen tights to spare him the amusement of the crowd and the cruelness of the newspaper men's pens. Bob was also almost six foot tall and unnaturally 'lanky' for the time and suffered from premature balding, which had left him with a thinning crop of reddish hair. Bob's considerable muscular development was also well concealed within the sharply tailored suits that he wore, so it was no surprise that Jack thought, as others had, that Fitzsimmons 'looked more like a parson than a prize-fighter.'

On this occasion, Bob appears to have spiced up his act a little for the appreciative Pontypriddians, asking which hand he should use on the punch ball. Whichever hand was used, the effect was exactly the same, and Bob sent another ball flying into the middle of the crowd. When leaving Pontypridd, 'Fitz' would do so in a manner that would leave many contemplating his astonishing physical strength, with Jack Scarrrott remembering that a porter had struggled to lift one of Fitzsimmons trunks at the train station, with Bob having been forced to come to his aid by helping move the trunk with one hand.

Chapter 19

The Resolven Giant

On November 23rd 1899, a Welsh bare-knuckle boxer by the name of Dai St. John would earn more fame in death than he had ever received in life, having died for king and country in a manner that would ensure that his name was recalled by his fellow Welshmen for a number of years after his death. An infantry man in the 3rd Battalion of the Grenadier Guards, St. John has served at the Battle of Omdurman before having been sent to the front at the Boer War, and it would be there that he would meet his end, although he had long been known as a boxing celebrity of some status in South Wales long before his untimely demise.

Born in the small village of Resolven on 1st April 1871, Dai would quickly mark himself out amongst his fellow miners for his bare-knuckle prowess, which would become the stuff of legend and he was said to have 'whipped man after man' in bare-knuckle contests while still in his teenage years. This was almost certainly due in

Dai St. John in military uniform

part to his imposing size and proportions, having stood six foot three inches and weighing over fourteen stone, at a time when such size and bulk was almost unheard of. With a natural swagger that came from his many victories in bare-knuckle matches, it was not long before Dai was a well-known man, and one that was feared by the booth boxers who appeared on the boxing booths to be found each year at Neath Fair.

One man who certainly should have known better than to rise to the challenge was Cardiff's John O'Brien, who was appearing alongside Jack Scarrott, Bill Lane of Cwmavon and Shoni Engineer on the boxing booths. Having been busy taking on all comers on the booth throughout the day, it was foolhardy for John O'Brien to think that he could meet the gargantuan miner in a match, and in the contest that followed, Dai St. John 'practically put him out'. It was an embarrassing defeat for John O'Brien, having been considered to be the Welsh heavyweight champion following a victory over Pete 'Dublin Tom' Burns inside three rounds, and having soundly beaten Shoni Engineer to take the title. A test to demonstrate his skills at Bob Habbijam's School of Arms in London was forthcoming for the young miner, although the opportunity to fight before a London audience was lost as no testing opposition of similar size could be found at short notice to meet the young miner in a battle.

With John O'Brien and Dai St. John's rivalry laid to rest for the time being, St. John found another challenger in the form of Tom James of Aberaman back on home turf. Being roughly the same age as Dai, and standing six feet tall, James was about as good an opponent as could be found for the young miner, now being known by the nickname of the 'Resolven Giant'. The two men would meet on the 5th November 1892 at Merthyr Drill Hall. The contest came to an abrupt end in the fourth round with a knockout victory by Dai St. John. The victory was one that Dai would celebrate in overly enthusiastic style by declaring himself 'Champion of Wales', which seems more than a little premature, having only met one challenger in a glove contest following his early fame as a bare knuckle fighter. The decision to call himself by such a grandiose title infuriated John O'Brien, who having proved himself worthy of the title prior to St. John's claims had been laid low with sciatica, and not Frank Craig, the 'Coffee Cooler', as claimed by Jack Scarrott. Scarrott would appear to be fairly unfamiliar with O'Brien's record, having only fought alongside O'Brien for a short period of time when both were working on the boxing booths, and did not ever engage John O'Brien to feature amongst his own troupe of booth boxers.

A rematch with Tom James was on the cards and the fight was fixed for the People's Park at Pontypridd, after an attempt was made for the contest to be brought off at the Kennington Club in London, which fell through. Dai was well trained for the match, having had both Sam Butcher and Morgan Crowther assist him in his training at Porthcawl. The bout was well fought throughout, but the beginning of the end would come in the fifth round when Dai landed an uppercut which lifted Tom James off his feet and sent him crashing back into a corner of the ring. James found himself knocked backwards into a corner in the sixth round, and before long he was smashed into submission by St. John's powerful swinging blows.

While it proved to be a good win, St. John had still not met anyone of any real standing in a glove fight, and decided to throw out a challenge to Jem Smith, the English champion. Given that he had only had two contests with the gloves, and both with the same man, it was no surprise that the challenge lay unanswered. St. John's audacity in proclaiming himself 'Welsh champion' did however, serve to inflame the anger of John O'Brien, and after some dispute the match was finally fixed to come off at the National Sporting Club in London for a purse of £50 and the right of the victor to call himself the 'Heavyweight Champion of Wales'. The contest would be one that would long be remembered by those members of the club that were lucky enough to witness it.

O'Brien was dwarfed by the superior size of the Resolven man, and gave away nearly 2 stone in weight, with the Cardiffian weighing in at 11 stone 13 lbs. to St. John's 13 stone 12 lbs. O'Brien made a valiant start, and was seen to feint and dodge in and out trying to ascertain St. John's weak spots. The second round saw both men step up the pace with a furious exchange of blows of the most determined nature. O'Brien put down his enemy in the third with a hard blow to the neck, but it was St. John's right hand that sent O'Brien reeling across the ring and off the ropes. Dai was waiting and dropped his great enemy in the exchange that followed. It was Dai that then came to the front, flooring O'Brien for the second time with a hard shot to the neck. Back came O'Brien, and after Dai's head had dipped through a concerted attack to the ribs, a quick right to the jaw sent the cumbersome miner down for a count of eight. Anticipating an end to the battle, O'Brien quickly moved in but was caught with an unexpected punch and he went down again but struggled gamely to his feet once more. In the fourth it looked as though St. John would triumph, having put O'Brien down twice before the end of the round. The fifth proved to be a show-stopper, and it looked for a time as if the great Resolven Giant would emerge triumphant through his sheer strength and weight advantage, sending O'Brien down for another count with a right hand to the chin. Pushing into close quarters, O'Brien landed a right to the chin which proved to be decisive with St. John having been counted out just before the end of the fifth round.

Following his defeat at the hands of O'Brien, Dai saw fit to issue further challenges to both Jem Smith and the Australian fighter Frank Slavin, but the challenge would fall on deaf ears. His challenge to Frank Slavin had come after an impromptu tear-up in a London bar-room which had seen St. John give the Australian a 'tremendous thrashing' and forced Slavin to concede defeat. A match would be made between Slavin and St. John at a Birmingham Club, but Slavin pulled out at the last minute, and so the contest never took place. Sadly St. John would appear to have been far from a success with the gloves, and encasing his huge fists in the "mufflers" appeared to make showing off his natural fighting skills a great deal more difficult. After boxing a few rounds in gloves, the Resolven Giant always showed a strong desire to tear off the gloves and go to work with bare-knuckles with the "no holds barred" rules that he had excelled under in his early career fighting his fellow miners on the mountainside. It was thought that had St. John come to the front in the times of the earlier pugilists, he might well have risen to become well known as a fighter, but due to his own rather clumsy style of fighting was unable to make his mark amongst the gloved fighters of his day.

His shortcomings as a boxer seemed to be acknowledged by St. John himself. One night Dai was drinking in a bar-room with several companions when a cat belonging to the tavern sprang across the floor and re-appeared with a huge rat quivering between her paws. The cat released the rodent and let it run for a few seconds before recapturing it again. Watching the display for a few seconds, St. John turned to his companions and remarked;

"The owl cat uses 'er paw well. Lor' if I could jab the left like that, Oi'd make 'em all look like rats'.

Following his defeat at the hands of John O'Brien, St. John was lucky enough to meet Peter Jackson at a social engagement at the National Sporting Club. Jackson was impressed enough by the physical development of Dai to ask the Welshman to go on tour with him, which proved to be a lucky break for the ex-miner, who travelled throughout England and Scotland and to Paris with the great heavyweight. Jackson's attempts to impart some of his ring experience to aid St. John in his further career failed to assist the Welshman. While Dai's physical strength had never been in doubt, he suffered from having been shown the finer points of glove fighting late in life, and was seen to be both slow on his feet and poor at judging distance with the gloves.

At the end of the tour, Dai St. John returned home to Wales, and found that another match against Tom James was waiting courtesy of William Samuels, whose boxing booth was stationed at Neath. Out of condition, Dai relied on his superior strength to carry him through, and although the decision was given as a draw, it was a disappointing performance for St. John, and one that received loud boos from the dissatisfied audience. Despite the irritation of the crowd, Dai was a friendly and likable man who appeared to make friends wherever he appeared. On one occasion he had been engaged to spar with one Mike Mahoney at a Dublin music hall over a week's visit to Ireland. On the second night of the engagement, Mahoney had got drunk and had collided with a blind man in the street. Inflated with a sense of his own importance, the Irishman had then given the blind man a sound beating. After having been locked up by the police for the night, Mahoney was unrepentant in court the following morning, claiming he would have beaten his own grandfather if he had dared to try and shove him aside and was fined fifteen shillings for the crime.

Just as Mahoney was being removed Dai St. John pushed his way through the crowd, and confronted his sparring partner;

"Thou'd beat a blind mon, eh?" asked St. John as he pushed the astonished officers to one side. "Well, lad, just see how I'll beat thee". Before anyone could interfere, St. John had his sparring partner on the floor and Mahoney was given a sound thrashing by the Welsh Giant. Mahoney was seen to be terribly beaten when he was finally released from St. John's grasp. His assailant was immediately arrested and then fined for creating a disturbance in court, but after paying the fine St.John merely laughed and remarked;

"Cheap at th' price, th' lad was of no account an' deserved the beatin'. Ah'm fit to whip such men every day."

It was at the Battle of Belmont that St. John would meet his untimely end. Standing at the foot an unforgiving battleground at the base of a steep hill of rock and stone with his comrades in arms, the troops were given the order to take the hill by their superiors, a task that would result in the deaths of many before the battlefield was taken, with St. John's actions being recounted with astonishment by one of the survivors;

'We were out in the open flat at the foot of the hill, and no guns there to shell the Boers loose for us. We had to do the whole jobs ourselves, and so we did it. The bullets did come thick, an' they got thicker, but we had to go up, and so up we went, with the bayonet. We charged, and it was all stones and steep; but we charged. And St. John he charged – by God! He did charge. He was ahead all the way up; he never slowed for breath; he never missed a stride. Up he went, an' in he got with the bayonet ahead of all of us. You should ha' seen him. He got eleven of them – killed eleven of 'em with his own bayonet, and then one shot him while he was at it. And when he'd shot him the Boer that did it dropped his rifle and threw up his hand, an' cried out 'Mercy!' for the rest of us were up then, an' he couldn't get away. The sergeant-major was nearest 'Mercy!' says he; 'I'll give you mercy!' an' with that he smacked the steel through his breast – clean through him – the bayonet and the barrel after it, clear through, till the grip of the left hand stopped it at the back-band. 'I'll give you mercy!' says the sergeant-major; 'I'll give you mercy!'".

Soldiers finding the body of Dai St. John

Following the battle, the valiant end of the Welsh Giant, Dai St John was recorded in full alongside numerous sketches of St. John's final stand against the Boers and the discovery of his body amongst those of the dead in the aftermath of the battle, ensuring that within a few days the name of the Welsh pugilist would be remembered throughout the United Kingdom. In one newspaper a poem was published, which would prove to be as fitting a tribute to the memory of Dai St. John as any;

How David St. John Fought His Last Fight

To read about this Welshman bold,
Is a romantic story.
As in the fray Dave fought his way,
For Duty not for glory.
In that grim fight on blood stained height,
Each soldier die or do man.
Dave met one Boer 'mong many more,
Who proved a worthy foeman.
With bayonet fixed they fighting mixed,
'Till burly Boer cried "Fain it!"
But bold St. John was taking none,
And drove right home his bayonet.
When David's blade in that Boer stayed,
And left him cold and senseless.
It went so hard past the cross guard,
That Dave was left defenceless.
Now, brave St. John with weapon gone,
Would to no Boer cry "Quarter,"
He fights in vain, for ball in brain,
Adds St. John to the slaughter.

Chapter 20

Skerrit's Boxers

There are very few indications of the exact movements of Jack Scarrott's booth prior to the turn of the century, and it might be imagined that as a fledgling boxing booth operator Scarrott certainly had his work cut out for him. For one thing, there was plenty of competition, with there being many boxing booths that had developed a far more established footing. Some had the advantage of a semi-developed pool or troupe of known fighting men and were able to do a stronger trade and offer more lucrative purses as a result. John Stokes, Patsy Perkins, Charlie North, and of course William Samuels, had all found that they could do better business further to the West at Port Talbot, Aberavon, and at Swansea and Neath. Their movements here were somewhat less hampered by the stern non-conformist attitudes of the tightly knit chapel communities of the valleys to the East, and less likely to incur the wrath of the local police forces as a result.

As always, it was the fairground that determined the route taken, with the booth owner developing relationships outside the fairground with local business people for lease of a piece of land either in accommodating towns or within close distance from them where they might be enabled to set up shop without too much interference from the moral majority. Judging by the entries of the 1901 census, in which his daughter, Phoebe (aged 6) is recorded as having been born at Aberavon, Jack Scarrott was pitching his boxing 'saloon' in the area as early as 1895. His son, John Scarrott Jnr. was born in Llanelly in 1900, where Jack had witnessed the fight between William Samuels and Bob Dunbar while travelling the fairground circuit with his parents as a young boy.

There is one intriguing record of a 'Scarratt' having appeared at the boxing booth of William Samuels at Swansea in April of 1895 seconding in the corner of Enoch Morrison along with one 'Beresford' in a six round fight against William 'Slogger' Hooligan, a well-known Swansea booth boxer. Morrison is recorded as having been based out of Cardiff at this time, and could be considered a contemporary of Jack Scarrott's having run a boxing booth as well as having previously performed as a boxer throughout South Wales, after having supposedly won some renown as the 'Champion of Shrewsbury'. Hooligan was seconded by members of the Swansea boxing set, with Dick Ambrose and 'Sullivan' appearing in his corner. Hooligan was seen to enjoy a great advantage in weight, and Morrison did not seem to be at ease in the contest, with Hooligan being much stronger throughout. Throughout the course of the fight, Enoch Morrison did show that he was a clever and skilled fighter, although he was seen to repeatedly go 'to earth', with the majority believing that he was seen to be fairly well beaten by the second round. Disaster occurred when Morrison launched a swinging blow, and landed a forearm on the head of Hooligan with such force that 'an ancient fracture gave way' and he broke his arm. Despite the injury, Morrison showed his pluck by finishing out the round, before finally conceding his defeat.

The only indication as to the movements of Jack Scarrott's boxing booth around this time period come from the few very brief printed entries in which Jack Scarrott's booth can be found namechecked alongside other travelling concerns touring on the welsh fairground circuit. Although reports are few in number, 'Skerrit's boxers' is recorded as having been one of the many entertainments jostling for space at Treorchy Fair in June of 1899, which also included snake charmers, strong men, no less than three of the developing cinematograph shows, one having been operated by early film pioneer, Walter Haggar, as well as a 'stereo fine art show' and two working colliery model exhibits. It was the start of an expansion of the pleasure fair on a scale that had never been seen before, with all of the show people paying their dues to the Studt family for their pitches. It seems plausible that Scarrott may have already been supplementing his booth income with other concerns by this time, as two weeks afterwards at Porth 'Skirret's athletes and boxers' is recorded as having been present, along with various other 'novelties' having been offered by 'Messrs. North, Shcen, and one 'Skerret', amongst the coconut shies, shooting galleries and the smaller enterprises on the fairground. All paled into insignificance alongside the magnificent rides being offered by the Studt family, having cornered the large scale entertainments market with six 'large concerns, including switchbacks, roundabouts, a tunnel railway and swings. Jack also set up the booth at Neath Fair in September the same year, with 'Scarratt's boxing saloon' having featured prominently amongst the amusements recorded as having appeared there.

By 1900, entertainments by 'Scarrott' were also doing business alongside William Samuels' boxing booth when stationed at the Treorchy Fair in June, and would also be name checked as having been present at the two 'back-end' fairs at Aberdare and Mountain Ash later that year.

Having set up shop in the near vicinity of Swansea, it was not long before Jack's booth was acquiring a better class of booth boxer. One of the earliest fighters that Jack recalls having fought on the booth was Pedlar McMahon ('McMann'), who he remembers as having been 'a real pocket Hercules' with a knockout punch. There are no records to show where Pedlar McMahon (sometimes 'Pedlar Pat') was born, although it seems plausible that he may have come from the Glasgow area. At one stage McMahon was residing in Haverfordwest, although his profession as a fur pedlar meant that he was by nature a travelling man, and would travel throughout the United Kingdom. Despite having been a very promising pugilist, the necessity for McMahon to work his day job meant that most of his contests would be made on the boxing booth and he picked up contests on his travels, fighting on numerous booths. Had McMahon spent more time pursuing a profession boxing career it seems likely that he would have become far more familiar to the public as a professional pugilist. McMahon first came to the attention of the press in 1895 in Swansea after having appeared on a bill at William Samuels' Gloucester School of Arms as the trainer of a Glaswegian pugilist by the name of 'Young' (Billy) Pearson ('Scotch Laddie') against a local fighter, Jack Cox, which was fought to a draw in the tenth round. McMahon would be taking on Cox himself a few weeks later at the same establishment.

Pedlar McMahon's first battle showed him to good effect, and he proved to be a harder proposition than his pupil, Pearson. The match was made for six rounds with small gloves, but in a hard fought battle, it was Cox that proved to be wanting. In the first round, both men hit out heavily but it was McMahon that had the best of matters. Both men went at it hammer and tongs, but the Pedlar had more success and was seen to be 'a long way in front' by the call of time. The second round began more cautiously although it was again McMahon that seized the advantage although Cox was quick to launch an assault to the body, scoring heavily with round arm blows that forced McMahon to show caution. The third round showed clearly how quickly McMahon had mastered his man, following his opponent all over the ring and forcing him on the defensive. Pedlar was seen to feint 'beautifully' with his left, puzzling Cox enough to drive home a powerful right which exploded on Cox's jaw, putting him to sleep for the full count. McMahon was deemed a deserving victor, having shown greater 'science' than his opponent in the course of the contest, and having proved to all that he was a powerful two fisted fighter.

Having shown himself to good effect before William Samuels as a boxer worthy of attention, McMahon was afterwards retained to meet Ormus Griffiths, also of Swansea, the following week. Griffiths proved to be a no show, and so one J. Birmingham of Greenhill was chosen to stand in instead. Despite having been staggered early in the first round, McMahon showed the cooler head under pressure. In the later rounds, he came back strongly, and at the end of six well contested rounds was deemed the better man in a close contest. Over the course of the next couple of years, McMahon proved to be a fairly frequent performer at Swansea, although he travelled to Aberdare to make his very first recorded appearance on Jack Scarrott's booth in December of 1898 when he fought George 'Punch' Jones of Aberaman in a contest billed for the Welsh 9 stone 6 lb title.

McMahon would also develop a strong rivalry against fellow booth boxer, Frank Lowry of London. Their first traced contest came off at the Niagara Hall in Swansea on the 20th July, 1899 for £10 a-side and a £10 purse with the prize money to go to the man who distinguished himself most over 10 rounds. Lowry appeared particularly confident of a victory, asking whether anyone wanted to take a bet of a sovereign on himself to win, but there were no takers. The contest began slowly, with both men showing a great deal of caution in the early rounds. It was in the sixth that Lowry began fighting with more enthusiasm, but it was McMahon that emerged the stronger, landing powerful blows on the jaw and body. The seventh round also showed Lowry to good advantage, but in the latter rounds the harder blows all came from McMahon, who, having woken up '…slogged at his opponent in sledge-hammer style, and displaying excellent form, time was called, and he was awarded the victory amidst cheers.'

The return fight came off at Jack Scarrott's boxing 'saloon' on the 6th September 1899, and attracted a great deal more interest, with the booth being crowded with a large number of local enthusiasts wanting to see how the six round match turned out. McMahon was seen to be in better condition, and was the driving force behind the action in the opening rounds. The match heated up in the third round, and both men gave all they were worth, and fought to a "standstill" in the final round. The match was too close to call and the referee had to order another round to come to a decision. Lowry staggered McMahon with a solid straight left, but on attempting to land the same blow again, the Londoner suffered a right counter for his efforts. At the end of a hotly contested match the decision was given to Pedlar McMahon.

Sadly, this appears to be the only contest for Pedlar McMahon that appears to have been recorded as having occurred on the booth of Jack Scarrott at Aberavon. It is clear from his record that the vast majority of his bouts on the boxing booths do not appear to have been recorded, although McMahon did fight on the booths of Harry Cullis and Felix Scott amongst others. McMahon also won a competition for novices at the National Sporting Club in London in 1897 and had a long boxing career, having appeared in the boxing ring as late as 1908. Little appears to be known of McMahon's movements in the years following, although it is believed that he emigrated to the United States where he is said to have set up a boxing school and supposedly became a good friend of the 'Manassa Mauler', world champion, Jack Dempsey.

With Jack Scarrott encroaching on William Samuels' turf, and his booth starting to develop to the point where he was attracting better known boxers, he was increasingly using boxers that had initially featured on the booth of Samuels. It was only a matter of time before the two showmen would fall out. The boxing booth proprietor Charlie North could probably have warned Jack Scarrott of the possibility of such an occurrence after having become the victim of the Swansea booth proprietor's wrath and fallen foul of Samuels' quick temper back in 1886 after a chance meeting on the day after the Brynmawr fair. Samuels had approached Charlie North in a confrontational mood and challenged North to do battle, putting up his hands and taking a fighting stance after stating that he was capable of killing North 'in a minute'. The two men had previously sparred together at Neath Eistedfodd, with the dispute having apparently occurred due to North's unwillingness to concede that Samuels had been the better man in their five round sparring exhibition. The dispute ended up being brought before Brynmawr police court, with Samuels having been let off the charges brought against him. Ultimately Charlie North ended up paying the price, and was ordered to pay all costs, as well as William Samuels' railway ticket from Pembrokeshire to attend the court proceedings.

Within a few years, William Samuels was also running a cinematograph show, having apparently been one of the first showmen on the Welsh fairgrounds to recognise the money making possibilities of moving pictures. This would lead to some conflict with the family of William Haggar, who had been touring the fairgrounds as travelling play actors before investing in a cinematograph machine of their own. William Haggar's son, Walter would long afterwards remember the rivalry between his father's show and William Samuels' boxing booth and would write of Samuel's confrontational manner in his 'Bioscope recollections' as recounted in the book *William Haggar, Fairground Film Maker by Peter Yorke (Accent Press, 2007)*;

'Bill Samuels of Swansea, the one-time celebrated Welsh pugilist, had a very fine boxing show and a small cinematograph show, and was very jealous of our intrusion in what might be called his own domain. Bill Samuels, God rest his soul, a good man in his own line, used to refer to Father as 'the old mummer', referring to his play acting days. On this occasion, we were standing next to Mr. Samuels Boxing Show, and when opening time came for us the night before the fair at about 7 o'clock, we turned out our little brass band to play some music to attract the crowd (we had by this time engaged a professional cornet player), but Mr. Samuels thought differently. Every time we turned out our band, Bill Samuels turned out his boxers, their raucous voices touting their own show. This rather took the wind out of our sails: we could not get the people to hear what we had to say, and in the end we retired into our own show in ignominy. But father's persistence would not be suppressed. 'Time to organise things,' he said to the cornet player. 'You have been in the army, haven't you?' 'Yes, governor.' 'When I say 'go', you go out and blow bugle calls towards Bill Samuels' show until I tell you to stop.

'Father was directing the battle: he waited until Mr. Samuels had finished springing his lines and had a nice crowd of people round him to listen to what he had to say, then he gave the word. With drum and bugle we surged forth and would not desist. 'Bang, bang, bang', we repeated until poor Bill Samuels was almost demented. He turned towards Father saying, 'Stop that ruddy drum!' But we did not stop, and Bill Samuels and his boxers in their turn retired into their show in ignominy. The crowds were enjoying this rivalry, and Father, ever ready to seize an opportunity, invited the public into his show free. We had a packed house and this proved to be an excellent advertisement: we did very well on the two following days.'

By 1900, Jack Scarrott was already quickly becoming a fixture on the Fairfield at Neath Fair, and it would prove somewhat inevitable that William Samuels would feel threatened enough by the presence of a rival boxing booth to stomp across from his own pitch to confront the competition. Finding Jack Scarrott sitting on the front of his booth, Samuels at once started verbally abusing the latest showman foolish enough to dare test his patience. Finding Scarrott to be a less than willing combatant, Samuels threatened to break his jaw. It was Jack Scarrott's refusal to react, and telling Samuels to go away that engaged the wrath of his childhood hero and pushed him past his breaking point.

In a fit of rage, Samuels tried to knock Jack over and started butting at him with his head. In the brief fight that followed, it would seem that Jack Scarrott was actually getting the better of Samuels for a couple of rounds. True to form, Samuel's fearsome wife Elizabeth Samuels was quick to defend her man, making her presence felt by threatening to 'stick' Scarrott with a knife. Reinforcements also arrived on the scene in the form of William Samuels' Jnr. who also started attacking Scarrott, along with one of their in-laws, further threatening Jack Scarrott's safety.

It was John Studt that proved to be Jack Scarrott's lifesaver, having appeared on the scene just in time to separate Samuels from a rapidly worsening situation. Having had almost as fierce a reputation as her husband, Elizabeth Samuels did little to calm matters, with a witness stating that the warlike Mrs Samuels had said, 'I will make you fight' to Jack Scarrott and implored her husband to 'kill him before he is done with.' Had it not been for the appearance of Henry Studt on the scene, the witness believed there 'would have been murder'.

When the case eventually wound up in court, neither William Samuels nor Elizabeth Samuels or any of the extended family would bother showing up. It hadn't been the first time that Samuels had fallen out with Jack Scarrott, and Scarrott was quick to state that he did not consider himself to be a fighter, and had never styled himself as a champion boxer, and had not contacted the papers with regard to the dispute, which seemed to have been the work of Billy Samuels.

John Studt effectively pulled a discreet veil over the event by saying that there hadn't been anything serious in the matter between the two showmen and that he had run across from the front of his gondolas as soon as the fight had occurred. Luckily John Studt had heard no threats, and had not seen Mrs. Samuels with a knife, although he did recall that afterwards Priscilla Scarrott had been holding a knife, as if she was going to go and peel potatoes. It was decided that William Samuels would have to pay peace sureties to the tune of £10 and agree to maintain the peace between them for six months. Both had sailed pretty close to having paid a greater cost, with it being suggested that those in charge of Neath fair might consider the desirability of excluding boxing shows from the fair altogether in future. Samuels believed that he had ended up wearing the victor's laurels on this occasion, stating before his booth audience on the evening after the assault that: "He is 26, and I am 63. And I satisfied him in two rounds." One thing was for certain, Jack Scarrott's boxing booth was slowly gathering a better class of champions to entice the crowds.

Chapter 21
Dai Dollings

The most famous of those to graduate from the boxing booth of William Samuels would not become best known for his skill as a pugilist, but as a trainer of boxing champions. David John Dolling, better known as Dai Dollings, would become a trainer of international repute, although he was initially known as just one of the many bare-knuckle fighters to be found in and around the area of Swansea. Born in February 1859, Dollings spent the days of his youth living 'a wild and carefree life at the ocean side' and excelled at swimming, stating that 'at 6 I could swim like a fish and was as hard as the rocks near the shore'. At the age of nine he was running errands, and by the age of thirteen he was apprenticed to a butcher, which helped him become 'familiar with each and every intestine of the cattle we disembowelled', and he afterwards deemed to be 'a great aid to me when I became a trainer and had to treat the ills of humans. I knew when a torpid liver or bad stomach was the cause of sluggishness.'

Dai Dollings and Matt Wells

Dollings was also lucky enough to have had a tutor in the use of medicinal herbs in the form of his mother, who taught him 'facts which I alone know about the proper mixtures and ingredients of certain herbs which have performed wonders'. In later years, Dai would claim that this knowledge of herb lore had helped him cure patients who doctors had been unable to assist, and would lead him to be called 'The Medicine Man' by many of those that found themselves aided by his use of herb craft.

Dollings' great-grandfather also appears to have had a formative impact on Dai's decision to become a trainer, having said to have been a 'famous trainer of humans, horses and dogs. He was remembered by Dai as having developed the famous greyhound, 'Master McGraw, winner of many a blue ribbon'. His great-grandfather apparently also had an interest in boxing, as Dollings would later claim that he had also 'brought forth Martin Fury and William Samuels'.

As an adult Dollings would find employment as a riveter in and around Swansea's growing dockyards, although he also competed as a young man in local running events and became well known as a gifted runner. At some point Dollings decided to try his luck at boxing, recalling that;

'…each class of tradesmen had its pugilistic representatives, and after seeing some of the battles I was persuaded to don the gloves against Bob Carter, champion lightweight of the butcher gentry. I weighed 116 pounds and never did scale above 126, even though I fought heavyweights. All matches during this period

were finish fights, I knocked out Carter in the second round and received £5 for my efforts'.

Dollings also fought in bare-knuckle matches, and said that '…in my first bare knuckle battle I met a heavyweight who weighed 200 pounds and put him to sleep in seven rounds.' Other men that Dai Dollings claimed to have beaten included George Lucas and Shamus Warner, both familiar fighters on William Samuels' boxing booth, as well as Shonney Shone, Jack Reese and Nunc Wallace, one-time bantamweight champion of England. Dollings developed a reputation as a hard fighter, which he claimed allowed him to win two purses of £500 without even having to raise his hands, as these substantial side bets ended up being awarded to him after two prospective opponents had backed out of fighting him.

Intriguingly, Dollings would also relate that in one match he 'whipped' Billy Samuels Jnr. when 'young Billy held the lightweight title of Wales'. The defeat apparently stirred the wrath of William Samuels himself;

'His father, William, demanded a bout with me with the desire of getting revenge. He was 40 at the time and fought until he was 60. We battled at bare knuckles and I was winning when the police stopped the match.'

Despite the battle, Dai Dollings would relate that 'Old man Samuels then became one of my best friends and organised fighting shows which I joined. During one of these boxing shows I knocked out seven men in one day.' Dollings later claimed that over the course of his career as a pugilist he fought a hundred bouts with the gloves and a further thirty battles with the knuckles, and only lost one contest to Morgan Crowther, who knocked him out in three rounds at Tenby. Dollings would remember that one of his best performances had been against Frank Crozier who later fought the heavyweight champion of the world, Jack Johnson, and who Dollings supposedly 'cut to ribbons' and knocked out in nine rounds, receiving just £25 for the bout.

In between fights, Dollings continued to run as an amateur, and 'was paid to win heats for bookmakers until the officials gradually made it so difficult for pros to compete with the amateurs' forcing him to quit. As a trainer of runners, Dollings had a great deal of success, the first well known man Dollings trained was Artie Collumb, who held the professional record for 1,000 yards at 2 minutes and 9 seconds. Artie Watkins, who made the world professional record for covering 11 miles and 1,000 yards within an hour was also coached by Dai. The world champion walker, Yeomans, who held the world record for one mile in 6 minutes and nineteen seconds, and the two mile record in 13 minutes and nine seconds was also said to have benefitted from Dai's assistance. Bob Derbisher, the first man to swim 100 yards in one minute was looked after by Dollings, as was Artie Lawson, the weighted club swinger, who he remembered having once swung three pound clubs for 101 hours without rest or sleep at Sydney, Australia. He also trained Harry Watkins and Arthur Manning, who were both well known as middle distance star runners in their day.

By 1895, Dai Dollings was regularly appearing in the corners of Swansea fighters, most notably acting as trainer and second to local fighters Dick Ambrose and

Billy Morgan on the occasions where they fought in the Alexandria Road boxing booth run by Billy Samuels and also at the Gloucester School Arms, while under the management of Patsy Perkins. In July, 1895 Dollings and local boxer Evan Davies seconded Dick Ambrose in a bout against Charles Palmer of America in which Ambrose was knocked out in the seventh round at the Gloucester School of Arms. In January 1896, Dollings seconded one Harris of Llansamlet against 'Barry' of Greenhill along with Tom James of Aberaman. Barry had the Swansea butcher, and veteran bare-knuckle fighter George Lucas and boxer Dick Ambrose in his corner. The match proved to be an exciting one, with it being declared a draw after ten hard fought rounds. The following month found Dollings back in the corner of Swansea man Billy Morgan when he appeared at the Alexandria Road sparring saloon of William Samuels to meet E. Osbourne of London for a ten round fight. The men had fought some time previously at the Gloucester School of Arms, when Morgan had won after about six or seven rounds after Osbourne had given in owing to an injured arm. Billy Morgan would end up getting the better of Osbourne throughout the re-match, and Osbourne received such punishment in the fifth and sixth rounds that he ended up going down in the seventh due to a very light blow to the face and was counted out. While Osbourne might have been within his rights to go down and avoid further punishment, the manner in which he did so became the subject of much ringside discussion as the blow which finished him was deemed to be hardly enough to 'have stretched an infant out'.

March 1896 also saw Dai Dollings appear in the corner of one 'Hartley' of Swansea when he emerged victorious in a twelve round bout against 'Phillips of Landore' with small gloves. Hartley was seen to be in much better condition and 'hit his opponent all over the shop' in the fourth round, forcing Phillips to give up the fight. On March 20th, Dai Dollings was back in business seconding Dick Ambrose in a contest against Tom Davies at the Alexandria Road booth alongside George Lucas. The ten round contest would end in tragedy with Tom Davies having died the following day of a blood clot on the brain. Dollings was taken into custody as having assisted in 'feloniously aiding and abetting, counselling and procuring' Dick Ambrose to commit a felony, along with seven others, including the referee, Tom James of Aberaman and the booth proprietor, William Samuels. The Bench was left to decide whether the contest was an exhibition of skill or whether it constituted a 'prize fight' as the contest had been advertised as having been "for a purse and a side bet of £10". The grand jury would later throw the case out, with Dollings and the other men having come close to being charged with having assisted in the accidental manslaughter of Tom Davies.

Dai Dollings resumed his training duties after the tragedy and was reported as having seconded Billy Morgan in an unplanned night-time knuckle fight on Swansea seashore that came off on the 2nd April, 1897 against Morgan Grey, a younger brother of well-known Swansea fighter 'Billum' Grey. Earlier on in the evening a discussion had occurred between the fighters and their friends about the difference between boxing and fighting. In the course of the conversation, Morgan Grey had asserted that Billy Morgan could not knock him out in ten rounds with gloves, but that he could finish Morgan within four rounds in a knuckle match, as he deemed that Morgan was 'no rough or tumble fighter'. Words became so heated that Morgan and Grey decided to go down to the sand to settle the matter at about 11.30pm followed by a crowd of approximately thirty onlookers.

It proved to be too dark to hold the match on the seafront, and so it was decided to hold the contest in an area illuminated by a large electric light. Before the contest could begin a police whistle was heard, and led the men to fear that police interference was imminent. The dock constable on duty could not leave his station and his call went unanswered, and so the men decided to continue. Billy Morgan faced into the electric light, giving a slight advantage to Grey. Grey lunged with the right, but Morgan dodged, making him miss. He then rushed in and held Morgan, who stuck fast to him, with both men falling down. In a fit of anger Grey foolishly punched Dai Dollings as he was picking Billy Morgan up. A few words were exchanged before the fight resumed again. The men immediately clinched again and went to the ground once more. Grey put in a couple of short-arm blows with his left but they did no damage, and was sent down by Billy Morgan with a hard right to the jaw. As soon as Grey was back on his feet, Billy Morgan landed on his face again with the other fist and Grey began to look beaten. He closed on Morgan hoping to throw his opponent, but miscalculated Billy's strength and was forced to observe the call to "break away". It was at this point that Billy Morgan landed an almighty right hand to the jaw, putting Morgan Grey to sleep for about twenty seconds. After having regained consciousness, Grey wanted to resume the fight, but was eventually persuaded by his friends that he had no chance.

Morgan Grey would receive a greater beating than he had planned on, as after the fight with Billy Morgan he was invited to step up and meet Dai Dollings, who was annoyed at having been struck when picking Morgan up. Grey accepted the challenge, but he 'received much more severe punishment in the rough and tumble that followed than he had got from Morgan, and his friends were soon glad to see the fight come to a close'.

In the years that followed, Dai Dollings would go on to more widespread acclaim after having become the principal trainer of Tom Thomas of Penygraig, who became British middleweight champion in 1909. Although Dai was travelling throughout the country as a trainer at this stage, he appears to have stayed a resident at his hometown of Swansea, appearing as a corner man at the Swansea Athletic Club as late as 1910, when he seconded Boyo Bradley the 8st 4 lb. West of England Champion in a five round victory over Jim Dermody of Ystradgynlais on June 30th. Dollings was by now spending an increasing amount of time in London, and had taken over the training of British Welterweight champion, Young Josephs, while also travelling to Paris to assist the American welterweight, Harry Lewis. Other boxers who would come under his guidance would include such well-known names as Bobby Dobbs, Digger Stanley, Jim Driscoll and Gunner Moir. Dollings would become regarded as having been one of the most talented trainers in Britain after having trained Matt Wells of London in his preparations to defeat Freddie Welsh for the British lightweight championship on the 27th February 1911. The Swansea trainer would afterwards accompany Wells when he travelled across the Atlantic to meet U.S. challengers in March of 1912. When Wells had first come under the care of Dollings as a middleweight he had been the recipient of a great deal of criticism from the ex-bare-knuckle fighter, who had told him "You're too bloody 'eavy lad. You shouldn't weigh no more than nine stone seven." Soon after, Wells became a lightweight, but didn't appear to lose any of his punching power along with the twenty seven pounds he shed due to the training regime enforced by Dollings.

Dai Dollings would place a great deal of emphasis on the importance of roadwork in the preparation of a boxer, and could often be scathing in his opinions regarding the inability of other trainers to train alongside their man, recalling that;

"Fighters today think they are doin' a lot of roadwork if they 'ave to run three miles. When I brought Matt Wells to America, we used to run 18 miles together, then come back and I'd put on the gloves with 'im. I'd like to see any of your bloody modern trainers do that. Trainers is what they calls themselves, but all they know 'ow to do is hang around the gymnasiums and wipe a fighter's face between rounds. Trainers ? Hah ! They're all mouth and no 'ead. They couldn't train a blarsted flea!"

By 1913, Dai Dollings had built a reputation as one of the best boxing trainers in the country after assisting Ted 'Kid' Lewis in achieving his goal to become the featherweight champion of Great Britain. In 1914, Dollings crossed the Atlantic for the second time to assist Ted 'Kid' Lewis in his fights in the United States, despite having been reportedly eager to return to his hometown in Swansea where for a while he had been considered for the position of trainer of the Swansea football team. Lewis would long remember Dai Dollings as having been an uncompromising trainer who was dedicated to his preparation of boxers;

"He was a very strict, conscientious trainer and, much as we all admired him, he had us all scared. He never spared himself when he was training a boxer and was a great believer in hard work. After meals he would take me on the road to cover an average of 12 to 16 miles a day, walking and running. It was stiff work and the call to bed was the sweetest music of the day for me."

Dai Dollings ended up settling permanently in the U.S. where he would become one of the most highly regarded trainers at Grupp's Gym on West 116th Street in New York. It was here that he would mentor a young Ray Arcel, who would go on to become one of the foremost boxing trainers of the 20th century after having first started learning the art of working a fighter's corner from Dai Dollings, who he would later remember as having been a particularly stern teacher;

'He was a funny sort of guy. He lived on 15th Street and he was so frugal he wouldn't spend the nickel to get on a streetcar to get to the gym. He'd walk from 15th Street to 116th Street where the gym was. That was about five miles, a hundred blocks. Rain, snow, hail, he'd walk. He'd come up to the gym and he'd say: "You bloody Americans, you're made of tissue paper." The truth was, he wasn't a particularly pleasant guy. He always seemed to be angry. When he talked to you, he'd always point his fist at you. I don't think he meant anything special by it, but you could

see even a fighter like Lewis being intimidated by it. But I didn't let that bother me. I was so interested in asking him questions, I'd walk down to his house with him, and since I didn't have the nickel carfare to come back uptown, I'd walk all the way back home.'

Dai was initially reluctant to take Ray Arcel seriously about his intention to become a trainer, *'Over and over he kept asking why I wanted to be a trainer. When I told him that was my ambition, he'd let it go for awhile, as if that was an answer, then come right back later on with the same question. At first the most I got out of him was along the lines of 'If you're going to be a trainer, be the best one or don't bother with it all.' Maybe I just wore him down and I don' think all those marathon walks down to 15th Street with him hurt. Anyway, I knew I'd made a breakthrough of some kind one day when he told me I didn't want to be a trainer. I wanted to be what he called an analyst.'*

According to Dollings the difference between a trainer and an 'analyst' lay in the ability to view each boxer under his care as individuals, whose care and training would differ according to their particular needs. Arcel would remember that;

"He'd tell me, 'See what the other guy has. See what his strengths are, see what his weaknesses are. See how you can overcome anything he has to offer. Just to train your fighters, have them hit the bag and skip rope and develop stamina, that doesn't mean anything. Get it out of your head this is just some blooming gymnasium. This is a school where these guys come to learn their lessons and where you should be learning them, too."

Patience would prove to be the key in analysing fighters, and Dai would tell Arcel that he;

'...shouldn't jump to conclusions too fast, I should have the patience to see if my first impressions were right. If I wasn't going to be patient, I wasn't going to be a trainer or an analyst, at least not a very good one'.

Ray Arcel would be greatly influenced by Dai's sage advice and would apply his understanding of fighters to all of the boxers he would handle throughout his long career, 'Every young man that came to me, I remembered what Dollings had told me. I made a complete study of his personal habits, his temperament, because there are some people you can scold and some people you have to be careful with. No two people are alike. And unless the kid was obviously not cut out for the ring, I always took my time figuring him out.' Arcel would become exceptionally successful as a trainer of champions by following Dai's advice. The first champion that was trained by Arcel was Benny Leonard, who would become world lightweight champion after his defeat of Freddie Welsh. In the years that followed Ray Arcel would train a total of eighteen boxing champions, with the last time that Arcel worked a championship bout being when he was 82, working in the corner of Larry Holmes, assisting Eddie Futch in a successful title defence against Gerry Cooney in 1982.

Dai Dollings was still training fighters in New York some ten years after his arrival in the United States, and remained as critical of many of those who would call themselves boxing trainers as ever, stating in 1926 that 'Unless a trainer can outdo or equal his pupils, prove the efficacy of his methods by his own physical condition, show that the strict application to his principles, as embodied in himself, is potent proof of his knowledge, he cannot truly claim he is a real trainer.'

It was through his willingness to undergo the same training alongside those boxers that he trained that Dai attributed much of the success of the fighters that had fallen under his care, and he would say that 'close personal contact is the only way to study your man' and that the trainer should 'become acquainted with his habits, his exercises, the food he eats, his character, personality and will power'.

As a result of maintaining a rigorous personal training regime, Dai was as physically fit as ever, so much so that he was prepared to throw out a challenge to 'any man my years in the world to a series of athletic contests comprising a 100 yard dash, one mile run, five mile race, ten mile run or walk, or to swim any distance up to and including five miles' despite having been 67 years of age. In 1917, Dai had proved his toughness through having supposedly swum five miles when the temperature was fifteen below zero at Rye beach.

Dai maintained that three quarters of the boxers that he had handled suffered from indigestion, with few having paid 'the least bit of attention to the selection of their meals' and having relied too heavily on meat as a staple of their diets. Dollings had given up meat over two years previously, and would try to impress upon his boxers the importance of a vegetarian diet, believing that 'meat causes more kidney trouble than alcohol. It inflames the organs and clogs the system, yet we frequently read that some great fighter had four or five steaks during the day. He rarely ever lasts long in the ring.' Dai believed that there was more nourishment in one pound of fresh green peas than in the same quantity of meat or eggs, and believed that parsley and leeks among other greens were an invaluable part of any diet.

Dai Dollings believed that he knew 'the capabilities of the men I work with better than any other trainer, because I do everything they do'. One heavyweight that could attest to the personal fitness of Dollings was 'Big' Bill Brennan, who would go on to fight Jack Dempsey and Luis Angel Firpo, amongst others. Brennan had heard that Dollings could run as well as any youngster, although Dollings would later recall that he had initially laughed when Dai had made his initial appearance at Brennan's training camp;

"'Why you poor old man," said he "you'd collapse after a half mile, come on and I'll kill you off." He started off at the lope most boxers use; I kept pace with him and when I had gone five miles Brennan was puffing and said, "They didn't lie about you, old-timer." Then I dashed in front of him away in the lead and had his dinner ready by the time he got home.'

Dai retained a great deal of faith in the ways of the old-time fighters, and believed that the boxers of the modern age were "to the old-timers like hothouse flowers are to posies that grow out in the open" and that the old-timers alone "can teach the modern fighters how to hit, block, duck and all the other ring knowledge needed by good fighters". Dollings would long maintain that 'Position is the secret of 'itting', bemoaning the fact that "'Arf the fighters today is too close to their man. They don't get no power into their punches. And the fighters of today ain't got the endurance. I've never seen a

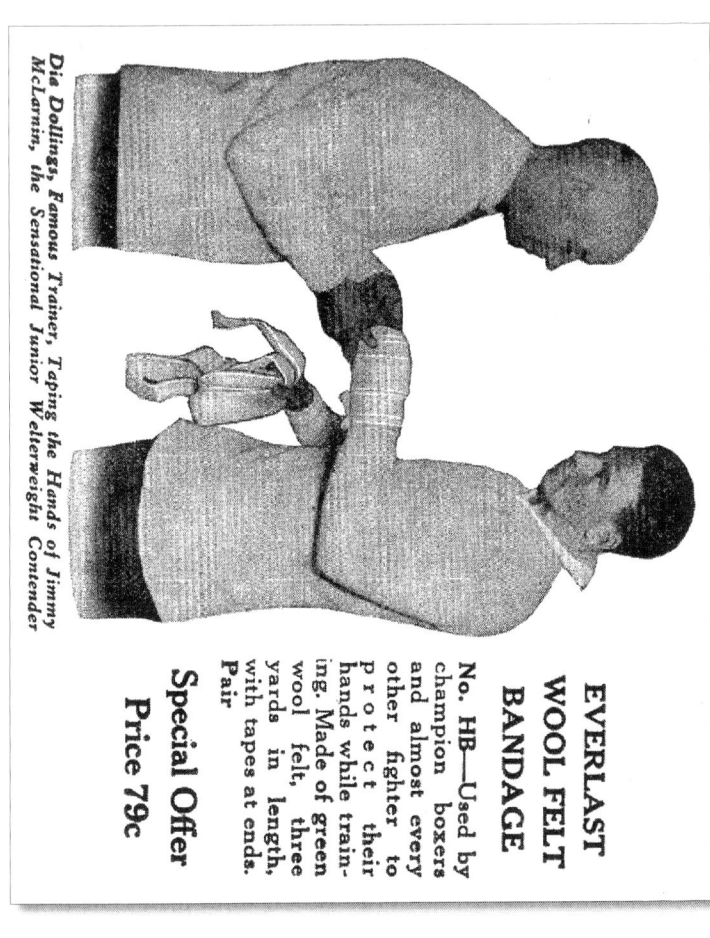

Dai Dollings advertising Everlast bandages

mon that's got the endurance I 'ave. I can knock a mon out wit' me 'ead – the Liverpool they calls it. I learned that un in the booths.' The veteran bare knuckle boxer believed that he owed his toughness to his schooling on the boxing booth of William Samuels which had provided the "best school of all" and where a fighter had to "learn all the tricks or you'll get bloody well done for."

Dai Dollings could still be found at Grupps in 1931 when he was interviewed by a reporter while having been engaged in training Dave Shade for his 420th fight against Joe Anderson of Covington. He had long since developed a reputation as being a talented masseuse as well as being one of the best rubbers in the business, and still found his skills in high demand;

" I rubs ten or a dozen a day and I never gets tired. I knows how to live, I does. Look at me body. Not much of me, but doctors says as I 'ave the finest physical machine they ever see in a man of my years. I'm 65, and only weigh about 110 now, for I just got over being knocked down by a motor car, but t's the truth I'm speaking when I say I can lick 'alf of them boxers out in that gym.

There was never a better heel and toe walker than Dai Dollings, if I do say it meself, nor a better trainer or second in the ring...Many's the belt holder I trained, boxing and wrestling. I trained Hackenschmidt, the rassler; 'n Ted Kid Lewis, Matt Wells, Digger Stanley, Owen Moran, Jim Driscoll, Gunner Moir, Tom Thomas, Frank Goddard, Phil Scott, Bill Brennan, Mike McTigue, Kin Norfolk, Harry Greb, Rocky Kansas, Jimmy McLarnin, and 'eaps of others I've forgot. I been in the States now off and on sixteen years. Here too long to be 'omesick. Got two kids on the other side. Well, maybe I would like to see the old docks again or the flower show in Shrewsbury where I used to run as a kid."

Dai Dollings was still working as a trainer and corner man in 1942 at the age of eighty three and was reportedly both 'lean and leathery' and as 'straight as a whip'. The Welshman still put in a six day working week in the gymnasium getting fighters ready for their contests, and retained enough vigour to also work several nights a week as a second. Until recent years he had no need to climb through the ropes, choosing to put one hand on the top rope and vaulting over it into the ring, it was only after having broken a leg that Dai was forced to duck beneath the ropes in a manner more befitting a man of his years. Despite having one leg two inches shorter than the other as a result of the fracture, Dai still routinely walked 10 miles a day except in extremely hot weather. His knowledge of how to assist fighters in reducing their weight meant that his services were in as much demand as ever;

"The principal thing is to get 'em perspirin' and then keep 'em perspirin'" he said *"Ow do I do it? Well, sor, I gives 'em an 'ot bath in washin' soda. That opens the pores and draws out the pizen. Then I makes 'em drink plenty of water while they're sittin' in the bath. It flows right through their system, like water flushing a street, takin' all the rubbish alonf with it, through the pores. No fighter of mine ever 'as to dry out. "E can 'ave all the water 'e wants while 'e's training, save when 'e's eatin' or before goin' to bed."*

Dai also excelled at rubbing and massaging his boxers and would claim that he could rub two pounds off the body in a single rubbing;

"I usually rubs 'em for an arf hour but I prefers an hour, I rubs in two directions at the same time, like this," (Here Dai made a series of fast passes through the air like a magician palming the ace of clubs.)

"You must 'ave a solid table for good rub. A bed won't do, cause it gives too much. I can rub all day and not get tired because I uses only me 'ands, not me body. I'm the best rubber in the wurruld."

Dai remained a prickly character into his old age, having reportedly recently floored a 'young squirt' who had dared to start picking on the Welshman in a New York restaurant. Dollings gave him a straight right which put his antagonist down, forcing the younger man to pick himself up before making a respectful exit. Unlike most of the boxing world, Dai did not emphasize the importance of the straight left as the most important punch in a boxer's arsenal, believing that "A straight right beats all the lefts in the wurruld". He felt that modern fighters showed an ignorance of the correct application of the art of boxing by hitting and then falling into a clinch, and that the best method was that taught by the old-timers, to hit and then get away before resuming the attack was the best formula for success.

Despite his advancing years, Dai showed no signs of slowing down or taking things more lightly, believing that "Six 'ours' sleep is enough for mon or beast, pervisin' he ain't disturbed". Some held the opinion that his longevity was such that he would end up working until a hundred, although Dai could only forsee himself working for a few more years, saying "I says meself I've got five more years and then I'll 'ave to start takin' it easy."

Dai Dolling's remarkable tale, from his humble beginnings in Swansea as a bare-knuckle fighter and graduate of the boxing booth of William Samuels to arguably one of the foremost trainers of boxing champions of the modern age would cement his memory in the history of boxing, with the old trainer having assisted the careers of more top-class boxers than he could remember on both sides of the Atlantic. It would be true to say that none of the Welsh fighting fraternity who had once rubbed shoulders with him in the boxing booths of Swansea would ever be remembered to the extent that Dai Dollings would, having become one of the best known trainers in the boxing world, over half a century after having first raised his bare fists at the start of one of the most influential careers in Welsh pugilistic history.

Chapter 22

Peerless Jim

When Bob Fitzsimmons had come to Cardiff in 1896, his manager Martin Julian was shown about the city, and was taken for a visit to Bob Wiltshire's School of Arms, to satisfy his curiosity at the quality of the local boxing talent to be found there. Bob Wiltshire had been retained to fight on the bill of the assault-at-arms prior to the first appearance of Fitzsimmons on the boards of the Roseberry Hall, and had developed a strong reputation as being one the most highly regarded boxers in Cardiff, having at one stage unsuccessfully challenged the well-known bare knuckle boxer and booth owner Patsy Perkins for the right to be called lightweight Welsh champion. Now at the veteran stage, Wiltshire had elected to go into business as a publican, whilst also running a school of boxing for youngsters on the side.

Intriguingly, Bob Fitzsimmons manager was reportedly 'highly delighted with the displays' of the young men under Wiltshire's care. One, in particular, would seem to have stood a little more highly above the common herd, with a reporter commenting, 'Wiltshire had a class that he has every reason to be proud of, for it contains some exceedingly smart youngsters, and in one case, at least, it would surprise me if a young 'un with a terrific long reach and a taking style did not manage to capture a competition or two. He has a bit to learn, of course, but he is still very smart, and, if he improves only a little he will eventually turn out a very warm handful for some poor unsuspecting amateur'.

Although the 'youngster' is not named in the piece, it is to be wondered if the teenager in question is not one 'Peerless' Jim Driscoll. Driscoll had been born to Irish immigrants who had found housing in Cardiff's 'Newtown' area, with the majority having been employed in the building of Cardiff docks. Just a few months after the arrival of Elizabeth and Cornelius Driscoll, young Jim was born on 15th December 1880. What was an already unquestionably hard existence was made dramatically harder by the loss of his father, Cornelius, the following August when he was knocked down by a steam train in the local goods yard and lost both legs before having passed away due to his injuries. In order to make ends meet and feed a young family, Jim's mother, Elizabeth was herself forced to seek employment unloading the potato boats from Ireland where loose potatoes were gathered up by women to be sorted ready for sale. To supplement this meagre income, Elizabeth would also buy fish early in the morning from the trawlers and then re-sell them on the streets of Cardiff.

Jim's developed an interest in boxing early on in life due to the tales told by his uncle 'Patsy' who kept the Duke of Edinburgh public house in Ellen Street, and who was also part of the Assault-at-Arms Committee for Nazareth House, a sizable charitable Roman Catholic concern in Cardiff run by the Sisters of Nazareth which had come into being to alleviate the suffering of Cardiff's poor and needy. The assault-at-arms demonstration often consisted of a display by members of the local military, showing off their skills and abilities with swords, foils and single-sticks, although the main bulk of the proceedings in later years would be made up of boxing displays. In time the event would end up becoming the main annual fundraising source for Nazareth House and was eagerly anticipated as one of the highlights of the year for the boxing fraternity. Many if not most of the main boxers that first appeared on the billing were actually more familiar as knuckle fighters, and included such men as William Samuels, Patsy Perkins, Dai St. John, Morgan Crowther, Redmond Coleman, and John O'Brien as well as Bob Wiltshire himself having appeared at the event in its early years.

There can be no doubt that Jim Driscoll was familiar with many of these leading lights from an early age, having later recalled that when, *'…the late John O' Brien was training to fight Shoni Engineer, he did so in our loft, and he used to have three pigs bladders hanging from the beams as punching balls! Being light, the bladders bobbed about in comical fashion, and John had all his work cut out to hit them. His "sparring partners" consisted of his trainer, who was a fellow named Jim Sullivan, and anyone who chanced to come along to see him at work. But visitors were very rare, as at that time we had very few boxers, and so O'Brien's staff was very meagre. They say that John could do ten miles an hour on the road easily, and I believe it, because his training mostly consisted of road work, and he must have done about 20 miles or more every day, whereas present day boxers do about seven.'*

In so many ways, Jim Driscoll would be amongst the first nationally known exponent of glove fighting to have stepped out of a background of Welsh bare-knuckle boxing, where the majority of the well-known 'gloved' boxers of the time had little national fame outside the narrow confines of the fairground boxing booths themselves.

As a young boy, Jim was an apprentice at the Western Mail newspaper, and it was here that he would first recall having first wrapped the waste paper round his fists and started to 'play' at boxing with his fellow printer's devils. Amongst these boys was one particular individual that Jim Driscoll was always falling out with, and in consequence they ended up having a few rough and tumble fights, with Jim having come off the better, which naturally worried his challenger who was said to be the best boxer amongst the Western Mail boys. The boy tried to persuade young Jim to enter a local boxing competition for boys under 7 stone, in order to prove his superiority at boxing, believing that his boxing skills were far superior to Driscoll's. The boy's father was also eager for the two to settle matters in the boxing ring, and so the father and son badgered Driscoll to enter the competition as he tried to make his way home that evening after work. The two boys afterwards met in the boxing ring, with Jim recounting that;

'There wasn't much boxing about it, you understand. He may have been very expert with the gloves, but I didn't give him any time to make use of his cleverness. Just went at him, with both arms whirling and chased him about all over the stage.'

It was soon after this that Driscoll entered an amateur competition for 9 stone boys which he won, and would then go on to win a number of small local competitions for small prizes, chief among them having been a silver cup said to be worth about £5, but one which was the '...sort of article....which you have to struggle hard to pawn for one shilling if you want to raise money on it.'

After having won another of these cups and a further cheap gold watch, Driscoll began settling into the idea of boxing more seriously, as he found he had a natural aptitude for the game, although he had not developed lofty ambitions with respect to his future in boxing; 'I was only a kid, who wanted to earn as much pocket money as he could. I wasn't thinking about becoming a champion either of England or of the World at that time, but was just boxing because I liked it and because I was picking up stray prizes and small sums of money, which either looked pretty on the mantelpiece at home or else came in useful in many ways.'

With the famous boxer Pedlar Palmer, known as the 'Box o' Tricks' regularly travelling down to Wales to run competitions and tournaments, Jim managed to take a number of further prizes, and quickly developed a name for himself as a prospect for the future. It appears that it was at this stage, Jim was also noticed by 'Professor' Harry Cullis, the Wolverhampton born proprietor of a well-known boxing booth, possibly while having been a pupil under Bob Wiltshire's care at Wiltshire's 'School of Arms'.

Harry Cullis was well known for having featured some of the cream of the domestic crop of boxers to be found in the country on his booth at one time or another, with some Welsh fighters having featured prominently on his booth front. Jim Driscoll, Tom Thomas, Jim Courtney of Barry as well as Johnny Owen of Aberaman, the one-time claimant of the Welsh and West of England Featherweight Championship all served their apprentices under Cullis' guidance.

Jim would later remember that he was a lad in his teens when he had first stepped up to meet all-comers at the country fairs that were then the only training school available for would be boxers from South Wales. Jim would recall that the formula in making matches had been largely the same as it had been throughout living memory;

'The method of making matches is the same for every booth. The proprietor introduces his champions from a platform outside, and he invites members of the crowd to have the gloves on with one or other of them. Directly there is an acceptance he slings the gloves to the spectator, who at once enters the booth and is generally followed by the crowd.'

On one occasion, Harry Cullis' booth was brought to a standstill and had to close shop at Troedyrhiw, due to the difficulties that Jim and two other members of the troupe, Jim Courtney and Tom Barnes of Merthyr had with meeting a tough collier known by the nickname of 'Cock Robin'. Having accepted Cullis' challenge, Cock Robin stepped forward to take on the hard hitting Jim

Courtney, who put the collier down three or four times each round, but could not make him stay down. He eventually broke the knuckles of both hands trying to finish off his opponent.

Having failed to get the collier to give in, Driscoll then stepped up, and found to his dismay that like Courtney, he could not finish the job. 'It was my misfortune to have to try and complete the task. For two rounds I dropped this cast-iron collier again and again, when suddenly he swung a vicious punch which landed on my wrist. That wrist had been broken some time before and been badly set, the result being that it again gave way, and for the remainder of the bout I fought him with one hand.' Jim took a serious beating in the final round, stating that, '…he hit me oftener in the last round than I have ever been hit in ten.'

At the end of the booth session, two of the main performers were out of action, and at the opening of the next 'house', Cock Robin was again awaiting Cullis' challenge. Tom Barnes then rose to the challenge, telling Cock Robin in no uncertain terms that the treatment he intended dishing out would make the '…gamest man living turn it up'. Cock Robin merely smiled back at him. Tommy appeared to get the better of their bout until part way through he yelled 'My hand is broken'. Somehow Cock Robin remained on his feet, forcing Barnes to walk back to Merthyr to find a bonesetter. Only Harry Cullis and a young lad remained on the booth, and so the booth was forced to shut down for the night.

On another occasion when the booth was pitched at Ferndale Fair, Jim's friend and fellow booth boxer

Patrick 'Boyo' Driscoll came in for a difficult time when he was matched with a local 9 stone collier. Boyo had been getting the better of things, when the collier decided to swing the balance in his favour, and started kicking out right and left, forcing Boyo to jump over the ropes and into the crowd for safety. Although Jim rushed to the rescue, the collier continued to kick out, forcing Jim to also leave the ring. In total there had been six members of the boxing troupe ready and willing to engage all-comers, but unfortunately the 'mule' refused to step out of the ring, forcing Harry Cullis to send for the police in order to continue proceedings.

The life of a booth boxer was constant variety, and Jim would meet all manner of opponents on Cullis' booth, and would remember that it was also while featuring as part of Cullis' show that he would receive additional payment for having disposed of a particularly annoying customer from an unlikely source;

'It was at Pontypool Fair. One of the quarrelsome kind came to the booth, and volunteered to have the gloves on with me. Naturally I obliged and right away we had a real fight. It was a grand slam until the second round, when I connected with his chin and put him to sleep. He lay in a corner for quite a time. Later that night came a startling surprise. A sergeant and constable came along and wanted to know which of us had knocked a man out during the evening. No-one would give me away, but fearing that the police would close our show I confessed. Imagine the shock I had when the sergeant slipped half-a-crown into my hand, saying 'Good boy; have a drink.' If that sergeant is still alive I hope he remembers the incident.'

One who would retain vivid memories of the boxing booth of Harry Cullis was Norman Clark, author of 'All in the Game' having been a regular patron on the occasional visits the booth would make to Wednesbury in the Black Country;

'Cullis' booth, like most of the others, consisted in the main of a sort of tent, at the front of which was an elaborate façade of gold and red, covered with the paintings of such fistic heroes as Tom Sayers, Jem Mace, John L. Sullivan, James J. Corbett, etc., etc. It was as well perhaps that the names were supplied with the pictures; for except that some had moustaches and were bigger than others, there was little to distinguish them by. In front of the façade stood a platform, and it was on this that 'Professor' Harry Cullis, always attired in a check suit and brown bowler hat, used to parade his boxers under the flare and splutter of the naphtha lamps.'

After the introduction of the various booth boxers, Mrs. Cullis would take her usual seat at the door of the booth, and the laborious process of filling the tent would be started;

'Walk up! Walk up! Gentlemen' old Cullis would shout. 'Show about to commence. Real champions to be seen in real contests.' And one or two of the boxers would leave the platform as if to get ready for the fray. But before the tent was filled this process had to be repeated time and again, of course, and usually it was not until those inside could no longer be pacified by exhibition sparring that a start was finally made.'

Intriguingly, Clark would remember that it was while fighting for Harry Cullis that Jim Driscoll appears to have become associated with an entertaining turn that would afterwards be recalled as the stuff of legend. When the booth did not attract enough challengers to put on a serious competition, one of Driscoll's favourite resorts was to offer '*...a guinea to anyone who could hit him a single blow whilst he went purely on the defensive, not hitting at all with either hand. Up the fellows would come one after another, and in the small ring they would slog away at Jim's head for all they were worth; but he would duck and slip, side-step and retreat, and, often without stopping or parrying with the gloves or arms, he would escape their blows in most exhilarating fashion.*'

The memory of the displays given by 'Peerless' Jim would long after convince Clark that even if at this stage of his career Driscoll was not yet a champion, he was '...probably as good a boxer as ever he became.' It was Jim's schooling in the boxing booth of Cullis, avoiding all blows while on the retreat that would make Driscoll such a past-master of defensive boxing;

'He always held that, against an average sort of opponent in his class, a boxer's skill ought to be such that, if for any reason he decided to restrict himself to defence entirely, he could manage to escape all serious punishment'. Certainly, for the most part, Driscoll's superior ring craft lifted himself above the abilities of the average booth challenger, and would appear to have received very little damage other than a 'cauliflower' ear over the course of his estimated six hundred booth battles.

It appears that around this time Jim had also drawn further interest at Cardiff for his boxing skills, and would come under the care of local sportsman Bob Downey, who was also a licensee of a public house in Cardiff Bay. The first true sparring partners of Jim Driscoll beyond those that he had boxed alongside on Harry Cullis' booth were drawn from the numbers of the black seamen that were engaged for sparring by Downey. In later times, Driscoll would have a more permanent series of partners made up of men drawn from a pool of eager young boxers including Boyo Driscoll, Maurice 'Badger' Brien, and 'Slam' Sullivan. Another of Downey's acquaintances, Albert Shirley would also see plenty of promise in the young boxer, and so agreed to lend his services as both manager and backer. Jim Driscoll's professional career is recorded having begun in 1901 with a defeat over Billy Lucas in February, although from later sources it appears that Driscoll was still regularly fighting in the booth of Cullis, and possibly other booth proprietors, and definitely fought other matches not recorded in the press of the time. The majority were 'money matches' all of which Driscoll won, although the syndicate backing him had been wise enough to make sure that his many victories would not appear too easy, and thus avoid reducing the odds and risk the size of their return.

On one occasion Jim Driscoll was facing a particularly smart young boxer from the Rhondda. Driscoll endeavoured to try and keep his opponent busy but without launching a committed attack, while his backers went around accepting bets. Unfortunately the ferocity of his rival was such that it was more than Jim was prepared to stand for more than a short period of time, and so he signalled to Bob Downey for instructions.

"Not yet," was Downey's whispered response, "We haven't got all the money on". In the next round the efforts of Jim's skilled opponent became even more

Jim Driscoll sparring with 'Badger' (Maurice) O'Brien

pressing, and Jim felt he could hold back no longer. "Money or no money, he is going out this round" said Jim in response. He afterwards put his opponent out so completely that he had still not fully recovered the following day, having asked a friend "What round is this?" while dressing himself.

It is interesting to note that Jack Scarrott would clearly remember the occasion of his first meeting with Driscoll, which shows conclusively that Jim did not tour with Jack Scarrott until quite late in his career as a booth boxer, contrary to popular opinion, having already come under the guidance of Bob Downey and Albert Shirley, as well as having toured extensively while featuring on Harry Cullis' booth as a teenager. Jack Scarrott first met Jim Driscoll when Driscoll was fighting on the undercard of a fight between Dave Peters of Treorchy, the middleweight champion of Wales, and Jack Palmer of Newcastle at the Prince of Wales Circus at Merthyr on Monday 23rd June, 1902. Said to have been for the 158lb and 160lb middleweight championship of England, the twenty round glove match ended in scenes of chaos after local champion Peters was sent sprawling over the ropes in the eighth round. As he failed to come up to the call of time, Jack Palmer was declared the winner. The decision was not well received, with the referee having afterwards been assaulted by the supporters of Dave Peters, and was forced to seek sanctuary from the crowds in the nearby Vanguard Inn. Driscoll had been defeated that night by his old injury to his wrist, with the wrist having broken in the course of his fight, forcing him to throw in the towel.

It was some time later that Jack Scarrott asked Driscoll to appear on his boxing booth, with Jim having become a familiar face at boxing exhibitions for charitable causes even at this early stage of his career as a professional boxer. Prior to boxing for Jack Scarrott, Jim returned to the boxing booth of Harry Cullis once more, having fought against Dai Stevens of Tonypandy on the booth when it had been stationed behind the Ivor Arms at Pontypridd the following month on July 19th, 1902. Driscoll would long afterwards remember the fight as having been one of the toughest that he had experienced;

'I was travelling the country with a boxing booth, and when we reached Llwynypia I met Dai Stevens, who was to give me a tough fight. The conditions of the contest made it all the harder for me, for my friends had agreed that if at the conclusion of the six rounds the referee declared a draw, the backers of Stevens won their money. In addition to the referee, two judges were appointed, and in the event of them disagreeing, the referee, of course, had to give his casting vote. Well, I was naturally anxious to get it over with as quickly as possible, and, therefore, to give myself a better chance of landing a decisive blow, I sailed in, leaving myself open. The result was that I was forced to take a lot of punishment. My opponent lasted the six rounds, and though I thought I had done quite sufficient to merit the decision, each of the two judges declared a draw, so that the referee had no option but to agree, and Steven's friends won their money. For a six-round bout I thought that was the hardest in my ring experience.'

After having met Jack Scarrott, Driscoll would appear to have infrequently fought on Scarrott's boxing booth over a fairly substantial amount of time. Certainly, Jack Scarrott recalls Driscoll having turned up on the boxing booth at Porth the very next day after his second defeat of

Joe Bowker for the British featherweight title as late as 1907. Jim had by this time fallen in with another future boxing superstar in the form of Pontypridd's future lightweight title holder, Freddie Welsh, and the two had become firm friends.

The two boxers actually met on the booth of Frank Gess, who would become one of Scarrott's main boxing booth rivals in the years that followed. Frank Gess, originally from Devon, had been a booth boxer on the booth of Harry Hughes prior to having become a booth proprietor. Gess had been given a trial at the National Sporting Club in April 1898 against Alf Green of Finsbury, and was seen to take the victory in a ten round contest, and afterwards improved his standing by winning a 10 stone competition in Glasgow. Frank Gess then went back to the boxing booths, where he proved himself to be a difficult customer for those that stepped up to challenge him. In later years, his boxing booth business would be taken over by his younger brother Joe, who was the first to see the potential of future world heavyweight championship contender, Tommy Farr.

At the start of September 1907, Gess' boxing booth had been the venue for a contest that would become the stuff of legend at St. Mary's Hill fair, when it was the setting for a six round contest between Jim Driscoll and Freddie Welsh. It has been claimed that Freddie had 'stepped up' and taken advantage of the barker's offer to stay the distance with Driscoll, and began setting about the Cardiffian with kidney and rabbit punches, which he had learned how to use to good effect when in America. Newspaper reports of the time do not bear out this claim. Indeed, Scarrott would recall that the contest had initially been offered to him, although the conditions didn't suit him, and it seems that he was less than impressed with the desire of Freddie Welsh to stand on the door and collect the money.

Jack had other customers anyway, with the Scarrott pavilion being reportedly 'tested to its utmost' by the Welshmen and the gypsies from the valleys. The 'cream of the talent' was reportedly to be found at the booth of Frank Gess, who himself was not present, having been lying in hospital at Cardiff due to illness. In his place the booth was being managed by 'Young Wilmot', one of Gess' booth boxers. The main bout that took place was the contest between Welsh and Driscoll. According to the *Mirror of Life* newspaper a 'very pretty set-to was seen, the footwork of both was very neat, and many of the old timers present said it put them in mind of the day of the Dan Thomas and Nolan fight.' No decision was given at the end of the bout, which would tend to confirm that Jack Scarrott was right in his belief that the two men merely put on a show for the money.

Despite his large number of appearances before the domestic fight fraternity, Driscoll was not given the nickname 'Peerless' Jim Driscoll until comparatively late in his career, after having travelled to America to challenge for further honours on the other side of the Atlantic. After having cut a swathe through some of the leading featherweights, and having beaten Leach Cross, 'The Fighting Dentist' of New York, Driscoll was matched to fight the American champion, Abe Attell with Attell apparently having agreed that the winner of the fight would be allowed to call himself the legitimate Featherweight Champion of the World. Ordinarily the decision as to the outcome would have been left open, with the decision as to who was the deemed the victor having been made by the newspapers the following day.

The fight had ended with the majority of the newspaper men putting their decision behind a victory for Driscoll, with the Welshman having made Abe Attell look foolish from the beginning. It was Attell that had led and attempted to clinch, but found the elusive Driscoll was out of his reach, and was sent sprawling through space. A ringside critic declared that from the beginning that Attell had looked as 'cheap as a lead nickel'. At the end of the ten round bout the decision could not be in any less doubt, with one newspaper having stated that;

'Abe Attell is no longer the premier feather-weight boxer of the world. Jim Driscoll, of Cardiff, gained the honour last night. The little Briton opened the eyes of the crowd and closed one of Abe's.' Another was quick to point out the lack of damage received by Driscoll at the end of the fight in contrast to that received by Attell; *'The winner left the ring without a mark, whereas Attell's right eye was bunged up and his nose spread over the face that for years had worn a championship smile.'*

Despite the best efforts of his management to get Driscoll to stay in America, and to capitalise on his new earning powers, nothing could be done to force the Welshman to stay. This was principally due to the fact that Driscoll had made a promise to attend the annual assault-at-arms exhibition for Nazareth House at which Driscoll had given an exhibition performance for many years. His American manager, Charlie Harvey, would later recall that Driscoll sailed for England the very next day on the St. Paul, and did not even wait to receive his earnings in America before sailing, with Harvey having to bring Jim's share of his winnings to Britain some time later.

Although Driscoll's health had often been in the balance throughout his professional career, having frequently been the victim of both stomach trouble as well as having weak lungs, no-one could have foreseen his early demise at the age of forty four. His health had been further weakened by his decision to sign up for military service at the start of the First World War. What had started as just another chill had rapidly developed into pneumonia and the famous boxer finally took the long count on the 30th January 1925. His funeral would prove to be a fitting memorial to a life which had been marked by his willingness to help others, with the army as well as the orphans of Nazareth House taking part. The funeral cortege stretched through the streets of Cardiff, with thousands having gathered to pay their respects to Cardiff's most famous fighting son, as the Union Jack covered coffin was slowly drawn through the streets on a military gun carriage to its final resting place in Cathay's cemetery.

The Times newspaper would be just one amongst many newspapers to have made room to marvel at the greatness of Peerless Jim's boxing skill and at the passing of a boxing legend;

'Driscoll, in fact, was merely the perfect featherweight and as modest in pretension as he was outstanding in skill and achievement. It may be, of course, that, if Driscoll's path to fame had been less severe, his wonderful combination of boxing and fighting would have been denied to a generation which sadly

needed and still needs every example of the classic style and the chivalrous manner. One is selfish enough to be thankful for the existence of a Jim Driscoll, whatever his own personal struggles may have been.'

Chapter 23

The Bullfighter

There had been a new customer doing the rounds of the boxing booths in 1894. The youthful stranger would trudge long miles to enter the flapping canvas doorway of any booth situated within walking distance of his father's farm in Penygraig. No-one noticed the heavy set teenager amongst the excitement of the crowd, but he paid more attention to the contests that followed than virtually any of the other customers. Tom Thomas was quietly learning through watchful observation long before his entry into a boxing ring, though it was necessity rather than a need to earn a crust that would ignite a desire in him to learn how to defend himself with the fists. Having attended the local school until the age of 14, Tom was sent to an uncle in Cardiganshire in West Wales for a holiday, and it was deemed it might be worthwhile for him to stay on with his uncle to allow him to further his education at a school in Newquay.

Tom had a reticence to continue his education and decided that he would run away, and it was while tramping on the road to Carmarthen, a distance of thirty miles, that he had an experience that would change his life forever when he met a group of gypsies on the road;

'These wandering Nimrods showed fight and began to set about me in a cowardly fashion, severely slashing me with a whip. It is owing to this hiding I then received that inaugurated the pugilistic spirit that had hitherto lain dormant with me. Ultimately I found myself at home, whence I was sent to school again, where my scholastic career was a very short one, owing to my thrashing other school lads who used to pick quarrels with me, finally finishing up on my uncle's farm as a ploughboy. On coming home again, I bought a set of boxing gloves, which I carried about with me, inviting anyone to have a couple of rounds with me.'

Despite having been a quiet and solitary boy, Thomas was devouring every book that he could find on boxing and was soon afterwards roaming the farm boundaries, looking for a reason to try out his developing skills;

'One day I met a big burly fellow on my father's farm, who was packing blackberries, and I invited him to don the hair bags. Of course he accepted the offer with alacrity, and we had a bout of fisticuffs there and then. Jabbing him a bit hard on the face, my big opponent lost his temper, and, landing me a terrific blow in the stomach, he completely knocked the wind out of me and sent me rolling in the hedge side. When I came to a bit, I wanted to continue, but my opponent was generous enough to cry off to another and more opportune time, seeing the state I was in.'

Within a short while, Tom Thomas was constructing his own makeshift gym in his father's barn, and slowly developing his powerful punches on a homemade punch bag, and was more than willing to swap gloves with the stranger the very next time they met, recalling that '…after this drubbing I began to train a little, and a short time after he turned up again, and so we had another set-to, this time in the barn. This time I turned the tables, and the big chap had to quit quickly.'

After having scoured the neighborhood, Tom Thomas found that his punches had developed sufficient force to scare away the competition, and he soon found that there was no-one left to tackle, although he did have one sparring partner, who was still willing to put up the gloves, despite having had a significant handicap;

'One of my sparring partners I used to practice with had the misfortune of only having one leg, his other being artificial. He was an exceptional man with the gloves, but on one occasion his artificial leg gave way, and it was only after a considerable time had been spent in searching for tools to patch up his 'leg' that he was able to walk home again.'

It was soon after this meeting that Thomas would venture down from the mountains to learn as a keen observer at ringside of the travelling booths, although contrary to Jack Scarrott's recollections, he was not quite as 'green at the business' as Scarrott's memoirs suggest. Tom Thomas was first retained on the boxing booth of 'Professor' Harry Cullis, and while his early record is quite poorly recorded, he is recorded at having travelled as part of Cullis' booth for a number of years prior to his first recorded appearance on Scarrott's boxing booth in 1904, with some sources believing that Thomas might have even started travelling on Cullis' booth as early as

1898/1899 in the company of such notables as Jim Driscoll of Cardiff, Jim Courtney of Barry, Johnny Owen of Aberaman, and Harry Mansfield of Bristol. Tom's first recorded contest occurred in 1902, when he met Archie Cook (the mountain fighting father of Gordon Cook, future Welsh lightweight champion) on the 8th November 1902 when the booth was situated between Treherbert and Tonypandy. Thomas also appeared on at least one occasion on the booth of John Stokes. More intriguingly, it appears as the first of his booth experiences might well have occurred under the canvas covering of William Samuels' boxing booth.

The boxing writer, Trevor C. Wignall would often muse on his formative years as a young boxing fan, and frequently recalled the days when he had been just another boy in the crowd at William Samuels' boxing 'saloon'. It was here that he first met Tom Thomas, and also fleetingly wondered at the influence that Samuels' himself may have exerted on the development of Welsh boxing, having apparently been doubtful of the truthfulness of William Samuels' 'tall' tales. At the time a young Trevor Wignall was handing over the few coins he earned as a lather boy at a local barber shop to witness members of Billy Samuels' 'staff' of boxers at his booth at Swansea, Samuel's career as Heavyweight Champion of Wales had almost certainly passed into a tapestry of time-worn tales. Wignall had no other sources to verify the truth of Samuels' brush with the lions or his early meeting with Heenan or his later days with "Toff"`Wall, or sparring with John L. Sullivan. According to one clipping remembering William Samuels' early contests, Samuels had at one point even beaten Jem Mace's one

Back row from left, Bob Berry, Tom Thomas, Jim Driscoll, 'Badger' (Maurice) O'Brien

time opponent, Tom Allen, in a match at Merthyr where Allen had been made to look like a 'third-rater' despite Allen having later claimed the Heavyweight Championship of both Britain and America. Wignall would say of Tom Thomas that;

'Thomas...was the father of boxing in Wales. He popularized a style – a blend of boxing and fighting – that was slavishly imitated by all who succeeded him. His boyhood was spent as a twenty-bouts- per-day fighter in a booth – and it was in a booth, curiously enough, that I met him. We were both children, standing side by side watching our first fights. I did not think then that Thomas would become a champion or that I was destined to chronicle some of his victories.

Nor, for that matter, did old William Samuels, the owner of the tent; a gnarled, harsh-voiced bruiser of another age who smacked us smartly on the ears for leaning too heavily on the ropes. I cherished what I fondly believed was a faint mark left by that blow for weeks; Samuels in my schooldays, was the chief of my heroes. According to himself, he had fought everyone from Cribb to Mace. He was not always truthful, but he could certainly tell thrilling stories. And it was a brave sight to see him standing on the platform of the booth, waving a pair of soiled gloves, and requesting the pop-eyed lads of the period to "step up and have a do." I wonder now whether Samuels was not the man who nurtured in Thomas the wish to become a fighter. If that is accurate, he did more for boxing in his own land than he realized.'

There can be no doubt that in Samuels' own mind, and in those who had been there to witness his long career as the first real Welsh boxing champion of note, with skills developed through long years on his travelling booth, that he would probably argue that he had acted as the pre-eminent nurturing force in Welsh boxing. He would undoubtedly have been more than willing to seize the opportunity to also claim that he had also assisted Wales' first Lonsdale belt winner in his climb to the top through his example, and through the boxing displays in his boxing booth long before Jack Scarrott, or even his ex-booth boxers, Bob Dunbar and Patsy Perkins had set up in business.

After having won a heavyweight competition outright at Ystrad, Tom Thomas felt sufficiently confident to enter another competition at the National Sporting Club in London, but was defeated by the Heavyweight amateur champion of England. After re-entering in the middleweight category it was another story and Tom Thomas won with apparent ease. It was after enquiring about the possibility of further fights that Tom was pointed in the direction of Harry Jacobs, the manager of Wonderland in Whitechapel. On asking whether a contest could be found, Jacobs, Thomas recalled, '…arose from his chair, and feeling my shoulders, remarked that I was a very powerful fellow, and that I was strong enough to tackle Harry Shearing, a very promising middleweight.'

With no-one to look after him, Tom's training was simply to walk the streets of London and wait for the following week, being a stranger in the city and knowing of no place to go to train. The eventful night soon arrived, and having heard of Wonderland's reputation as a place frequented by pickpockets and the criminal element, Thomas deemed it best to take some precautions and '…left watch, chain and money with my landlord, who resided near Tottenham Court Road, and proceeded to Wonderland alone. Going into the hall, I was placed amongst the boxers, who occupied one corner near the dressing rooms, some waiting their turn to go on, and their trainers rubbing them down. I also heard some of the boys remark, "there's that Thomas of Wales, he'll get a tousing tonight with (Harry) Shearing.'

Excitement turned to worry as in the opening contests some of the fighters were carried from the ring, although self-doubt turned to determination as Thomas vowed inwardly to fight for his life. After tearing into the first and second rounds, Thomas' opportunity came in the third, after hearing Harry Shearing's seconds shouting 'Swing your left up, Harry', Thomas beat him to the uppercut, landing it squarely on the jaw. Shearing fell to the floor, motionless, and had to be carried to his corner. It was the making of Tom Thomas at Wonderland, where he would afterwards become very popular.

By 1904, Thomas was bowling them over on home turf as well back in Wales, although despite being to all appearances a picture of health, Thomas was already suffering from acute rheumatism, a condition that would cast a dark cloud over his life and future boxing career. The wonder is that despite the excruciating pain from his joints, Tom continued to train at all. If Tom had a secret weapon in his armoury to help swing the odds back in his favour, it was in the form of his trainer, Dai Dollings of Swansea. It was Dolling's skill at massage that proved to be a gift from the gods for Thomas, and it must be wondered without Dai's 'golden touch' whether he would have been able to continue in his chosen profession at all.

Through his studies in herbalism Dai had also 'invented' a strange and disgusting mix of herbs, which he had mixed into a solution which he would carry around with him in a champagne bottle in his second's bag. Despite swearing by the mixture as an elixir that would assist his boxers in achieving optimal health, Dai's fighters remained unconvinced and would try anything to avoid drinking the horrible mix.

It is most likely that it was around this time that Thomas first joined up with Jack Scarrott, having developed considerable power, but having lacked the finer skills that could only be developed through ring experience. There was no greater training ground for developing skill than the booth, where the necessity to 'beat all comers' meant that all manner of opponents were met, from the powerful ironworkers, eager to blast punches at close range, to the amateur boxers or active mountain fighters who had already dropped a few hard men around their town or village.

Despite having appeared to have fully learned the finer points of 'slipping and dodging' by this stage, the Penygraig farmer had found a novel way of working on his weaker points in-between labouring on the fields at his father's farm. Tom Thomas had engaged the services of one of his father's bulls as a novel 'sparring' partner, with one newspaper commenting, 'Tom would dance around sparring while the bull pawed the earth. Then, when at last the temptation grew too strong, the latter would charge, and Thomas would slip aside. It was nervy work, but it was excellent practise.' Tom never laid punches on the bull, but lacking a sparring partner, it proved to be the best solution available at the farm to increase his speed, although on one occasion the bull proved that it hadn't completely forgotten the indignity of those early sparring sessions;

'Tom, it seems, was leading his friend out of the yard once to his grazing ground, and was opening a gate to let him through, when the bull took a mean advantage. Tom's back was turned, and his thoughts were centred on other subjects, til they were brought back to hard facts by the shock of a heavy charge from behind. The horns missed him, fortunately, but Tom remembers that charge to this day.'

News of Tom's methods soon spread, and it wasn't too long after that the local fight crowd were referring to him by the nickname, 'The Bullfighter'. Tom was a gentle, quiet man, and appears to have enjoyed spending his time away from the gym working his father's fields, and while he would develop a reputation for being 'tight' with money, it might easily be seen as caution for what the future might hold. Tom enjoyed walking as a means of getting exercise, particularly as his rheumatism often prevented him from undergoing more strenuous roadwork, and it was this that probably earned him the reputation for not wanting to spend a penny to ride a tram, usually preferring to walk to his destination. As Thomas' career took off, he would appear at many charitable events to assist in collecting money for any worthy cause, usually performing a polished ball routine to raise funds, which does not ring true of a truly tight fisted individual. Tom, on balance would appear to be a man who took enjoyment in simple pleasures, and was known locally as 'Farmer Tom' and could be found working the land when not fighting. The quiet farmer's boy was never to be found amongst the usual flotsam and jetsam surrounding the London ring, nor did he have time for boastfulness or the crowing of would-be champions. For the promoters he was a Godsend, there was no quibbling or arguing over purses, he appeared to fight simply for the love of fighting, and in-between fights he was always toiling back on the farm.

Tom had a joke that he liked to play of writing his correspondence backwards using a mirror, which would appear to have confused some of the recipients of his letters. James Butler, the well-known boxing writer was completely taken aback at the gibberish that appeared in a letter addressed to him by 'Farmer' Tom from Wales, and appears to have been duped by the middleweight's offbeat sense of humour;

'He used to write me the most curious letters. They were written in beautiful script, for Thomas was a well-educated man, but I gave up trying to decipher the first one, thinking it must be in Gaelic. Not until later did I discover that to read his writing you had first to hold it up to a mirror! Thomas whose sense of vision must have verged upon the freakish, formed every character backwards. That was the only way he could write!'

When not practising backwards writing, Thomas also found he had plenty of practise at dodging on the boxing booths, having laid out a Blaengarw mountain fighter who came at him in a manner reminiscent of his father's bull, with Thomas only having to plant one on his chin as he 'floundered by' to put him dead out. This event would have had to have occurred some considerable time after his earlier contests, as Scarrott recounts that he had to ask Jim Driscoll along with other booth boxers Harry Mansfield and Dave Wallace to speak up on Thomas' behalf to his father who was unhappy about him becoming a booth boxer. Jack Scarrott did not meet Jim Driscoll until 23rd June 1902 after the match between Dave Peters of Treorchy and Jack Palmer in a match that was billed for the English middleweight title at the Prince of Wales Circus in Merthyr. Thomas' first appearance on the boxing booth must have been some time after this, as Jack recounts that at the time Driscoll, Mansfield and Wallace were 'three of the best men in England, and Driscoll had still been employed as a boxer on Harry Cullis' booth for some considerable time after this date.

The next challenger on the booth proved a little trickier, and was well known as a man willing to strike up a match with either the knuckles or the gloves. 'Bullo' or 'Buller' (Dai) Rees was a well-known footballer at Aberavon, who had recently beaten Bill Lane of Cwmavon in a forty round match held on the mountainside, according to Scarrott's recollections. They had long been rivals, despite Bill Lane having long reached the veteran stage of his boxing career. Both were ex-army men, with both men holding the respective championships of their regiments. Due to arguments between their followers as to who was the superior fighter, and a few 'minor' scraps which failed to settle matters once and for all, a match was made for them to meet on the mountainside near Cwmavon in July of 1900. The stipulations for the fight were, for once, well laid out. The match was made for £10 a-side with the knuckles, being two minute rounds with a minute's

Jim Driscoll, Tom Thomas, and Freddie Welsh

interval, 'to a finish'. Despite Bill Lane having been forty-two years old to Bullo's twenty one, betting favoured the veteran at 3 to 1 on Lane.

The opening rounds started well, with both men showing their skill to good effect, with the greater hitting power of Rees being balanced against the 'better science' of Lane. Bullo was steaming ahead until the sixth round, when a right cross-counter under the heart caught him napping, and it seemed as though the tide might turn in Lane's favour. Bullo Rees came back with all the strength of youth, and punished Bill Lane with impunity. It was in the thirteenth round that Lane received a crushing blow and his arm gave way. Bullo continued bashing away until the plucky Bill Lane could take no more, although the contest continued until twenty seven rounds had been fought in a knuckle fight that lasted over an hour and twenty minutes. Presumably their rivalry was never fully laid to rest. Tom Thomas had a far easier time of things with Bullo Rees, having taken Jack Scarrott's advice and successfully side-stepped the knuckle fighter turned glove boxer, and put him out in the second round with a hard punch to the chin.

With Tom Thomas taking on all comers and improving all the time, it was only a matter of time before the money men came calling, and he would soon leave his booth career behind, although he did fight at least one match for John Stokes at Tonypandy fairground, having met and defeated Bill Griffiths of New Tredegar on Stokes' booth on August 15th 1904. The stage was set for a showdown for the middleweight championship of Wales, and on the 22nd July 1905 at the Queen Street Hall, Cardiff, Thomas had his chance against Harry Dunstan, the middle-weight champion of the British Navy. Thomas found the bout to be a step up in class and a trial by fire, using 4 oz. gloves for £25 a-side and a purse offered by the promoter. Despite having been put down twice in the second round, it was Thomas that came out on top. The third found them both throwing leather without any regard to defence, but it was Dunstan that was left more battered from the encounter. At the start of the fourth, Dunstan held out his hand in token of his defeat. Thomas was soon afterwards being picked as a likely candidate to fight for the British middleweight title. The chance became a certainty with Thomas having been picked to meet Charlie Wilson of Aldgate in London for the title, and the very first Lonsdale gold belt on the 20th December 1909.

Tragedy struck while in training when Tom's knee gave way while undergoing his roadwork, with the unfortunate boxer having been overcome with rheumatic pains. The resulting injury was so bad that a horse and cart had to be used to relay him back to his training quarters. Only the close attention of Dai Dollings in massaging out the affected area helped to ease Thomas' misery. There were grave doubts as to whether the afflicted boxer would be able to go through with the contest in the event that the old malady took hold, particularly as the area had to be massaged by Dollings at the end of every round of practise with his sparring partners.

Even before entering the ring, there were concerns that Thomas might have his chance of taking the championship belt taken from his grasp through these cruel turns of fate. Despite these worries, it was Tom that came out firing on all cylinders, shooting out a left that landed flush on Charlie Wilson's nose. A retaliatory left from Wilson was checked by Thomas' raised arm, and Thomas was straight back at his taller opponent, landing three left hands to the face without reply. It was at this point that Wilson switched his attentions to the ribs, and dashed in to punish Tom, but with little effect. The 'Bullfighter' was pulling out all the stops, and despite the injury to his knee, was seen to be slipping Wilson's deliveries in 'grand style'. Each time Wilson found his opponent was out of distance, and even his better shots were 'only just grazing his objective'.

Getting to close range it was all Tom Thomas, landing to the throat and then ducking underneath a counter, and scoring again to the face. He blocked and parried, slipped out of the way and let his left fly for the face and throat once more. As the round progressed it was Thomas that scored again and again as he targeted the face, with Charlie Wilson eagerly trying to land on the body. Each time, it was Thomas' footwork that took the sting out his opponents work, making it impossible for him to land with any real force. At the end of a fast round, practically all the real work had been done by Tom Thomas, while Wilson returned to his corner having suffered from the effects of Thomas' hard left, with a trickle of blood starting from his left ear.

In the second round Charlie Wilson fared no better, with Tom Thomas continuing to launch a heavy handed assault with his left to his opponent's rapidly reddening face. Attacking to the body again, the majority of Wilson's hooks fell short, and he paid the price, receiving a series of hard jabs in reply. Shaken, Charlie Wilson launched a hard left hook, which sent Thomas back, but within seconds he had recovered and started jabbing to the face once more. The Welshman then launched a powerful left hook that caught Wilson on the chin, sending his stumbling backwards across the ring with his head up and hands down. Tom was straight after him, finishing his man with a crushing right to the chin. The effect was plain to see, as Charlie Wilson was spun in a circle and dropped like a log onto his back with his arms extended. At the count of five, Charlie turned over with his nose to his knees and showed the crowd he had plenty of guts, trying to push himself up using his hands three times, but his efforts were in vain and he slipped down on to his face. The fight had ended in just 5 minutes and 27 seconds, and Tom Thomas of Penygraig was the British middleweight title holder, and was afterwards given the first solid gold Lonsdale belt to prove as much.

Sadly, due to Thomas' recurring problems with rheumatism, Thomas was unable to secure the belt and ended up getting beaten by Jim Sullivan, who relieved him of both the belt and the title the following year. To add insult to injury, Thomas had invested in a case for the belt, so sure was he that he would make it his own after two more successful defences. He was forced to sell it to Sullivan at a knock down price. Although he would appear in the ring a couple of times afterwards, it was clear that Thomas was no longer the man he once was. No-one could have then guessed that he was so close to the end. A few weeks before his death, Thomas took part in a benefit performance at Ogmore Vale, and deciding to travel late across the mountains he lost his way, getting caught in a shower of rain, which would appear to have led to a recurrence of the rheumatic fever that had dogged him throughout his career. His heart finally gave up the fight on 13th August, 1911. He was only thirty one years old.

Chapter 24
Gentleman Joe

It was some time in 1901 that Jack Scarrott decided to set up shop back at Pontypridd, where he had spent so much time as a boy. The census of 1901 records Scarrott's occupation as having been an 'amusement caterer' a catch-all occupation, covering all manner of fairground based employments. Jack Scarrott appears to have been doing quite well for himself, having made enough money at the boxing booth trade to purchase a travelling caravan, in which he lived with his expanding family, the latest addition having been John Jnr., born in Llanelly the previous year. One can assume that Jack's caravan was stationed in an area often used by the travelling brigade, with Jacob Studt having featured prominently amongst his neighbours.

There are few indications in the local press as to the size and scale of Scarrott's growing booth at this time, although it can be gleaned that the booth still remained a travelling enterprise. It would appear that Jack Scarrott

Joe White

often employed transient fighters who could also frequently be found on the boxing booths of other proprietors. One of Jack Scarrott's more regular fighters was the black boxer, Frank Reed of Cardiff. On 14th September 1903 Reed knocked out Billy Morgan of Swansea, a regular on the booths of both William Samuels and Patsy Perkins with a 'terrific stomach blow' in the third round at Neath, on an unnamed boxing booth, but which appears likely to have been that of 'Professor' Harry Cullis.

Frank Reed had featured prominently in the early days as one of Jack's black booth boxers. In his day, Reed had made a name for himself as a boxer of some standing, and was well thought of, being more than willing to appear on the behalf of numerous charities alongside other boxers to assist in raising funds through his boxing skills whenever he was able. Sadly, Reed would afterwards become a figure of some pity after a boy had thrown a stone at him and destroyed the sight in his left eye. The sight in his right eye had also become affected, and some time afterwards he lost the use of his right eye as well, with the end result that he had to be led about as he became completely blind. Reliant on the charity of well-known local sportsmen, Harry Wheeler and Bob Downey, a benefit event was arranged at Andrews Hall, Queen Street, Cardiff late in October 1906 for the unfortunate ex-booth boxer. Many prominent Welsh boxers would make an appearance in order to raise funds for Reed, including Tom Thomas, Dave Peters, Joe White, Billy Morgan, Ivor 'Butcher' Thomas, Johnny Owens of Aberaman, and Jim Driscoll amongst others.

It appears as though Frank Reed's situation would not end up being greatly improved, despite the efforts of the boxing fraternity to help him. In August 1908, Reed was brought up in court after having been accused of assaulting one Elizabeth Cops with a stick. Reed had previously threatened her after she had taken offence to him begging at her door, and had apparently lost his temper and struck the lady in question on the forehead with his walking stick. Despite having lost his eyesight, the booth boxer was too quick for the husband of the lady in question, who appeared at the door after hearing her screams and Reed tried to lay about the husband as well. Having had no previous record, Frank Reed was afterwards let off lightly by the court, having been ordered to pay £10 in costs or receive two months imprisonment, and was also given a month in which to find the money.

By 1903, 'Mr. J. Scarratt's Pavilion' had set up shop at Pontypool. In April of that year, a special twelve round contest for £20 a-side and £15 prize money was arranged between another of Scarrott's regular performers, George Roach of Rhymney and Young (Frank) Dixon of America. Both had attendants familiar to the majority of the crowd, with Jack McCarthy of Rhymney standing in Roach's corner, and Dai Thomas of Neath and Syd Russell of Cheltenham supporting the American challenger. Dixon appears to have been well beaten, having gone down in the second round, and was floored again on attempting to rise. Dixon's seconds failed to secure a foul from the referee and timekeeper, one John Cameron of Ebbw Vale, and the decision was given to George Roach.

The following month, the well-known sporting newspaper, 'The Mirror of Life' stated that Jack Scarrott's booth was visiting the Rhondda valley after an absence of six years with his team of boxers which consisted of Frank Dixon of Boston, U.S.A (11st. 6lbs.), Mike Riley of Liverpool (10st. 10lbs.), Syd Russell of Cheltenham (9st. 12lbs.), 'Darkey' Thomas of Neath (8st. 4lbs.), Frank Reed of Cardiff (11st. 8lbs.) and George Roach of Rhymney (11st. 6lbs.). Sadly there appear to be no accounts of the fights that Scarrott's booth boxers engaged in over the course of their tour, with local newspapers having reported on contests within the boxing booths on a very infrequent basis.

Of the men appearing on Jack Scarrott's booth at this time, very little is known. Perhaps the most familiar name to fight fans was 'Darkey' (Walter) Thomas who originally hailed from Melincrythan and was well known to Swansea fight crowds, having defeated Dai Morgan, the brother of the well-known Swansea champion, Billy Morgan in 1899. The rematch between the two men was fought on 27th October 1899 at the Niagara Hall in Swansea, with Pedlar McMahon seconding Darkey Thomas. The initial rounds were 'pluckily' fought out, with both men having been seen to receive much punishment from each other. In the fifth round the tables turned in Darkey's favour and only the call of time saved Dai Morgan from being counted out. By the seventh round, Darkey put paid to Morgan's hopes, and Morgan was knocked out amidst considerable excitement. After having beaten a fighter by the name of 'Diamond', who also hailed from Melincrythan, Thomas also went on to meet Dai Morgan's brother, Billy, on the booth of William Samuels when it was stationed at Neath fair the same year, although he was unsuccessful in beating the more experienced Swansea champion.

Darkey had been a fixture on the boxing booths for a number of years, and appeared at the Ivor Athletic Club in Swansea as late as 1910, when he was matched against Eddie Carsey, an American boxer and travelling companion of Freddie Welsh in an eight round contest. The contest turned out to be a disappointing affair with neither man showing at their best, and with the crowd appealing for the men to fight instead of killing time. It wasn't until the seventh round that either man began to show anything like their true form. Carsey was seen to good advantage in the eighth round, exhibiting 'rare skill and vigour' and was 'easily the better man', although Darkey was visibly much lighter and stuck 'gamely to his task'. At the end of the contest the referee would give the decision as being a draw.

By 1905, Jack Scarrott had attracted a new boxer to stir the interest of the crowds, a travelling Swiss-Canadian middleweight boxer by the name of Joe White. After arriving in the United Kingdom, Joe White had shown early promise after beating the boxing booth owner Alf Harry in a twenty round contest at Liverpool. Joe White appears to have touched down in Wales for the first time in 1902, having defeated the well-known middleweight champion, Dave Peters of Treorchy on the booth of Harry Cullis in August of that year. White afterwards met and drew with the great black American boxer Bobby Dobbs at Cardiff and Mountain Ash Pavilion. Another attempt to beat Dobbs at Liverpool saw

White go the distance in a twenty round bout, but the decision went to Dobbs.

On the 2nd January 1905, Jack Scarrott had engaged boxing sensation, Frank Craig, another visiting boxer from New York, who would become better known as the 'Harlem Coffee Cooler'. Craig had beaten a large number of the leading domestic boxers on his arrival in 1894. His first victim had been the Cardiff born booth boxer John O'Brien, who in a humiliating defeat had been schooled by the 'coloured' middleweight champion of America inside two rounds. Jack Scarrott promoted a ten round contest between Frank Craig and Joe White on 31st December 1904 at Newport which was won by Joe White on points. The elation at the victory against Craig led to a renewed sense of confidence in Joe White, who afterwards stated his desire to travel back across the border into England, telling the local press that; 'I consider myself capable of beating anyone in England, and I am open to fight any one of them'. Surprisingly, Jim Courtney of Barry would also pull off a spirited stand against the Coffee Cooler a few days later on 2nd January 1905 surviving a six round contest of two minute rounds. Having made such a great showing against such well-regarded opposition, Jim Courtney was retained to fight a fifteen round contest the following Saturday, and was offered the startling sum of a golden sovereign for every round that he survived. Sadly no record appears to have been made of the outcome of the contest.

Joe White became a popular figure in his adopted hometown of Cardiff, being widely known by the nickname, 'Gentleman' Joe due to his unusual attire, consisting of a silk hat, frock coat, spats and gloves. With the nature of Joe's work providing an inconsistent pay packet, he often found himself either homeless or near penniless, and so out of necessity could usually be found either going into or coming out of one of the local pawnshops, with his unlikely dress suit providing a few coins to keep White's head above water until his next contest. When he had received a purse, White would make his way back down to the pawn shop to be re-united with his favourite outfit.

After having settled more or less permanently in Cardiff, Joe White had fallen in with no less a local celebrity than 'Peerless' Jim Driscoll, who was quick off the mark to see some opportunity for merriment at White's expense after he had 'liberated' his favourite outfit from the pawn shop once more. White's silk hat would be snatched by the mischievous Driscoll, who would sprint off up the road with the hat perched on his head at a jaunty angle, with Joe White chasing along behind threatening all manner of punishments unless his hat was returned.

On another occasion, Jim Driscoll met up with White at a local dance where White had been fortune enough to engage two young ladies in conversation. After having spotted his friend, Joe White drew Driscoll aside and confessed that he had no money, and suggested to the featherweight boxer that he might find his way clear to inviting the three to have some refreshment. Seeing his opportunity for a practical joke, Driscoll strolled up to the group and entered into conversation. After some time had passed, White began to signal to Driscoll that the time was right to make the invitation. Driscoll was quick to seize the moment; 'Joe, why don't you ask the ladies to have a cup of tea?' White pretended not to hear, but Driscoll spoke louder, and as White found his pockets quite empty, he had nothing to say. 'Ah, well' Driscoll remarked, 'if you won't stand the ladies a cup of tea, I will' and promptly ushered the two ladies in the direction of the refreshments, leaving Joe White behind.

One contest that does not appear to have been recorded in either the records of either Joe White or Frank Craig occurred around the time of White's earliest days in Cardiff. White had found himself down in the gutter after having fought at Liverpool and had been forced to walk the best part of the distance back to Cardiff, and was dependent on the charity of Jim Driscoll and others after his arrival. Shortly afterwards, Frank Craig drifted into the town, having taken on the name of 'Battling' Craig. His entrance into the sporting life of the town was a dramatic one, after he had walked into Ye Olde Dolphin Hotel and had agreed to a bet that he was willing for a man to smash a ginger beer case on his skull for a round of drinks. The stunt was performed successfully and apparently without any injury to Frank Craig whatsoever.

Jim Driscoll and a few others afterwards made a match between Joe White and Frank Craig, which came off in a large marquee a short distance from Cardiff Arms Park. New chairs were hired specially for the occasion, and the straw from the marquee floor was taken up and placed under the ring, with the promoter, Johnny Thomas stating that it might come in handy later. While there was a crowded attendance, the boxing itself did not satisfy the paying public. The preliminary bouts proved to be disappointing, and the main contest also failed to live up to expectations. It was in the second round that Driscoll, having become frustrated by the wild swinging blows of Frank Craig, shouted 'Now!' which was the signal for White to skilfully avoid one of the Coffee Cooler's swings, and immediately countered with a sharp blow to the chin.

It proved to be the winning punch. Frank Craig stood erect for a second, shivered from his head to his heels with the effect of the right hook and then fell like a tree before a woodsman's axe onto his nose. White had won. The suddenness of the ending did not go down well with the crowd, and the man in charge of the takings decided it was best to total up the money in the promoters house, where he was joined a short while later by the others. The takings were good, and the promoter was eagerly discussing the prospect of further shows when the party broke up. Coming out into the street, they noticed a bright glare in the sky, and had not proceeded far when they discovered that the marquee was on fire. Evidently some of the dissatisfied spectators had chosen to make their displeasure known, and had used the straw that they found under the ring to set the marquee ablaze.

Having received the winning end of the purse Joe White was for once able to pay his bills, while also benefitting from the generosity of his friend, Jim Driscoll, who would often lead a crowd of his boxing friends into his mother's house for a slap up meal. It was at this time that another contest was made against Dave Peters of Treorchy, and was fixed to come off at Pontypridd. The contest was something of a tame affair which caused a great deal of concern to one of Joe White's main backers, the ex-featherweight bare-knuckle champion, Morgan Crowther. Crowther shouted at White to get busy while White was caught up in a clinch, and White not feeling the same sense of urgency as Crowther replied, 'There is plenty of time, I told you the seventh round'. Joe White won, and after having received the verdict he called out to Crowther, 'Did you get 3 to 1? I told you I would beat him'.

Joe White would afterwards progress in quick fashion, having regularly appeared in Jack Scarrott's boxing booth in 1906. At the start of September, White was receiving 'considerable interest' from fight fans at Aberavon Fair field who paid their entrance fee to Jack Scarrott in order to see how White would fare at the hands of local pugilist, Patsey Sullivan, who it was believed would give White a hard contest, and who endeavoured to beat 'Gentleman' Joe within eight rounds. That Sullivan failed to beat White was not entirely unsurprising, as White was considered to be at 'the top of his form' having reportedly won 'no less than fifty hard-fought fights' over the course of the summer. Joe White would appear to have attached himself to Jack Scarrott's booth for a uncertain amount of time in 1906, and also served as a second in a match between the 'well known 9st. champion' Jack Jenkins of Port Talbot and Dick Williams of Cwmavon, billed as 'a powerful local exponent, who scaled nearly 13 stone'. Jenkins had been seconded by Will Jones, a popular footballer from Aberavon and Bill Griffiths, the well-known boxer from New Tredegar with Williams having been seconded by Joe White. Despite the near 4 stone weight disadvantage, Jack Jenkins 'proved the cleverer' man and was awarded the verdict by the referee, Ted Jones of Merthyr.

Joe White would have one other recorded appearance on Jack Scarrott's Pavilion at Llanelly on the 6th October 1906, when he took on the referee of the Jack Jones vs. Dick Williams bout, Ted Jones of Merthyr, for £10 a side and a purse in a twelve round contest. A capacity crowd turned out for the event, with the battle having been a 'severe struggle' for supremacy. In one round, White had been knocked over the ropes, but was seen to be a convincing winner. By 1907, Joe White had sealed his reputation as having been a cut above the average booth boxer after having beaten Andrew Jeptha on points in a fifteen round contest billed to be for the 144lb Welterweight title at Merthyr Tydfil. It was after this that White was engaged to be the test by which the skills of a rising boxing star by the name of Freddie Welsh could be gauged. With the local talent having heard of Freddie's rapid rise to the top in America, no-one could be found at his own weight to fight him and so Joe White was engaged to put the young Pontypriddian to the test. On September 16th 1907, Welsh met Joe White at Pontypridd, conceding the veteran nearly a stone and a half for a stake of £100 a side and a purse. There was no doubt that Welsh would be meeting a difficult customer, with a newspaper reporting that Joe White was '…nearer forty than thirty and for his years a phenomenon. He has won his fights through his extraordinary reach and his signal skill in avoiding punishment.' In Freddie Welsh, White would find a twenty one year old possessed with greater speed and stamina, with a persistent nature and a great deal of variety in attack, although in the early rounds White outpointed Welsh with his long left hand, and clinched effectively to avoid punishment.

White would find that youth would be served, and discovered that Freddie Welsh was a boy who could utilise all the resources of a lighter man fighting a heavier and considerably older one. Welsh forced the pace in every round, with the strength exerted in keeping up with the younger man inevitably taking its toll on White. In the final rounds, Joe White found the pace too hot to keep up and at the close of the sixteenth round, White's right eye was very quickly closing up. Realising that the victory was now beyond him, in the minute between rounds, White quickly consulted with his seconds and afterwards crossed over to Welsh's corner and told Freddie Welsh of his willingness to retire, and congratulated the victorious lightweight as having been the best man at his weight that White had ever seen.

Although Joe White would afterwards fight a number of contests against lesser opponents, it was undoubtedly the swan song to White's professional boxing career. Joe White would remain a proud 'adopted' Welshman to the end, and when in 1919 he became a victim of tuberculosis and was nearing the end of his life, he chose to return to Cardiff to die, with his last words from the carriage that took him to the sanatorium being that he hoped that his feelings of gratitude for the kindness that he had received in Wales would be passed on to those who might remember him.

Chapter 25

The Mighty Atom

The first thoughts of any onlooker who had stumped up his entrance money to enter Jack Scarrott's Pavilion in 1908 was that he was witnessing a boxing demonstration by a freak or a fake. Nothing could prepare the casual observer for the appearance of Jimmy Wilde. It was quite by chance that Wilde had even found himself standing on the platform of Scarrott's boxing booth and taking challenges from the crowd as the 'boy champion' at all. From his earliest days he had spent his days fighting on the streets while spending whatever pennies he could find to gain entrance to the boxing booths where he would witness challenger after challenger being slaughtered by the boxing booth champions, and had imagined that one day he would be the challenger to step up and wipe the floor with them. Right from the beginning Wilde had found his spindly four stone frame could withstand any amount of pressure from boys weighing up to nine stone, over twice his weight. It would set a precedent that remained throughout his boxing booth career.

It had been after having already been sent down the local pit that Wilde's luck changed when he was apprenticed to Dai Davies, an old mountain fighter, who would later become Wilde's father-in-law. It was Dai who would give Jimmy his first brief 'lessons' in boxing, taking advantage of brief lulls in their work to demonstrate such basic punches as the '….upper-cut, the straight left, the essentials of defence: virtually all he knew.' These impromptu fighting tips soon gave way to bedroom boxing lessons in Davies' tiny Tylorstown house, where after pushing the bed against the wall and piling all the furniture on top of it, Jimmy quickly learned how to fight in an exceedingly small space, and the necessity of quick footwork and bodywork in turning such cramped boundaries to his advantage, an essential skill in the 12ft ring of a boxing booth.

It was a short time afterwards that Jimmy Wilde found himself haunting the boxing booth of Jack Scarrott when he was not working down the coal mine. Jack Scarrott, Jimmy would remember, was 'a grand fellow', although at first Scarrott found difficulty believing that the youth was already able to meet and defeat men twice his weight, and initially refused Jimmy's request to fight on the front of the boxing booth and would only consent to giving him a job keeping the boys from sneaking in under the canvas at the back of the booth. The boys that routinely congregated there thought that Wilde would not represent any opposition to their entrance, but found that the skinny waif that blocked their path was more than they could ever have bargained for;

'I had to start a fight with one and before I knew where I was a dozen of them had started to mill towards the tent, and with my back towards it I was having the stiffest ten minutes of my life. Boys went down like ninepins, the crowd grew rapidly, youngsters joining in and older men roaring at the spectacle. But Jack Scarrott's roar terrified my opposing army at last and scattered them.'

It was after this early introduction into life on the booth that Wilde would become one of Jack Scarrott's booth boxers, with Jack frequently making disparaging remarks about Jimmy's skinny arms and legs, and the fact that the boxing gloves looked like pillows on him. Still, with the knockouts piling up, and with each one representing five shillings a time for Jimmy, Scarrott soon found the booth was busier and more lucrative than ever. The first boxing writer to have witnessed the startling abilities of Jimmy Wilde was Trevor C. Wignall, the Swansea born sports reporter who had worked on local paper, *The Cambrian*, before having received an invite to write for London based newspaper, *The Standard*. 1908 had seen Wignall enter Jack Scarrott's booth for no other reason than to shelter from the rain. Boxing booths had long held a fascination by Wignall since his earliest days at Swansea, although he had only once dared to enter the ring on one occasion as a challenger himself;

'I held up my arm when old Billy Samuels, a boyhood idol, dared my gang to have a do. Only once. I was hit with everything save the tent pole…And after I crawled away from the Samuels' booth I was prepared to vote for the instantaneous suppression of boxing.'

At Jack Scarrott's boxing booth, Wignall found that the booth had only moved on a little from the days when Samuels had been introducing such notable members of his staff as Dick Ambrose, George Lucas and Pedlar McMahon for the entertainment of the crowd, Scarrott's booth, he deemed, was 'typical of its period', with Scarrott's reverberating voice being strong enough to drown out the roundabout organs as he invited the crowds to step up and challenge one of his champions. Inside the booth was nothing more than 'a small sawdusted ring, illuminated with the smoky gleams of naphtha lamps' and it was here that Trevor Wignall would witness the giant-killing properties of Jimmy Wilde for the first time;

'He was so tiny, so frail, so lacking in everything that connotes strength and endurance that, instead of creating interest, he produced in the onlooker a feeling of pity. He was no more substantial than a wisp, or a shadow. He appeared to be about ten years of age, his babyish face held an expression of child-like innocence, his arms and legs were pipe stems, his body was no thicker than a weight-lifters biceps, and he was said to weigh exactly 84lb. I paid four admission fees to that booth, so fascinated was I by this odd apparition, who, I felt, would have been better off in a cot, or in his mother's nursing arms. And four times I saw him crack down grown men twice his size with punches that travelled only inches.'

It was after having beaten a flat footed and hunchbacked but eminently capable local scrapper by the name of Dai Chips that Jack Scarrott began to take the boy skeleton seriously enough to ask whether Wilde might consider travelling to the town of Caerphilly when he deemed it was time for the booth to move on. It was

*Jack Scarrott, Jimmy Wilde and trainer,
George Ballieau with his daughter, Peggy*

at Caerphilly that the legend of 'The Ghost with a Hammer in his Hand' was further strengthened. One night a particularly vocal onlooker insisted that the knock outs that were now piling up around Wilde's feet were fakes. After having made his suspicions known, the heckler was invited to step up and meet the boy champion. Approximately seventy seconds later, the challenger was stretched out on the ring floor.

"What have I been doing?" he asked on joining the land of the living once more.

"You've been boxing Jimmy Wilde."

"I have been boxing, d'ye say?"

"Yes."

"And who's won?"

"You haven't"

"I haven't, but that little ---- Wilde couldn't hurt me."

"Well, I don't know about that, you are certainly not on your feet."

"Who isn't on his feet?"

"You aren't"

"Then where am I?"

"You've been knocked out."

"You're a ---- I haven't started with him yet!"

The enraged opponent then jumped to his feet and made for Jimmy shouting "Let me get at him". Seeing the confused state of his antagonist, Wilde side-stepped, with the result that the confused challenger dived through the ropes and knocked himself unconscious for a second time. A bucket of water was used to revive the man once more, and he left shortly afterwards with a disgusted look on his face.

On another occasion after having knocked out another challenger who refused to accept that Wilde's knockouts had been on the level, the unfortunate victim suddenly came back to life and started going berserk. A number of the booth spectators as well as the referee and the doorkeeper all found themselves punished by the confused man's fists before he returned to the ring docile and unaware of his actions before lashing out at Wilde and then collapsing in a heap. Another bucket of cold water was needed to revive him. It would take a full half an hour to convince him that he had been beaten and he afterwards rushed round the booth lashing out at anyone in his path. Bewildered and saddened after his actions had been explained to him, he left the booth without challenging a second time to try and win his money.

It was to be a number of years before Trevor C. Wignall would hear of the wondrous Wilde again, after having settled into a job as a news-editor for a sporting paper in London. By this time Wilde had progressed far enough as a boxer to seek out new opportunities beyond the limited opposition on offer on Jack Scarrott's booth and had approached popular sportsman and athletics handicapper, Teddy Lewis of Pontypridd. Teddy had been the manager of a venue known as the 'Millfield Athletic Club' at Pontypridd where hundreds of local miners would pack into its tight confines to witness displays of local boxing talent. The two men would strike up a friendship as well as a business partnership that would last throughout Wilde's professional career.

Having been told that a couple of callers were waiting on him by a porter, Wignall was ushered in, and discovered that Ted Lewis was already waiting for him. At this stage, Teddy Lewis was already quite deaf, with his ear trumpet having provided no aid in furthering the conversation. Almost hidden behind him was Wilde, who appeared to have grown no larger in the time since Wignall had first seen him. He was however, now clad in what Wilde imagined might be thought of as the height of London fashion at the time. Wilde was wearing a worn rusty black suit, a shabby bowler hat and brown boots, with a thin bamboo cane hanging over his left wrist. It transpired that Ted Lewis had hoped that Trevor Wignall might be able to use whatever influence he possessed to enable Wilde to get a contest at The Ring in Blackfriars, which was a pugilistic venue of the lesser variety for the vast bulk of London fight fans who would never have a hope of passing through the doors of the exclusive National Sporting Club.

Having heard Lewis' pleas, Wignall found himself sufficiently intrigued by the re-appearance of the Welsh booth boxer to take Lewis and speak on his behalf to Dick Burge, who was at that time managing The Ring. Burge agreed at once to give the newcomer a trial, although as he later admitted, had he known how fragile Wilde had looked prior to agreeing to allowing him to fight at the venue, both Wignall and Lewis would have been shooed clean out of the building. When Jimmy actually stepped foot inside the building for the fight against his opponent, 'Matt Wells' Nipper on January 20th 1912, a meeting was quickly called between Burge and his associates. They were deeply concerned that their pint-sized pugilist had arms and legs like sticks and looked as though he might end up broken in half by a single punch. The Nipper, by comparison, was an experienced fighter, who had been in with some of the leading lightweights, and had already earned a reputation for putting down a line of challengers that had been placed before him. It was a long time before it was decided that Wilde should be given the opportunity to show what he was made of, with Dick Burge and his associates fearing the possibility of prosecution for manslaughter in the event that Wilde did not make it out of the ring alive.

At the beginning of the bout, when Wilde appeared and ambled on down to the ring, he was accompanied by utter silence, the disbelief of a crowd that finds it hard to comprehend the spectacle that it is witnessing. The silence was broken by the sound of a spectator hooting with laughter, and within minutes the place had erupted with the sounds of merriment from all corners. For Wignall, at ringside, it was the only occasion he ever witnessed when a fighter would have been forgiven for walking out due to the hilarity that his appearance had created. The 'Nipper' skipped lightly to his corner, believing that he would quickly bring an end to the contest. He could not have been more wrong. According to the newspaper, 'Boxing' 'Nipper was 'out-boxed, out jumped and beautifully polished off before the gong had sounded for the first round.' Wilde flicked a punch at the face of Nipper, which his confused opponent tried to counter, but Wilde side-stepped and scored heavily in return with lefts and rights to the head. The Welshman proceeded to throw hooks and jabs and swings on Nipper with carefree abandon, finally putting his confused opposition down with a right to the chin. Three times the Nipper went down before he was finally out for the count in the very first round.

Despite the dramatic manner in which Jimmy Wilde had beaten his man, there was not an abundance of column inches written to tell of the launch of a new fistic superstar. Enquiries by Trevor C. Wignall as to whether Wilde might be perceived as being a fighter of sufficient quality to warrant a showing at the National Sporting Club were icily received by the manager of the N.S.C, Peggy Bettinson. Ultimately the door was shut, with Bettinson growling, "Do you want me to be pinched for manslaughter? Get him to grow a bit before you speak to me again".

This refusal to accept that Wilde had crossed the threshold into boxing stardom persisted into 1914, when Peggy Bettinson finally relented, against his will, to match Wilde against the French champion, Eugene Husson. Wilde won, in devastating fashion in the sixth round of a fifteen round contest and finally convinced London that this most unlikely of boxers had a quality denied to almost all of his peers. His first defeat would come the following year in a contest against hardened Scotsman, Tancy Lee. Jimmy proceeded with the fight despite having been taken severely unwell with influenza just a few days before. This was despite the protestations of Ted Lewis himself, who begged Jimmy to pull out of the contest, "You haven't a chance" Lewis shouted, "Not a chance in a thousand, Jimmy; be wise and call it off." Jimmy was adamant, stating that he had never missed a fight and never would. At the weigh in, Wilde was wearing an overcoat and a thick scarf, which in itself was not deemed as unusual as his weight was invariably so marked in contrast to his challengers that he could afford to weigh in fully clothed. To the casual onlooker he also appeared to be no paler than usual, as he was usually as pale as a sheet anyway.

The decision to fight proved to be disastrous, and while Wilde lasted seventeen rounds against a very capable opponent before his trainer, George Ballieau threw in the towel, it was clear that he was not himself from the outset of the very first round. Simply put, the handicap was too great. After the contest, even Peggy Bettinson could not fault the heart of the little ex-miner, telling a newspaper that it was too much weight for Wilde to have given away, 'Years ago we used to grumble at a couple of pounds, and he is giving twenty. Why, even middleweights, yes – and heavyweights would object to that. He is a game boy and a wonder.' Jimmy would make no excuses for his failure to topple Tancy Lee, although he was quick to take manager Ted Lewis to task for having told Ballieau to throw in the towel, remarking, "No matter in what contest I am engaged hereafter, please understand that however bad a time I may be passing through, under no circumstances is the towel to be thrown into the ring. If the other fellow can put me down and out, then let him have the full credit for it. Please don't forget this."

It wasn't until 1916 that Jimmy Wilde won the nationwide adulation that he so richly deserved, after taking the British flyweight title, and with it the first ever Lonsdale belt offered at the weight. The first six rounds would see Symonds develop a long lead on points, and hit the Welshman so hard in the stomach that Wilde would afterwards say that "I thought the end of the world had come. My eyes went round and round, and for a moment there was only red and grey mist in front of me." Wilde fought back with great determination in the seventh round and was cheered throughout. The stinger had come for Symonds in the eighth round when he had stepped back to avoid a punch and caught it full on his Adam's apple, knocking all the fight out of him. He had difficulty breathing afterwards and it was only his overabundance of both heart and courage that kept him on his feet for the remainder of the fight. By the twelfth round it was all Wilde, and he fought with such terrific dedication that Symonds was brought to his knees, and Jimmy Wilde of Tylorstown had lifted the British flyweight title. It was a moment of glorious celebration and one long remembered by Jimmy Wilde;

"I remember grinning round as John Douglas lifted my arm, Johnny Basham darting into the ring and kissing me, Ted Lewis looking as though he had broken the bank at Monte Carlo, and the glorious realisation that the English flyweight championship and Lonsdale belt were mine. Hosts of Welshmen were on their feet and singing 'Hen Wlad fy Nhadau' and 'Land of my fathers.'

It was after this crowning achievement that Jimmy Wilde would return to fight for Jack Scarrott one last time, in which Jimmy would perform a feat that would afterwards be remembered as the stuff of legend;

'It was grand to see Jack, although it was strange to accept an offer to fight for him. It was at the Tredegar fairground, Pontypridd, and Scarrott asked me to box four hours for him – four hours ! – for a purse of forty pounds. I seemed to be back in the old five shillings days when I put on the gloves, but the welcome I had from the crowd warmed my heart.

In three-and-a-half hours, without taking the gloves off, I had nineteen knock outs to my credit. Then half an hour's rest, and another four. The booth had been emptied for the interval, and another admission fee was charged, but I think it was more crowded than for the first show, and I have rarely known a crowd to rise to me as that one did.'

Jimmy Wilde would afterwards wipe out the mark that had been put against his record by Tancy Lee, after having beaten his old adversary in eleven rounds. By 1919, and with the First World War over, it would be truthful to say that he was alone in his weight division. Perhaps one of the highest points of his career at this stage was when the Prince of Wales stepped into the ring, the first time that royalty had done so, in order to congratulate the diminutive Welshman when he beat the American, Joe Lynch, on points. In many respects he had already achieved the honour of being thought of as the world champion long before he began to trade gloves with such American stars as Jack Sharkey, Pal Moore and the Zulu Kid, but the contest that would remain in memory longest was that against American opponent, Pete Herman that was held on January 13th 1921 at a tournament that was held in London that went wrong from the start.

Jack Sharkey (U.S.A) and Jimmy Wilde prior to their fight in 1919

Wilde's opponent, Pete Herman, a dangerous fighter, was many pounds overweight, and refused to weigh in at ringside. Wilde had been advised not to risk his health against a skilled boxer who was allegedly 20lb heavier than himself, principally by his protective manager, Ted Lewis. Unfortunately, by the time the vast weight difference came to light, the Prince of Wales had already taken his seat. Once this had been pointed out to Wilde, nothing could persuade him from entering the ring, so eager was he to see that his Prince was not disappointed. The resulting fight was a tragedy that should never have happened, had it not been a twenty round bout, the result might have been different as Wilde was afterwards shown to be ahead by the fifteen round. By the seventeenth it was all over, with Jimmy having been knocked down with a terrific punch.

Sadly it was the beginning of the end for the great Jimmy Wilde. The fight that he should never have entertained was his last, coming after a long layoff and having lost the abnormal reflexes that had raised his star so highly. He was over thirty years old, and had been out of the ring for a long time. The magic that had accompanied his ring performances had long deserted him, although the guaranteed financial reward of £15,000 had proved enough to tempt him out of retirement to meet Pancho Villa in New York in 1923. Wilde would be shockingly beaten down to the floor inside seven rounds, but what was thought outrageous at the time was that after the close of the second round, Jimmy was smashed sideways by a vicious right hand punch after the bell, which would have been declared foul, and the match called to a halt, had Jimmy's seconds protested more strongly. He never fully recovered from the beating that he received that night, and would fail to recall what had happened to him long after his body had been dragged to his stool.

It might be wondered whether Jimmy Wilde had a secret that helped raise him above the standard of his contemporaries. For Jim Driscoll, who seconded Wilde in many of his famous contests, and who had taken Wilde under his wing at the start of his professional boxing career, it would be a combination of factors that would make Wilde one of the greatest pound for pound boxers the world has ever seen. Firstly, Jimmy's brain was faster than the majority of boxers, allowing him to see an opening and take immediate advantage, whilst also being fast enough to cover up or retreat with minimal risk to his own safety. Secondly, Jimmy had phenomenal strength for a man of his size, no doubt developed in his early days, where like so many others he had cultivated unnatural strength in his upper body and arms through his use of a heavy pick and shovel in the early days when he had toiled for a living alongside the other coalminers in Ferndale pit No 8. For Jim Driscoll, the speed of Wilde was key in ensuring that few men could stand before his punch;

'His hitting power…comes naturally with his strength and his speed. Besides he punches properly, so with his speed he is bound to hit hard. It is like a racehorse kicking. A racehorse can do as much damage with its kick as a heavy carthorse entirely owing to the speed of the kick.'

Jimmy's reflexes were so sharp that he could avoid a blow with the slightest twitch of the head, and it is this perhaps that also assisted him in his many victories by the knockout route. He had a natural ability to time his blows when his opponent was moving in, and so the weight of his opponent was added to the considerable force of his own fists. Others believed that Wilde was a genius in strategy of a kind rarely seen in the ring, one whose fast brain enabled him to think what might be possible and might be expected three moves ahead, 'like a man playing chess'.

His ring record would be disputed for many years after his retirement from the ring, with Jimmy once having supposedly calculated that he had fought an astonishing 864 times over the course of his career. It seems likely that when his first pit-head bouts and boxing booth challenges were added in, the total could conceivably be over 1,000. Perhaps it was his schooling in the boxing booth of Jack Scarrott that had assisted in making Jimmy Wilde the greatest flyweight of all time, Jimmy would later acknowledge as much himself;

'Scarrott, in the early days, had helped to make me, as he had helped to make many other champions. Little known, hardworking, certainly not wealthy, it is Jack and his fellow booth owners who prepare the champions of the boxing world. I have always believed that the booths get too little attention, and that many world-beaters in the making never get more than a pound a fight.'

Chapter 26

Scarrott's Pavilion

In the years that followed, Jack Scarrott's Pavilion remained a travelling enterprise, although following the discovery of such a lucrative asset as Jimmy Wilde, it would appear that Scarrott's funds improved greatly. By 1907, Jack Scarrott had enough funds at his disposal to secure the services of a very special boxing star to appear on the boards of his booth at Neath Fair in September, with Jem Mace, the ex-bareknuckle champion of Britain and the World having been retained to showcase his skills. Over the course of his exhibition, Mace had a 'set-to with a couple of youngsters' and was seen to perform as brilliantly as ever, despite having been seventy six years of age. He afterwards refereed a six round contest between Jack Williams of Skewen and one 'Walters' of Pontypool, with Williams having emerged victorious on points.

One sign that Jack Scarrott was on the up and up comes from a few brief accounts in local newspapers of a number of run-ins with the law beginning in April of 1908. Having apparently purchased a showman's traction engine to assist in pulling his travelling vans, boxing booth and associated equipment, Scarrott would end up being charged at Newtown with having taken his engine over the Brynderwyn bridge without a licence in contravention of the County Council by-laws. Jack Scarrott had crossed the bridge despite the fact that he had been warned on a previous occasion, and was subsequently fined £1 including costs.

Jack Scarrott was also in trouble the following month in Montgomeryshire, when he again decided to use the engine to pull several carriages through Llanfyllin without the necessary pass, having been meant to have renewed the licence for each day of travel. The lack of paperwork was uncovered by P.C. Parry of Meifod who had checked at the license office at Welshpool and found that Scarrott had not filed any request to travel that day. Worse than this, Scarrott had also been charged with similar offences at Welshpool, Berriew and Newtown. To add insult to injury, P.C. Parry had asked Scarrott for his license at Meifod, and had received 'a good cursing on a Sunday' for his pains. Jack Scarrott hadn't bothered to appear for the hearing and in his absence was fined £2 and costs. Intriguingly, like so many other showmen around this period, Scarrott is recorded as also having gone into business as the proprietor of a travelling cinematograph, which would no doubt have also accounted for the increase in takings and allowing Scarrott to expand his boxing booth business and other entertainments to a greater degree than he was previously able.

Throughout this time it would appear as though when not running the boxing booth, Jack Scarrott was still resident at Pontypridd with his occupation having been listed as 'Master Showman' on the Census of 1911, and was apparently away 'on tour' at the time that the census was taken. His daughters, Annie Maria and Phoebe Scarrott are listed as having been engaged in 'Assisting in business domestic' at this time. He certainly did travel far and wide while running the booth, with the booth having appeared at Brynmawr and Bargoed in 1909 and Troedyrhiw in November of 1910. With the transient nature of Scarrott's business, and few reporters having made it their business to report on boxing matches held in a local fairground, there are only a few short reports to be found regarding the development of 'Jack Scarrott's Pavilion' around this time period.

Pontypridd would depend on Jack Scarrott's booth for the majority of its fights around this time, with the booth having had a particular attraction for an aspiring young boxer by the name of Frank Moody, who was regularly haunting Scarrott's booth with the hope of getting in. Moody would go on to take both the British and Commonwealth middleweight title as well as the light-heavyweight crown in a career spanning twenty years in which the 'Pontypridd Puncher' as he became known would meet over two hundred opponents, but it was Jack Scarrott's boxing booth that had initially drawn him to boxing as he would later recall;

'Whenever Jack's booth was pitched in Ponty, and he had several seasons of a few weeks each during the year, I spent all my spare time hanging about outside, looking for a chance to get in. That big tent, with its life-sized posters of famous fighters on the

outside, fascinated me. Later on I was to become very familiar with the inside.

He always had a coloured man or two among his performers. With shiny black faces and glistening white teeth they would stand with beaming smiles on the platform outside the booth before the show commenced, and they always drew a crowd. Out Jack would swagger, a cane in his hand with which he would strike one of the coloured boys on the back and ask the spectators,

"Well, who's going to black his eyes tonight?"

He would then give each of his scrappers a tremendous build up, finishing his flowery speech by brandishing a pair of gloves "Well, who wants them?" he would ask and toss them into the crowd. Not once did I see those gloves tossed back again. Always there was someone anxious to put on the mitts with one of Jack Scarrott's boys.

I used to long for the day when, without fear of being laughed at, I could snatch the gloves and walk boldly into the booth. Of course, I always pictured myself as a hero of the ring – what boy wouldn't? Standing outside the tent I wold conjure up visions of myself battling with one of the coloured boys before a wildly excited audience and then winning with a spectacular knockout. The prospect of being beaten never occurred to me.'

February of 1912 proved to be a disastrous month for Jack Scarrott when a fire broke out in one of his show vans while he was travelling on the road from Tonyrefail to Gilfach Goch. Having driven the engine pulling a wagon up the hill, the wagon was unhitched and Scarrott and his two of his men started to make off in the direction of Tonyrefail with the intention of getting another van. Before they had progressed far, one of the employees noticed smoke coming from the wagon that they had just left. Jack Scarrott ended up running to a house a quarter of a mile away to get buckets to use in dowsing the fire from a stream near the burning wagon. Unfortunately it was too late to save any of the contents, and the show wagon was quickly turned into ashes due to a strong breeze. Jack would lose his musical organ, scenery and stage properties in his fire, which was only partly covered by insurance. Scarrott believed that the fire had probably started due to sparks from his engine falling on the covering of the wagon and burnt through, setting light to its contents.

Despite this setback, 1912 would turn out to be the breakthrough year for Jack Scarrott after he set up shop at Tonypandy in July. In addition to more well-known future champions, Scarrott's was also featuring a host of less well known boxing talent. Principal amongst these had been Evan Evans, who was better known to the crowd as 'Pom Pom' due to the frequency with which he landed his blows. Pom Pom had been widely perceived as having been the 'middle-weight champion of the Rhondda' after having knocked out Walter Parfitt of Pontypridd. His claim to the title wouldn't last long, as the following week Billy Rosser of Porth rose to the challenge, despite having been out of condition and much shorter and lighter than Evans. In a brief but dramatic fight, Pom Pom was sent down for a count of nine in the opening round, but recovered well enough to launch an attack with a 'stiff left that almost did the trick'. At the start of the second round, Pom Pom landed again on the jaw, but Rosser was seen to bore in, and drove the champion to the ropes. Rosser punished Pom Pom as he liked, and amidst great excitement Pom Pom sank to the floor and was counted out. It was a disappointing night for Pom Pom, it having been the occasion of his twenty eighth fight and his first ever defeat.

August would see Scarrott lay himself open to a night of problems while acting as both promoter and referee in a match between Lewis Williams of Penygraig and Shad Lewis of Ystrad, who appeared to be about a stone heavier than Williams. The contest had been fixed for eight two minute rounds for a small purse of fifteen shillings. Both men had asked Jack Scarrott to referee the contest, and the men reportedly went at it 'like game cocks' as it had been agreed that if both were on their feet at the end, the contest would be declared 'no decision'. After six strenuous rounds, in which Williams was seen to have the advantage on points, both were very weary. Scarrott, who was performing the duties as referee, suggested that he would stop the contest and divide the money equally. The crowd yelled their disapproval at the decision, forcing Scarrott to respond, "Very well, I won't take the responsibility, find another referee."

Another referee was found, but one of the men objected to a new referee being appointed at such a late stage in the contest, and so Jack Scarrott consented to allow the bout to resume. The match was fought to its full length with Williams finishing up with the lead on points. Jack Scarrott again tried to judge the contest as being one of 'no decision' which led to further disagreement on the part of the crowd. Hoping to pacify the spectators, Scarrott then suggested that as Williams had a slight lead on points that the purse be divided with ten shillings going to Lewis Williams and five shillings going to Shad Lewis. Williams objected to this state of affairs, saying that if he had won the contest he wanted the full fifteen shillings. Realising the difficulty in persuading Williams to accept his decision, Scarrott was forced into calling the contest a draw.

By September, crowds were descending on Tonypandy in such numbers that Jack Scarrott was forced to lease the Tonypandy Hippodrome, a large building that had previously been used as a circus and a music hall. The decision to open a permanent venue in the heart of such a bustling town proved to be a wise one, and 'at least 2,000 people' paid over their entrance money to witness a number of boxing contests at the venue. The crowds quickly grew week on week, and by December crowds were being turned away despite the addition of extra accommodation to allow a further 1,000 people to enter the building, with Jack Scarrott featuring Percy Jones of Porth and Jimmy Wilde as the main attractions.

The bumper houses continued until March of 1913 when Jack Scarrott decided to make good on a lucrative offer to sell out his interests, and elected to set up his travelling boxing booth business anew at Pontypridd. Within a month, he was back on the travelling circuit, having set up his booth at Mountain Ash, and taken a great deal of the local talent with him. By November, Scarrott had set up shop at Treherbert and would afterwards return to Tonypandy by December.

January 1914 saw Jack Scarrott try to repeat his earlier good fortune at Tonypandy by leasing the Pavilion Rink, which housed an astonishing 4,000 spectators, although he would find that he now had competition from across the road at the Hippodrome that was being run by a syndicate with his one-time referee, Ralph Lile at the helm. Thankfully, with his long familiarity with the local boxers, it was not long before Scarrott would be competing with the syndicate on equal terms, having attracted well known boxers Young (George) Dando of Merthyr and Charlie Yeomans of Pontypridd to appear on Saturday January 10th 1914 in a fifteen round contest. A crowd of approximately 3,000 turned up to find out who would emerge victorious. The contest had begun cautiously with Yeoman's scoring with his left and cleverly avoiding Dando's dangerous right hand. Evidently he was not cautious enough, having taken a count of nine in the fifth round, and was then sent down again after a light right hand. The contest warmed up in later rounds with Dando being seen to advantage with hard right hooks, while Yeoman showed his worth with the straight left throughout. The tenth round proved to be a showstopper with Dando having turned an unplanned somersault after having thrown a punch that was successfully ducked by Yeomans. With both boxers having shown a clever defence, the decision was given as a draw, which was seen to be an unpopular verdict by Dando's supporters.

It was not long before the increase in boxing activity in the town would draw the attention of the East Glamorgan Baptist Association, with the Reverend J. Nicholas of Tonypandy being keen to address the problems at the Associations half yearly meeting. He was quick to condemn the contests as lowering ' the morals and habits' and 'prostituting the ideals of young people' and called upon the twenty thousand Baptists of

'Young' (George) Dando of Merthyr who appeared on Scarrott's Pavilion in January, 1914

Glamorgan to stand behind him. His stance would be supported wholeheartedly by Principal Edwards of the Baptist College in Cardiff, who agreed that it was essential to make the protest as powerful as possible, believing that 'one boxing booth did more harm to the young people than twenty public houses'.

The attack would lead Jack Scarrott's current referee, Mr. Sam Williams, to make a protest on behalf of Jack Scarrott from the ring at the end of the month, stating that the aim of the management was to show boxing in its most 'scientific aspect'. The contests were intended to show 'a sense of justice and fair play and admiration for a true and quick arm and a love of that pluck which had made Britain what it was'. Williams was also quick to point out that since the hall had been opened there had been less drunkenness and no hooliganism in the district. They would therefore continue to endeavour to provide 'clean sport in the ring' and would '…provide it undeterred by any outcry from tyrannical killjoys'. To reduce the risk of further attack, Williams also made the offer that any objectors should send a deputation of three onlookers to claim three free seats in order for them to witness the contests held there themselves before condemning the sport based on second hand information.

Jack Scarrott does not seem to have been greatly affected by the protest, having apparently decided that it made more sense to follow the same formula that he had worked so lucratively at the Hippodrome the previous year. Having established another permanent boxing venue, he quickly sold out his interests and moved to the Drill Hall at Merthyr, where he put on a return match

Dai Roberts (Caerau), Lightweight Champion of Wales

between Young Dando and Charlie Yeomans. Scarrott would appear to have still had enough influence despite the pressure from the Hippodrome and the Pavilion Rink at Tonypandy to attract a good class of boxers, having put on contests featuring Merthyr based boxers Eddie Morgan and Billy Eynon in February.

Curiously, the match that Jack Scarrott recalls as having come off when he was in charge of the Pavilion Rink between Dai Roberts of Caerau and Joe Johns of Merthyr appears to have come off on Saturday February 7th, 1914 after Scarrott had already moved to the Merthyr Drill Hall. Possibly as the matchmaker for the month previously Scarrott may still have had a financial stake in the outcome of the battle. Over four thousand spectators turned out to how Roberts, the lightweight champion of Wales would fare against Johns. Joe Johns was seen to show good form throughout, and while Dai Roberts scored in fine style at times, Johns exhibited superior defence and the use of his left hand was very good. At the end of the sixteenth round both men appeared fresh, but the bout came to an early end in the following round when the referee brought a premature end to the contest on the grounds that he had been continually annoyed by the appeals from one of Johns' seconds and could not therefore give a just decision owing to the fact that his attention was being continually diverted from the boxers. Despite the announcement being met with a hostile reception, the referee insisted on the bout coming to an end, and no winner was named. The match would stand as the highest point of Jack Scarrott's permanent boxing booth, and while the takings were probably the most that Scarrott would earn throughout the lifetime of his booth,

From left : Joe Johns (Merthyr), boxing booth proprietor Alf Harry, and Tom Bates (Neath)

he would appear to have had no desire to settle permanently in either Tonypandy or Merthyr and by August Jack was setting up his booth at Aberavon beach once more.

Chapter 27

Scarrott's Amusements

No record of the movement of Scarrott's boxing booth appears to have been found in 1915 until July 10th when Scarrott set up shop at Ferndale and Billy Fry met and beat Sam Coombes, both of Tylorstown, in a well contested fight. A six round draw between Dai Chant and Eric Jones also gave some indication as to why the district was producing so many good boxers, with one of the boxers stating, "I am out of condition, mun, I have not done any trainin' only mountain fighting" to the bemused referee, Charles Barnett. Ivor Day and Billy Eynon also met at the Pavilion the following week in a twenty round contest consisting of two minute rounds for side-stakes of £50. Day did well in the early part of the fight, but Eynon, who had the benefit of Jimmy Wilde in his corner, put his rival down for a number of counts with the result being a draw.

With the First World War in full swing it might be imagined that there was a lack of men available to fight on the booth, and a lack of spectators able to pay over their money in order to witness a contest. Newspaper reports would indicate that Jack Scarrott was quick to divert his attention from boxing towards more lucrative entertainments, and followed in the footsteps of such showmen as the Studt family, investing in roundabouts and other amusements. Scarrott appears to have done exceedingly well, having been in a position to make significant donations to various bodies supporting the war effort while stationed in Bargoed. In July, Scarrott donated the whole of the proceeds for one evening's entertainment, a total of £31, to the 'Welcome Home Fund'. Jack Scarrott would hold another benefit evening in August on the McDonnell field for the local lodge of the Royal Antediluvian Order of Buffaloes (R.A.O.B) raising £11 3s. and 6d., and contributing the money to be used for the benefit of the Starving Prisoners of War Fund run by the Evening Express newspaper in Cardiff. The amount donated to the cause by Jack Scarrott would make up over a quarter of the funds collected at the McDonnell Hotel and passed onto the Hanbury Lodge of the R.A.O.B since the start of the war.

By November 1916, Jack Scarrott had decided to settle in Bargoed for the immediate future, electing to open the Skating Rink Pavilion near the Bargoed railway station to further expand his business. The building was remodeled at considerable expense. There were roundabouts, with music supplied by Scarrott's brand new organ, shooting stalls, which it was hoped would 'form a great attraction to the young men and intending volunteers for our home defense' as well as refreshment stalls and further entertainments for the children. Dog shows and baby shows had also been scheduled to be held at the venue, while a large room had been earmarked for boxing as well as fencing displays, with it being hoped that the contests held there would '...make men of conscientious objectors and fit them to face their opponents without the stamp of cowardice visibly deciphered on their countenances'.

Jack Scarrott had already earned a reputation for his generosity since April when he had given a benefit night every week in order to raise funds for military hospitals and the war effort, and had handed over the considerable sum of £400 to be used to assist wounded and disabled soldiers. Over the course of his stay at Bargoed, Scarrott also announced that he would continue with the benefit evenings once a week, and by this means hoped to increase the amount of money donated to a total of £1,000 which earned Scarrott the accolade of having been '...a personality of generous disposition towards helping those who are disabled and wounded in their discharge of and devotion to duty, who so nobly fought in protection of our native land'. The money raised by Scarrott was to be shared out to provide presents for the troops on the battlefield and amongst the prisoners of war, with the necessity for Christmas puddings to be provided for the men in the trenches having featured highly in Jack Scarrott's aims.

Jack Scarrott would fall foul of the law again in January 1917, and faced a heavy fine for permitting the use of gaming machines on the premises of the Bargoed Skating Rink the previous month. Scarrott on this occasion would appear to have been oblivious to the fact that two showmen, Henry Mills and George Williams were breaking the law by using a room at the Pavilion for gaming. One Police Sergeant Row had visited the rink on the 26th December and witnessed twenty men and boys using one of two slot machines. Over the course of twenty five minutes only two people were successful in winning cheques from one machine to the value of 2d. Seventeen people had used the other machine and only one had been successful in winning a prize. In order to win, the player put a half-penny in the slot which would send a series of figures passing across. Amongst these figures was one of the Kaiser, and if the player was quick enough with a pistol, he could shoot him down to win a cheque. Scarrott believed himself to be innocent of the charges laid against him, having been told by Henry Mills that "they were not against the rules and regulations of the country". Sadly the law didn't see things the same way, with Scarrott having been blamed for permitting the use of the machines after having been previously warned not to allow their use by Police Inspector Canton. Henry Mills was fined £5 (or 28 days in jail), George Williams £1 (or 11 days) and Scarrott £10 (or 41 days).

Despite the problems with the law, Jack Scarrott remained at Bargoed Skating Rink throughout 1917, and continued to raise money for good causes. In March, Scarrott put on a supper for the benefit of the National Reserve men, and would also raise funds for the benefit of the Bridgend Cottage Hospital, the Bridgend Nursing Association and the Neath and District War Hospital. The regular benefit events at the Skating Pavilion appear to have been held as late as May 1918, after which time Jack Scarrott decided to move on once more.

The decision to do so would result in further legal difficulties after Scarrott had stationed his travelling business at Neath and Aberdare and had issued a post-dated cheque to William Evans, a billiard hall proprietor based in Pengam for the use of a piece of ground at Fleur-de-lys which Scarrott had let on previous occasions to set up his travelling fair. In March, Jack Scarrott had agreed to let the ground and had issued a cheque for £32 to cover the use of the ground for two years. In April the cheque had been refused. Jack Scarrott stopped the payment after he had requested a plan of the ground which he never received and therefore chose to stop the payment. Despite the Judge having requested an amicable arrangement to the dispute be found, this was not forthcoming and so the following month, payment was awarded to Evans with costs.

With the end of the war in November 1918, Jack Scarrott was eager to enter the boxing business again, and by December he had leased the impressive Mountain Ash Pavilion, which was capable of holding 12,000 people and on the 22nd of December attracted approximately 2,500 spectators to witness a fifteen round contest between Jim Jenkins and Private Frank Evans, who had only been released from a prisoner of war camp by the Germans two weeks previously after being imprisoned for nine months. Although he was not in condition for a long contest, Evans was shown to possess a 'superabundance of pluck' although took the count after a right cross from Jenkins in the thirteenth round. The lease of Mountain Ash Pavilion would appear to have been a short one as by May 1919, the booth had again travelled to Tonypandy, and afterwards continued to show at various other towns throughout the valleys, having appeared in Tylorstown and then Mardy in July, and afterwards travelled on to Aberavon in August.

The great days of Jack Scarrott's booth had passed and in the years that followed, his boxing booth would be recorded as having made occasional appearances at fairgrounds and towns throughout South Wales, but without the frequency that had characterized its movements prior to the War. In 1921 Scarrott re-started as a boxing booth proprietor at Caerphilly. The following year found the booth situated at Blaenrhondda in May where Joby Culverhouse of Treherbert met Jim How of Newcastle and outpointed How in a twenty round bout. Culverhouse and How would meet again at the Opera House in Treherbert in April of 1923, where Culverhouse once more demonstrated that his boxing 'science' was such that he would usually triumph over simple punching power. Prior to the war, Joby Culverhouse had been seen to be one of the most promising boxers in the Rhondda, but after being seriously wounded at the front it was thought that he would never again be able to pull on the gloves. Through sheer grit, Joby had made a wonderful recovery, despite having not quite matched his pre-war form. Both Joby and his brother Jim Culverhouse, better known as a local wrestler of some repute, would appear on the booth of Jack Scarrott a number of times over the years that followed.

Intriguingly, one individual who assisted Scarrott in locating new boxing talent in the 1920's was Teddy Lewis of Pontypridd, the boxing manager who had played such a vital role in having brought the boxing talents of Jimmy

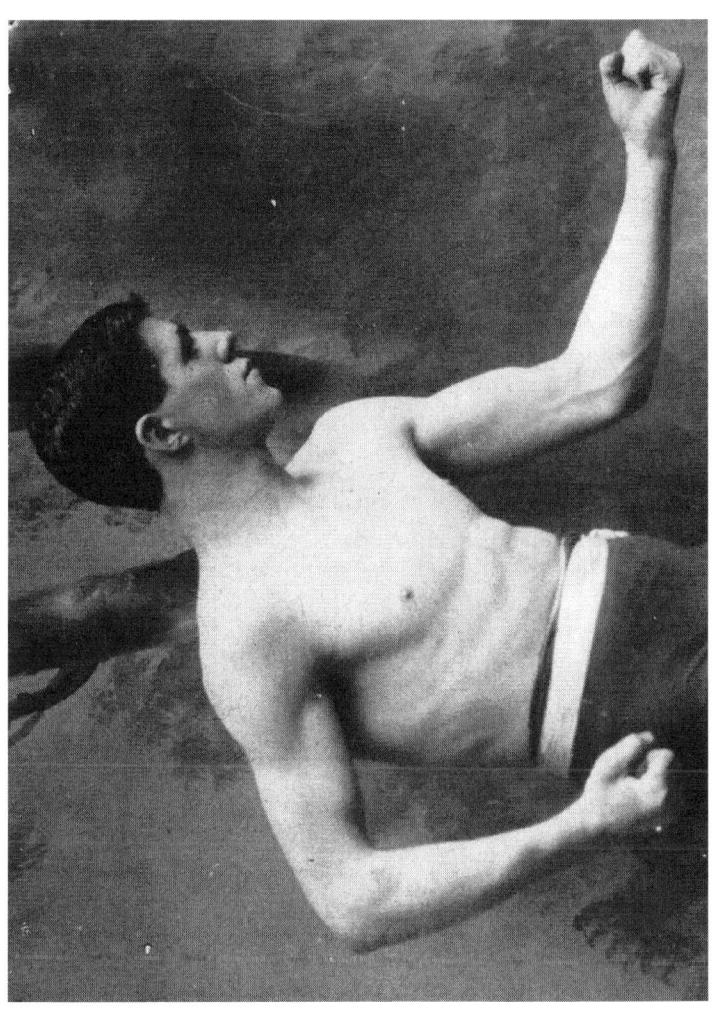

Joby Culverhouse of Treherbert

Wilde, Llew Edwards and Percy Jones to a wider audience. A contract between Ted Lewis and an unknown boxer by the name of 'Johnny' dating from the 1920's is open ended enough to allow the boxer to seek contests himself with the 'Hall Treharris' or with Jack Scarrott to pick up extra money, outside of contests arranged by Ted Lewis.

At this time Jack Scarrott was still running his boxing booth alongside his travelling pleasure fair, which had taken second stage alongside the more lucrative roundabouts and entertainments. Sadly, although he still talked about the days when he had filled the Tonypandy Hippodrome with thousands of spectators, and he still dreamed of opening another hall which would be capable of accommodating up to 3,000 boxing fans, nothing appears to have come of the idea. Certainly in the years that followed, Jack remained as eager as ever to pursue the boxing booth game, but the decline of industry in the valleys in the post-war years would mean that his dreams of boxing booth glory would never achieve the same size and scale again. The booth would appear for the odd contest in locations here and there as late as the 1930's although Jack's principal means of income would become the roundabouts and pleasure rides that ensured his travelling way of life would continue, long after the days when other boxing booth proprietors such as Jimmy Day and John Stokes had given up the ghost.

Even such well-established boxing booth proprietors as 'Professor' Harry Cullis would feel the pinch in the post-war years, and bemoan the fact that the boxers of the modern age seemed less hardy than the booth boxers of old, telling 'Boxing' magazine in 1926 that;

'...if all the boxers started in a booth, which is the only real boxing school, where the boys have to learn or get out, we should not have the retirements when lads find the battle going against 'em. They only have to hurt one of their little fingers to entitle them, they think, to retire, and this against foreigners. It makes me very ill when I read of it. I have seen, in my booth, boxers take all the gruel a man could take with my old 'tools' (gloves), *teeth knocked out, both mince pies* (eyes) *closed, 'beak'* (nose) *broken, and very likely a fractured arm, and then they were ashamed to give in. I've seen such wonderful things happen in that there booth of mine that folks would not believe if I took my oath on it.'*

Harry Cullis would remember that some of the best houses had come not as a result of any great champion featuring on his booth front, but often as the result of rivalry between two men over a woman;

'Young chaps who had fallen out most likely over a gal, would come to me and ask me to let 'em fight it out with the smallest and hardest gloves I had. I used to tell 'em that they could have four rounds, but they'd better wait til the night and bring their pals with 'em...Up they'd roll, and if a gal was at the bottom of it, she'd be there likely enough shouting advice to the chap she wanted to win, and taking his attention off his man and very likely getting him a good hiding.

This happened many times, but once a factory girl who had quarrelled with her young man promised to walk out with another one if he would beat her old flame with the gloves. He did so in my booth, but no sooner had he 'outed' his rival and left the stage to escort 'the woman in the case' from my booth than she turned round on him, called him all the uncomplimentary names she could think of, told him that she would not trust herself in the

Jim Culverhouse (Treherbert), boxer and wrestler

company of such an unfeeling brute, and turned to where her original flame was having his bruised features bathed, kissed him and assisted in making him presentable. Then arm-in-arm they left the booth, but what happened afterwards I don't know.'

These sentiments of loss for a dying age would be echoed by Joe Gess, younger brother of Frank Gess, who had taken over Frank's boxing booth in later years, and would say in interview in 1937 that the last ten years had been the 'most trying' of his career;

'My wife has stood by me loyally, and has shown great courage in 'heavy going'. The unemployment in the coal field has played havoc not only with the boxing booth, but with amusement catering generally, and, of course, there is the competition from the talkie cinema. Sometimes I have organised our shows and have fixed up good fights, but getting the people to see them has been like trying to force blood from a stone. And you must remember that we are not like ordinary boxing promoters. It is the sole means of our livelihood, not a pastime, as is the case with most of those who stage fights in Wales.'

Jack Scarrott's time as one of the foremost boxing proprietors, so closely linked to the boxing champions of the pre-war years had passed, with the old booth proprietor's business having lasted longer than a great deal of others. Jack Scarrott would recount the highlights of a lifetime spent in finding and promoting the cream of the boxing talent to be found in South Wales in 1936 to the journalist William Hughes, having outlived many of the men whose deeds he recalled.

Shoni Engineer, the Treorchy blacksmith who had risen to fame following his defeat of Pete 'Dublin Tom' Burns in forty seven rounds, and had fought an astonishing eighty five rounds against Jem Guiderell, died of erysipelas on January 17th 1894 at his lodgings in 22 Havelock Street, Cardiff, aged just 31. The condition had been brought on as a result of an injury sustained to the head after he had struck his head against a kerbstone while engaged in a street fight that had taken place on Boxing Day night in St. Mary's Street.

His great rival, John O'Brien of Cardiff, had also passed away in 1911 at the age of 43 at Cardiff Union Infirmary due to alcoholism. In his youth he had fallen under the wing of William Samuels, rapidly developing into one of the most feared fighters on Samuels' boxing booth and had toured the country, taking on all comers. As a bare-knuckle fighter he had excelled, having earned the right to call himself the bare-knuckle middleweight champion of Wales following his defeat of Shoni Engineer back in 1889. He was perhaps one of the most successful of the early bare-knuckle and boxing booth men to make the transition into gloved boxing, where his victories had secured his status as one of the most promising boxers on the domestic scene. O'Brien's glorious triumph over his great rival, Dai St. John, for the Heavyweight Championship of Wales at the National Sporting Club in London in 1894 had forged his reputation as being one of the best fighters at his weight to be found anywhere in the country, and would result in him being viewed as a potential candidate to fight for world honours. Sadly, fortune did not favour him, and after a series of demoralising losses, O'Brien returned to the boxing booths, where he would earn a meagre living as his pugilistic skills declined with the passing years. John O'Brien descended into criminality, supplementing his income by 'shebeening' – selling alcohol from his Cardiff home without a license, and drifted back into the underground world of the mountain fighters, where he would occasionally earn a few coins as a referee. He would spend his last years drunk and destitute, a shadow of his former self.

His mentor, William Samuels, the pioneer of the Welsh boxing booths, would outlive O'Brien by a number of years. Samuels remained full of vigour and maintained his colourful character into old age, frequently earning himself column inches in the local press through his exploits throughout the 1890's. Despite having supposedly fought his last 'official' contest in which he had demolished his one-time pupil, Shoni Engineer at Neath Fair when Samuels was already past his fiftieth year, Samuels was as willing as ever to raise his fists should occasion demand it. In 1893, William Samuels had taken his travelling booth on the road to Bridgend where he took an interest in a finely bred horse owned by a horse dealer named Henry Gardiner. After haggling with the seller for some time, Samuels successfully purchased the horse for the princely sum of four sovereigns and placed it in the harnesses attached to his living van. The horse proved to be a flighty specimen and quickly ran the veteran showman's van into a wall. One of Billy's children was lucky to escape without serious injury and his wife Elizabeth also had a close call, with one of the shafts having nearly harpooned her. After a few other skirmishes with disaster, the unpredictable temperament of the animal resulted in its early demise when it jumped off a cliff and plummeted to its death.

William Samuels bumped into Henry Gardiner at Bridgend some time later, and took the horse dealer to task for having taken advantage of a friend by selling him a horse of such highly strung temperament. Gardiner was unsympathetic to Samuels' sense of fair play, replying that he personally cared too much about his own wife and children to put them at risk by entrusting their safety to an untested horse. This slight on the paternal and conjugal responsibilities of William Samuels was enough to ignite his anger, and Samuels promptly knocked Gardiner to the floor with a single blow, leaving the horse dealer spitting out his two front teeth. When the matter ended up in court, Billy was unrepentant, commenting on Gardiner's youth and burly physique, and stated that he believed the matter should never have come before the court. "But he is not the proprietor of a boxing booth" said the Chairman. "No, sir, but I am 55 years of age, and he is 27", replied Billy proudly. Samuels ended up paying a fine of £1 including costs, with it being suggested that he keep his boxing skills strictly limited to within the confines of his boxing booth in future.

The following year in January of 1894, Samuels was quick to step up at Cardiff when he opened his boxing booth at the World's Fair and an Australian pugilist, Tom Ball, refused to meet John O' Brien in the ring. No doubt seeing the aging showman as an easier option, Ball accepted his challenge. Despite having been much the heavier man, Ball was seen to be unable to parry the skilful blows of William Samuels, who sent Ball to the floor in the very first round. There was no let-up in the second round, with Billy defying his years and sending

Ted Lewis

TELEPHONE - № 50
TELEGRAMS - "TED, PONTYPRIDD"

Penuel Road,
Pontypridd.

PRIVATE ADDRESS:
"DAN-Y-COED" 2, LAN PARK ROAD.

192

1. THIS AGREEMENT allows Johnny to be trained by whoever, and whatever way he and his friends may decide. I dont interfere in that, all I ask is for him to be fit to meet the engagements that I arrange for him.

2. Also I give him, and his friends, the privilege of fixing up on their own, any small engagements in and around this way - say with Scarrott, or at the Hall Treharris, and such like, where he can earn say £10 to £12 and for which I do not want any commission.

   But it will be necessary that I should be notified in such cases, so that they wont clash with fixtures that I am negotiating for.

Contract between Ted Lewis (Pontypridd) and an unknown boxer hard blows 'right and left into the Australian's face', knocking him down twice more. After the second round, Tom Ball could take no more and held out his hand, unable to continue the contest. The fight would appear to have re-invigorated Samuels' pugilistic spirit, in December of the same year, rumours were rife in Swansea of an impending fight between two local men, who had seemed undecided as to whether to fight or not. Samuels had little patience for the situation, coolly telling them he'd happily fight either of them for £25 a side whenever they liked. Neither of the pugilists appear to have been eager to accept the veteran bare knuckle fighter's challenge. Having maintained his strength long into advanced age, Billy held a low opinion of any man that had lost his vigour early in life, stating that he would like to see any men who felt old at forty confined to a large emporium where they could break stones all day until they felt young again.

Another boxer to have regularly featured on Samuels' booth, Tom James of Aberaman, engaged one of Billy's old opponents, Tom Vincent of Plymouth, at the People's Palace in Vincent's home town in January of 1895. It turned out to be a disappointing performance for the Welshman, with the call of time having saved James from being knocked out in the first round. While he fought better in the second round, his blows were seen to lack 'power and strength'. The third saw Tom Vincent have things all his own way, and he continued knocking the Aberaman fighter all over the ring in the fourth round. A 'slashing uppercut' saw James go down for good in the fifth. The victory was added to Tom Vincent's record, with it having been noted in the newspaper reports that followed that Tom Vincent had also previously recorded a win over Tom James' mentor, William Samuels.

Samuels' reaction was somewhat predictable, with his selective memory remembering only the first few rounds from his contest with Tom Vincent at Barnstaple fair in 1889, in which he had been seen to be the better man. Billy had conveniently forgotten the later rounds, when events had turned in Vincent's favour, forcing the Welshman to concede his defeat after a valiant struggle at the start of the fourteenth round;

'Hearing of the fight between Tom James and Vincent of Plymouth, I deny that I have ever been beaten by Vincent, as stated in one of the Cardiff papers. Five years ago I sparred him three rounds at Barnstaple, and beat him down in the third round, thought at that time I was laid up with erysipelas, I am prepared now to meet him at any time he thinks proper, at his own weight, for the biggest purse that may be offered for six three-minute rounds'.

Perhaps remembering the strength of Samuels' punch, and his skill at managing much younger men over a shorter contest, there was no reply issued to the veteran's challenge from Tom Vincent. Undeterred, Billy Samuels proved eager to duck back between the ropes of his High Street booth the following month on his home turf at Swansea. Samuels had stated his willingness to meet William 'Slogger' Hooligan, following Hooligan's unanswered challenge to Dick Ambrose, a dockside labourer who was a frequent performer in Samuels' boxing booth. A big crowd turned out eager to witness the old champion pull on the gloves again, but were disappointed to find that the contest was cancelled after Hooligan had injured his ribs and was unable to turn up. Undeterred, shortly afterwards, William Samuels put out a challenge in the local press stating his willingness to meet any boxer in Swansea for three three minute rounds with small gloves for any amount of money they wished to stake on the outcome. There were no takers.

Boxing regular exhibitions before the main contests on his travelling boxing booth with such notables as Billy Morgan and Dick Ambrose evidently kept Billy's arms strong, his punches crisp, and his eyes keen. He was sufficiently unimpressed by the fighting skills of Tom Harris of Llansamlet to throw out a challenge through the Welsh papers to the boxer to meet him for six three minute rounds at Cardiff for a purse of £5. Samuels was so sure of victory that he stated that he was willing to fight using just one hand. Tom Harris apparently wasn't too eager to engage Samuels in a contest, replying that he didn't want to be tried for manslaughter – but that he would be willing to take on any of Samuel's booth boxers instead, regardless of the willingness of Samuels to fight one handed.

Now nearer sixty than fifty, Samuels continued to hold such faith in his abilities that he also proved willing to step into the breech and offer his services to fight either Frank Lowry or Pedlar McMahon in 1899 after both fighters had been engaged in a dispute over a rematch following their contest on Jack Scarrott's booth at Aberavon. Although nothing would come of it, his willingness to engage such active, top rank professional boxers so much younger than himself bears testimony to Samuel's faith in his abilities, exemplified by his personal motto, which could be seen proudly emblazoned above his travelling boxing booth in bold letters, 'Strength and courage conquer all' and which had remained a frequent sight on its regular travels around the fairgrounds of South Wales.

Billy was still a popular figure on the fairground and took some interest in the new breed of glove fighters that were rapidly consigning the days of the mountain fighters to the pages of history. He continued to enter the ring to demonstrate his skills, which he seemingly maintained throughout his long and active life. As a spectator, he remained sceptical of the superiority of the gloved boxers to the bare knuckle fighters of his early days. The veteran rarely had anything complimentary to say about the modern champions who did battle with their fists enclosed in "pillow slops" as he contemptuously characterised the padded gloves now used in twenty round boxing contests of just three minutes duration. His long years spent in open ended bare knuckle contests, where tens of rounds which had only ended when one man had gone down had been a far harder school, and one in which he had repeatedly proved his grit in scores of battles. Some of his fellow early bare-knuckle men who had been lucky enough to have survived the mountain fighting rivalries of their youth could now be found paying over their coins to watch the younger booth boxers challenge each other inside the boxing booths. Many were keen to advise the bemused young glove fighters to keep up the old traditions and would relate the best ways to pickle the fists. William Samuel's expertize with dealing with facial swellings which he had learned through the course of his bare-knuckle career also meant his skills were often called upon to help with bloodletting in the corner of injured boxers. Perhaps showing his vintage, Samuels was well known for carrying a bradawl about his person to puncture the affected area, rather than use a straight edged razor.

His wife, Elizabeth Samuels, remembered as a fearsome and somewhat attractive woman who was undoubtedly the business brain that had enabled Samuels to run two permanent boxing booths at Swansea, a flourishing cinematograph business and the King's Head public house, passed away early in October of 1911 at their home at 9 Orchard Street, Swansea, leaving Billy somewhat broken. He consoled himself in the years that followed by remaining active on the pugilistic circuit, continuing to travel to Neath, Aberavon, and even as far afield as the Rhondda valley where he was a frequent visitor to the boxing booths of younger showmen and could still be persuaded to enter the ring on occasion to challenge amateurs and even professionals to 'get under his guard' in exhibitions of skill. Samuels remained exceedingly proud of the fact that although he had been fighting since the days of his youth, no-one had ever knocked him out in his fifty years of experience. He would often relate with amusement that he could only recall one occasion on which a challenger had even come close to achieving the feat. Billy had been taken off-guard by a farm-hand from the village of Marloes in Pembrokeshire, with Samuels apparently not having expected to take such a tremendous blow from such a lowly rural "clod-hopper" as he caustically termed the challenger. At the age of 73, the 'evergreen' William

Samuels entered the ring for the last occasion, having paid a visit to Harry Taylor's School of Arms at the Ivor Athletic Club, where he entertained the crowds and was seen to put up a 'spirited three rounds' against a young boxer by the name of Guppy Thomas.

William Samuels passed away at the same house in his hometown of Swansea, where Elizabeth Samuels had breathed her last on the morning of the 8th March, 1916, having supposedly reached the age of 77. According to his landlady he puffed away on his cigars right up until his last, and enjoyed watching the local children at play, giving away the last of the coppers in his pockets to the children before he died. Only two or three weeks previously he had been sitting at the ringside watching the contests held at the Olympic in Swansea where as usual he was heard to comment loudly on the merits and demerits of the modern school of boxers.

The announcement of the death of perhaps one of the most famous Welsh bare-knuckle fighters, and boxing's most committed promoters would recall memories of the highlights of his long career with both knuckles and gloves throughout Wales. At Pembrokeshire, many remembered the days of his youth when he had visited Portfield Fair, then in its infancy, at a time long before John Studt's glorious electrically illuminated gondolas and scenic railways, when Studt had been forced to propel his roundabouts by hand. At this time, it had been the appearance of Billy's 'broad, good humoured face' that had been 'hailed with delight' by the local people, and Billy's boxing show had proved to be the most popular entertainment on the fairground.

It would be recalled that it had been in these early times that;

'…Billie Samuels, then a comparatively young man, full of vigour, and with the strength of an ox, first began to visit Haverfordwest. The counter attractions at this time were few and simple in character, and usually consisted of the fat woman, the dwarf, and giant, so Billie's show cut a prominent figure, and was always sure of generous patronage. Billie was noted for his happy disposition, and he was a clean honourable fighter, and although occasionally some of the locals who took on for a bout would imagine they were taking a rise out of the show-man by getting in a smart blow, Billy was in reality "having them on," and the smack on his hardened skin, while it might appear very terrible to the onlookers, was in reality only feather taps to the seasoned pugilist. He would, however, mostly get his own back, but only in a good humoured way, and although he did not resort to hard hitting he had other methods of contributing to the discomfiture of his opponent, and his elusive tactics always turned the tables and evoked laughter in Billie's favour.'

On his travels throughout the country down the years, Samuels had discovered many promising young fighters, with a number of them having received sufficient schooling to have developed into well-known champions. John O'Brien, Dai St. John, Sam Butcher, Patsy Perkins, Bob Dunbar, Pedlar McMahon, Dick Ambrose, Tom James, Frank Craig, Dai Dollings, Billy and Dai Morgan and countless others had all appeared in his booth at one time or another. He had arguably done more for the development of the sport of boxing in his own country than any other showman of his time.

At Swansea, where Samuels had founded two permanent booths, some recalled the tremendous strength of Billy's stomach punch, remembering with amusement the occasion when he had met his rival Pete 'Dublin Tom' Burns at Sophia Gardens in Cardiff. Samuels was not showing his best form, and was seen to be suffering at the hands of the Cardiff fighter. Things were looking bleak for Samuels until Elizabeth, standing on the stage outside the booth, shouted 'Billy, final this round'. It was all the encouragement that Samuels had needed, and in the next moment '...Dublin Tom described an arc as he collapsed from the effects of a terrific body blow'. For others, the occasion when Samuels had met John L. Sullivan had proved to be the highlight of his career, when he was seen to stand up manfully against one of the most feared heavyweights in the world for three rounds, despite having been past his prime and being greatly outweighed. Many remembered the day on which Samuels had proved his fearlessness in the face of certain death and had been carried through the streets of Swansea, after having walked into the lion's den at Bostock and Wombwell's circus. No doubt whatever period of Billy's long and colourful life the people of Swansea individually remembered, all could agree with the sentiment expressed by the *Cambria Daily Leader* that;

'Billy's heart was good, and his hand strong. He will be missed by many. His proud soul was of the Viking type, his Valhalla lies with the champions of a bye-gone day.'

The mystery as to what had happened to William Samuels' pupil and the one time lightweight champion of Wales, Patsy Perkins, would become clear many years later when Perkins passed away at Merthyr on December 20th, 1933, leaving behind a widow and a daughter. In the course of his long career, Perkins reputedly fought over 300 times in the ring after having started boxing as a boy of just twelve, working for the travelling showman, Jack Steward, who he joined at Newport, being paid 5 shillings a week and his board. His wage was increased to 10 shillings when he reached the age of 18. Steward would offer £1 to anyone on Perkins's weight who would dare to take him on. The money was never claimed. After leaving Steward, Perkins threw in his lot with Alf Ball, then middleweight champion of England, in a twelve month tour. Perkins was routinely backed for £5 against all comers for six or ten rounds. Nobody ever won the stake, despite Perkins fighting at a weight of just 8 stone 6lb to 9 stone.

After this time, Perkins's services were retained by ex-soldier and boxing booth owner, Harry Hughes with whom he was associated with for many years when Hughes's booth was pitched at Canning Town in London. Perkins pugilistic expertise was renowned, having been billed as the champion of Canning Town, and open to fight any 10 stone man in the country. The challenge went unanswered and so the weight limit was removed. It was at this point that Charlie Bartlett, a black meat carrier from Smithfield market was matched against him. Perkins reportedly knocked out his opponent in sixteen rounds and one hour and five minutes of 'terribly hard fighting', despite having conceded 2 stone and 10 lbs. He would then go on to knock out Bill Coulsten of Canning Town in ten rounds.

One of very few defeats in Patsy Perkins's long career occurred when he was matched to fight J. Young of Mile End, who held the championship of England at 11 stone 7 lbs. The verdict was an unfortunate result with Perkins having been forced to give in after falling in the twelfth round, breaking his ankle. After returning to Wales in 1890, and falling under the wing of William Samuels, Patsy Perkins quickly made a name for himself on the Welsh pugilistic scene, beating all his opponents by knockout. 'Shumeck' Thomas lasted one round at Swansea, Tom Rooney was beaten in six rounds at Merthyr, and Perkins also supposedly fought and defeated Shoni Engineer at Newport in ten rounds, and Enoch Morrison at Merthyr in five rounds. Perkins was finally crowned lightweight champion of Wales after his knockout over his great rival Bob Wiltshire of Cardiff at Bob Habbijam's School of Arms in London on the 22nd March, 1895.

Patsy's parallel career as a boxing booth owner was not quite as successful as his boxing career. Perkins had been at the centre of a national scandal after having founded a boxing booth in a converted slaughterhouse at Aberdare and David Rees had been fatally injured after falling from the in the middle of an unruly match against Thomas 'Twm' Edwards on May 17th, 1894. Following the outrage of the local church people, Perkins had been forced to leave town and elected to open a new boxing booth at Swansea, in direct competition with his old mentor, William Samuels. It was not long before the two men came to blows, and while Perkins operated for some time in Swansea, he would leave the town after falling victim to intense police scrutiny following scenes of disorder at contests held within his boxing booth.

Perkins took to the road, running a travelling booth, but the enterprise met with disaster in 1898 at Southampton, when a labourer by the name of James Parsons died in his bed the day after being knocked out on Perkins's booth. In the time that had elapsed since his last professional contest, matches had become scarce and Perkins's last big fight was against old rival, Dido Plum of London, regarded as a coming champion of England. Perkins did not appear to have lost any of his skill, and reportedly knocked out Plum inside nine rounds, getting his revenge for two recorded losses to the Londoner recorded on Perkins record back in 1890. After a brief period as a boxing promoter on his return to Merthyr, in which he looked after the interests of the famed bare-knuckle fighter Redmond Coleman, Perkins took to the road again, ending up in Leeds where he would become a boxing instructor. Patsy was apparently still fight promoting in Yorkshire when the First World War broke out. Discreetly forgetting his age, he enlisted in the Army Service Corps and spent two years in Salonika where he was matched against Sergeant Saunders of the Royal Engineers. Although Saunders lasted ten rounds, he was decisively knocked out by the 53 year old ex-lightweight champion of Wales. On his return to Merthyr, Perkins quietly slid into obscurity and started work as a collier, the remarkable story of his pugilistic career having largely been forgotten until his death.

Bob Dunbar of Newport, who had fought William Samuels on a muddy field near Llanelly in Jack Scarrott's youth back in 1882 and was remembered by Scarrott by his early alias of 'Sam Lane' would pay the heaviest price for his long career as a bare-knuckle fighter and glove boxer. Following his defeat of William Samuels, Dunbar continued to share a great rivalry with the Swansea showman. A prize fight was organised between the two men just a few weeks later at Carmarthen that failed to come off, with a stake of £50 on the outcome having been put up by a 'gentleman' farmer. Early in the morning, police spotted a crowd of 50 people making their way through a field named Parkwaen, towards a marsh near the gasworks. Having spotted the police approaching the gathering, the crowd quickly split up, taking the stakes and the ropes for the ring with them. The police cornered Samuels and Dunbar and issued them with a warning not to continue with the contest. One of the two would-be combatants was quick to state that as far as he was concerned he would consider the match having been "off", not "brought off" in battle, but "declared off", and so with matters postponed for another time, both men wisely elected to leave town shortly afterwards. The interference by the police ensured that Samuels and Dunbar would end up locking horns at a future point. Things finally came to a head when William Samuels heard that Bob Dunbar had been running down Samuels' pugilistic abilities in his hometown of Swansea a few weeks later following their aborted contest at Carmarthen. It ended with a street fight in which Samuels ended up getting collared by the police and taken to gaol, and Dunbar took to his heels, luckily avoiding the same fate. William Samuels' pride ensured he continued to challenge Bob Dunbar into meeting for a rematch, eventually forcing Dunbar off the Welsh fairgrounds altogether.

Shortly after his last meeting with William Samuels, Bob Dunbar was the unfortunate victim in a terrible firearms accident, which left a lead ball lodged in his left eye socket. He was forced to go to London to seek medical assistance to have both the lead ball and his eye removed. Despite the severity of this injury, Dunbar continued to fight on, and had a long and 'creditable' record, fighting a great many middleweight men in the prize ring, although was perhaps better known for fighting four rounders in London. Bob Dunbar frequently performed in the capital, sparring twice before the Prince of Wales, as well as fighting exhibition matches with his good friend, Charles 'Toff' Wall. In 1883 he reached the semi-final of a competition for 9 stone men at Shoreditch before having been beaten by Harry Solomon of Mile End. Despite labouring under the disadvantage of having one eye, Bob Dunbar continued entering competitions, reaching the final of a 126 lb competition in January of 1887, when he was beaten by formidable opponent, Sam Baxter, at the Royal Aquarium Theatre in Westminster in the second of three scheduled rounds. Despite the setback, Dunbar was back in action the following month, fighting unsuccessfully in a 120 lb competition at the same venue.

Bob Dunbar settled in his hometown of Newport, although his relocation was not without problems, with his notoriety ensuring that there were plenty of local hard men who wished to further their own reputations by engaging the famous fighter in battle. Dunbar ended up in Newport Police court in September of 1887, having been charged with public disorder after fighting in Dock Street. Dunbar had been walking past the Old Green public house when he had been called over by a labourer named John Wallace and a friend. Both men had grown sufficiently courageous through drunkenness to threaten to throw Dunbar off a nearby bridge. The first man closed on Dunbar, who promptly knocked him out, and then meted out the same punishment to his companion. Wallace had his collar bone broken in the confrontation. At court the charges against Dunbar were thrown out after it was established that the one-eyed boxer had acted in self-defence.

He continued to run a boxing booth, frequently meeting all comers, in spite of the risk to the sight in his one remaining optic, and was well regarded enough as a boxing instructor and trainer to have been engaged by Harry Briggs when Briggs was in training for the Heavyweight Amateur Championship. Having already claimed the lightweight title of Wales by this time, a title he would later claim to have held for an astonishing ten years, he unwisely elected to continue in full length glove fighting contests. Bob Dunbar would meet Jockey Saunders of Birmingham in March of 1888 at the Ropery in Clarence Place, Newport for a prize of a silver cup valued at 20 guineas, despite Dunbar entering the ring with three fingers badly injured and conceding a stone to a formidable opponent. The event proved to be a particularly brutal affair;

Round 1 – *After a few preliminary spars, Saunders got home one on Bob's cheek, and then sent him to ground. A lot of heavy milling ensued, with little advantage to either side. Both men were in turn forced on the ropes, and when time was called both had quite enough of the fight. Saunders's weight so far had stood him in good stead though Bob was game.*

Round 2 – *The men soon got to work, both landing heavily on the head. First blood for Saunders, who drew the claret from Bob's right eye in a heavy stream. The fighting was very heavy and fast, and it was apparent at this early stage that no child's play was meant. Towards the close of the round, Dunbar hit heavily on Saunders's face, but Jockey kept well up, and running round, forced his man to the ropes. The round ended in much excitement.*

Round 3 – *Dunbar came up fresh, and hit heavily with his left. The fighting was now a little slower. Getting Bob to the ropes, Jockey planted a heavy one on Bob's head and upset him partly. The local man, however, recovered and went on family. The hitting towards the end of the round was of a truly slogging order. Saunders looked fagged, but did not heed the shouts of his opponent's partisans to this effect.*

Round 4 – *Dunbar came up much the fresher. A few preliminary parries ended in a hug, and then came a couple of marches round. Bob's eye bled copiously, but he dealt some heavy hits on Jockey's face, which, as yet, was kept thoroughly intact. Saunders meant to drop a lot of stingers on Dunbar's head, but Bob smartly parried, and then gave his opponent a sanguinary mouth. Dunbar's face, however, was now quite crimson with gore. Jockey Saunders smiled as he followed his man around, both being a little fagged. The close was somewhat slow.*

Round 5 – *Saunders came up blowing hard, and received a dangerous one from Bob's left. The referee gave the decision of a foul for a blow dealt by Jockey Saunders below the belt.*

The police had been present in the audience throughout the fight, and after the crowd dispersed, Bob Dunbar and his seconds were taken to the police station surrounded by a large contingent of police men. In the chaos that ensued, Jockey Saunders and his supporters took to their heels and escaped. At Newport Police Court, Dunbar was charged with engaging in a prize fight as opposed to a boxing match, and having committed a breach of the peace. The police had waited until the contest had gone beyond the point at which it might be deemed a boxing contest, and believed the brutality which had characterised the bout suggested it bore more resemblance to a prize fight.

While police believed that the contests preceding the main event had been harmless sparring matches, they maintained that the gloves used for the Dunbar vs. Saunders fight were 'of a very different kind from those used in the earlier contests', but in cross-examination, Police Inspector Winmill stated that he had not been able to inspect the gloves that had been used. At this point, Bob Dunbar contemptuously produced the gloves used in the contest and cast them onto the solictor's table, stating that the referee, "Brummy" Meadows, had offered them up for police examination before the contest began. They were ordinary gloves which he had previously used to give boxing lessons. Regarding the ferocity of the fight, Dunbar offered to undergo an examination, telling the court that if he was found to have been injured at all he would willingly put £2 in the poor-box.

Seeing the obvious injury to Bob's remaining eye, the Magistrate's Clerk asked Dunbar how he had received the injury. Dunbar claimed that the scratch had been the result of coaching one of his pupils who had accidentally brought the glove against his eye. To indicate that he thought nothing of the injury, he slapped the eye a couple of times with the palm of his hand. Dunbar's asserted that he saw nothing wrong with the legality of the contest, as a man had been knocked out senseless at the Albert Hall in London a few weeks before, and maintained that had the police approached the fighters before the competition and told them of their concerns, the fight would have been stopped. The court determined that as this was the first case involving the men that had come before them, the defendants would not be committed for trial, but were instead bound over to keep the peace and ordered to pay costs.

Bob Dunbar elected to fight on, and it was suggested by one newspaper in February of 1889 that he had engaged in a prize fight against Bob Wiltshire of Cardiff near Carmarthen. When approached on the subject, Bob Dunbar wisely decided that he should deny all knowledge of the matter, stating that while he had been away from Newport for some time, he was nowhere near Carmarthen on the day in question, that he had not fought Wiltshire, and as far as he was concerned the 'whole story is a myth'.

Whether or not Dunbar and Wiltshire met on this occasion isn't clear, although the following month a statement was issued to the newspapers stating that a proposed contest between the two men had been postponed. On the very same day, a ring was quietly pitched about four miles outside Hereford, while Bob Dunbar and Bob Wiltshire waited in a house nearby for their supporters to arrive. The ring had been pitched and the men were about to strip for battle when a trap containing four police officers under the command of the local Superintendent suddenly drove into sight. The ring was quickly taken down and put in a boat, and the spectators dispersed. Dunbar and Wiltshire took refuge in a barn where they hid for a number of hours. The various supporters of the two men retreated to a secondary location where it was decided to try and bring the battle off at an alternative venue. After a few hours spent dodging the fifteen strong police force that were hunting for them, the men were brought together in a large barn, with some suggesting that a nearby warehouse might make for a more secure place to hold the fight. Unfortunately, both places had hard stone floors, and so it was decided that the men would fight outside the barn, while the spectators would look out from within, in an attempt to avoid drawing the attention of the policemen roaming the countryside. Unfortunately, the agents of the law appeared to be everywhere, and so after much wandering up and down the Wye River looking for a suitable spot to hold the fight, the men reluctantly agreed to abandon the affair altogether.

Few details regarding Bob Dunbar's movements in the years that followed appear to have been recorded, although he was still running a travelling boxing booth as late as 1894, having set up shop at the market place in Ebbw Vale in February. Nothing more seems to have been heard of Dunbar until August of 1899 at Newport when he was once again taken before the police court, although by now he had paid a terrible price for his near twenty year career with both knuckles and gloves, having turned completely blind after losing the sight in his remaining eye. He was found guilty of having assaulted the owner of a boxing booth, Dunbar had wanted to spar on the booth, but '...his blindness was naturally an obstacle. Dunbar, a well-known ex-boxer, complained that the showman made capital out of his name and that angered him.' The court would find Dunbar guilty and he was bound over to keep the peace.

Bob experienced further tragedy the following month when his wife, Amelia Dunbar, passed away from cancer at London on 1st September, having been taken to a hospital there for treatment from their home in Newport. She would be buried near the graves of her mother and brother in the East London cemetery at Plaistow. Where Bob Dunbar went after the death of his wife in the decades that followed is a mystery. Unbeknownst to Jack Scarrott at the time he recounted 'Sam Lane's' tremendous battle against William Samuels at Llanelly some fifty five years previously in 1936, an elderly 'Sam Lane' lay bed ridden at Monmouthshire Mental Hospital in Abergavenny. He had been moved there from Swansea mental hospital in May of 1935, with his last known address having been at Riverside in Merthyr. On March 9th 1938, after forty years of blindness, Bob Dunbar died after falling out of his bed and banging his head on a chair. As far as anyone could remember, he was 79 years old. He had outlived his bitter rival William Samuels by twenty two years and one day, all of which had been spent in darkness.

At Pontypridd, James Frederick Dean, perhaps better known as Pontypridd's 'Cast-iron man', who had once appeared on Jack Scarrott's boxing booth, was also in poor shape. Jimmy Dean had reportedly reached the age of 66 in 1937, although he was deaf and almost blind after years fighting on the fairgrounds where he had earned some fame for a part of his act in which a man smashed stones on his chest with a sledgehammer. He was also remembered as having crossed fists in a few prize fights in the days of his youth, having most famously once beaten an unnamed black challenger over 65 rounds when he was 17 years old. Some thirty six years previously he had found love in the arms of Miss Norah Ryan of Ebbw Vale after appearing on the fairground in the town and both had travelled together to the United States with one of the travelling shows. He came back to Wales two years later, with Norah Ryan having stayed on in the U.S. for a longer period of time. By the time she returned to Wales, he had married another woman, and so she returned to the U.S. heartbroken. Despite her sorrow, Norah Ryan never forgot her one-time sweetheart, and Jimmy Dean would discover through a newspaper advert asking for information of his whereabouts that she had left him £1,800 in her will, after having been left a small fortune by her father who had run a bicycle shop in Fishguard.

March of 1937 would also see the death of one of the most renowned of the old bare-knuckle mountain fighters in Sam 'Butcher' Thomas, of Ynyshir Road, Ynyshir at the age of 75. After an early career with the knuckles he had served his apprenticeship with the gloves under the tutelage of William Samuels. Butcher achieved notable wins over such well-regarded opponents as Hopkin Williams of Ferndale, Pawdy McCarthy of Cardiff and Tom James of Aberaman, and had even appeared in the ring at the famous National Sporting Club in London on one occasion.

Even some of the boxers of the modern age, who had ushered in the popularity of boxing as a sport from their unlikely beginnings on the fairgrounds of South Wales at the turn of the century would be forgotten in the years that had followed. There were few, if any names of prominence that Jack Scarrott had not helped in their first steps towards their professional boxing careers through the schooling that they received in his travelling booth down the years. Jack Scarrott would himself outlive many of the famous Welsh boxers who he had known and assisted in their path to boxing glory at the start of the twentieth century, including Jim Driscoll, Freddie Welsh, Dai Roberts and Percy Jones. Although no longer the force that it had previously been in bringing the boxing talent of South Wales to the attention of the public, Jack Scarrott's amusements would continue to tour the show grounds of Wales until 1947 when the old master showman passed away at the age of seventy seven on the 6th October at the Caldicot fairground, he was afterwards buried at the Glyntaff Cemetery near his adopted hometown of Pontypridd. It would be said after his death that South Wales would never see his like again.

Appendix

William Samuels vs. Robert Dunbar

Llanelly & County Guardian 5th October 1882
'Fight at Llanelly Between Two Leading Pugilists'

Two professors of the "noble art of self-defence" settled their differences in the old fashioned way on the Fair Ground, Llanelly, on Monday morning last. Few frequenters of local fairs do not know "Bill Samuel". For many years he has claimed the questionable honour of being the champion fighter of South Wales. He is a fine built man, and apparently rather fond of showing off his fistic accomplishments. His boasts of thrashing half-a-dozen Llanelly at the same time, after beating a Felinfoel collier at Carmarthen have rankled in the minds of a good many local admirers of the "art," who frequent his boxing show on the occasion of its periodical visits. As is well-known to the supporters of the "magic ring," these travelling shows are accompanied by two or three reputed good boxers, who regale their patrons with exhibitions of their skill in pummelling visitors who have a try at the gloves and occasionally each other. This visit, Samuel's show boasted the presence of a young fellow named Bob Lane, hailing from that favourite haunt of Fistiana's heroes, Birmingham. A day or two ago, this Bob, who is about 22 years of age had his knee dislocated by a fall off one of Samuel's horses, and wished to break off his engagement. He produced a medical certificate, but Samuel refused to pay his wages, some £3, unless he would keep on over the fair, as his non-appearance would occasion him some loss.

Monday morning, Lane proceeded to his employer to demand his money. It was refused. Words led to blows, and the result was a fight. The various camp followers of the fair kindly formed a ring, and "to be or not to be" paid, became the subject of a fistic argument. Lane, much to his disadvantage, by reasons of his injured leg, could not "trip the light fantastic toe." Six or seven rounds were fought with great gusto, Lane being awarded the palm by the hundreds of judges who surrounded the contestants. Then a short armistice took place, to enable Lane to undress and he soon appeared in the regular naked-to-the-waist costume. Before resuming the argument, Samuel is said to have remarked, "Leave the little ---- have another round, and I'll kill him." But the little one had apparently a decided objection to such a fate and refused to be killed. To give the result of the half-dozen rounds which followed, in the proper parlance, Samuel's hitting powers were devoted principally to his opponent's "bread basket" and sides, while Lane paid his attentions to the other ones "mug" and soon the "cognac" began to flow from Samuel's "tap" and he gave signs of "going into mourning" by "putting the shutters up." Ultimatcly, after half-an-hours fighting, the cry of "police" was raised, which ended the encounter. Samuels it seems was severely punished, his face being dreadfully battered to which leeches had to be applied. Lane had only one wound in sight, a bruise to the side of the head. In justice to the "champion" it must be stated that the sympathy of the crowd ran strongly in favour of the "little one" who was warmly encouraged. Subsequently Samuel left for Carmarthen, while his opponent strutted about "cock of the walk" receiving with becoming modesty the congratulations of his admirers, who after the fight made a collection for the victorious "bruiser," with which he got a "big drink."

Fired by her husband's wrongs, Mrs. Samuels shortly afterwards started from her car across the road to settle a grievance with one of Studt's servant girls and threatening dire vengeance if she could come within reach of her arms. The threatened one was in a car, and Mrs. Samuels was told to wait a few moments as "Lizzie was not afraid of her and was willing to fight." But the crowd was baulked of its prospective fun, for the invader retraced her steps and shunned the fight.

How a fight could have taken place so near a street in the heart of the town without interference from the authorities is explained by the fact that the police were in the police station being drilled at the time. But surely the Superintendent should see that all his men were not off their beat during fair time.

Bibliography

Through the course of writing this book, the following publications and sources were consulted at various points.

Books

Butler, James – *Kings Of The Ring*, Stanley Paul, 1936

Clark, Norman – *All in the game*, Methuen & Co, 1935

Davies, Lawrence – *Mountain Fighters: Lost Tales of Welsh Boxing*, Peerless Press, 2011

Edwards, Wil Jon – *From the Valley I Came*, Angus and Robertson, 1956

Mace, Jem – *Fifty Years a Fighter: Bare-knuckle Champion of the World*, edited by Lawrence Davies, Peerless Press, 2013

Seymour Vesey-Fitzgerald, Brian – *Gypsies of Britain*, David & Charles, 1973

Sullivan, John L – *Life and Reminiscences of a Nineteenth Century Gladiator*, George Routledge and Sons Ltd, 1892

Wignall, Trevor C. – *Almost yesterday*, Hutchinson & Co, 1949

Wignall, Trevor C. – *Ringside*, Hutchinson & Co, 1940

Wignall, Trevor C. – *The Story Of Boxing*, Hutchinson & Co, 1923

Wignall, Trevor C. – *The Sweet Science*, Duffield and Co, 1926

Wilde, Jimmy – *Fighting Was My Business*, Michael Joseph Ltd, 1938

Wilde, Jimmy – *Hitting and Stopping: How I Won 100 Fights*, Peerless Press, edited by Lawrence Davies, 2012

Yorke, Peter – *William Haggar Fairground Film Maker*, Accent Press 2007

Newspapers

The Aberdare Leader, The Aberdare Times, Abergavenny Chronicle, The Abergavenny Mail, Baner ac Amserau Cymru, Barry Dock News, Barry Herald, Boxing, The Brecon Radnor Express Carmarthen and Swansea Valley Gazette and Brynmawr District Advertiser, Birmingham Daily Post, The Brecon County Times Neath Gazette and General Advertiser for the Counties of Brecon Carmarthen Radnor Monmouth Glamorgan Cardigan Montgomery Hereford, The Brecon Reporter and South Wales Generl Advertiser, The Cambria Daily Leader, The Cambrian, The Cambrian News and Merionethshire Standard, The Cardiff and Merthyr Guardian Glamorgan Monmouth and Brecon Gazette, The Cardiff Times, The Carmarthen Journal and South Wales Weekly Advertiser, The Carmarthen Weekly Reporter, County Observer and Monmouthshire Central Advertiser Abergavenny and Raglan Herald Usk and

Pontypool Messenger and Chepstow Argus, Edinburgh Evening News, The Era, Evening Express, Frank Leslie's Popular Monthly, Glamorgan Free Press, The Glamorgan Gazette, Haverfordwest and Milford Haven Telegraph and General Weekly Reporter for the Counties of Pembroke Cardigan Carmarthen Glamorgan and the Rest of South Wales, Herald of Wales and Monmouthshire Recorder, The Leeds Mercury, Llanelly and Country Guardian, Manchester Evening News, Lloyd's Weekly Newspaper, Sunday The Merthyr Express, The Merthyr Telegraph and General Advertiser for the Iron Districts of South Wales, Merthyr Times and Dowlais Times and Aberdare Echo, Mirror of Life, Monmouth Guardian, New York Times, North Devon Journal, Nottingham Evening Post, Pembrokeshire Herald and General Advertiser, The Penny Illustrated Paper and Illustrated Times, The Pontypridd Chronicle and Workman's News, The Rhondda Leader, South Wales Argus, South Wales Daily News, The South Wales Daily Post, South Wales Echo, The South Wales Star, Sporting Life, St Pauls Daily Globe, Surrey Mirror, The Times, Weekly Mail, The Western Mail.